SELECTED WRITINGS ON PHILOSOPHY AND ADULT EDUCATION

Second Edition

Edited by

Sharan B. Merriam

Krieger Publishing Company
Malabar, Florida

Original Edition 1984
Second Edition 1995

Printed and Published by
KRIEGER PUBLISHING COMPANY
KRIEGER DRIVE
MALABAR, FLORIDA 32950

Copyright © 1995 by Krieger Publishing Company

FROM A DECLARATION OF PRINCIPLES JOINTLY ADOPTED BY A COMMITTEE OF THE AMERICAN BAR ASSOCIATION AND COMMITTEE OF PUBLISHERS:

This Publication is designed to provide accurate and authoritative information in regard to the subject matter covered. It is sold with the understanding that the publisher is not engaged in rendering legal, accounting, or other professional service. If legal advice or other expert assistance is required, the services of a competent professional person should be sought.

Library of Congress Cataloging-In-Publication Data

Selected writings on philosophy and adult education / edited by Sharan
  B. Merriam. — 2nd ed.
      p.   cm.
  Includes bibliographical references.
  ISBN 0-89464-887-X (alk. paper)
  1. Adult education—Philosophy. I. Merriam, Sharan B.
LC5219.S44 1995
374'.001—dc20   94-24355
                                                                      CIP

10 9 8 7 6 5 4 3

Contents

Preface

Since its original publication in 1984, there have been a number of developments in the philosophical foundations of adult education that warrant this updating of *Selected Writings on Philosophy and Adult Education*. In particular, critical theory emanating from the Frankfurt School and Jurgen Habermas, feminist theory, and phenomenology are philosophical frameworks that have been adopted by adult educators as tools in the continuing examination of the knowledge base and practice of adult education. These orientations are represented by selections included in this revised edition of *Selected Writings*. In addition, several substitutions of newer material have been made in writings representing other, more traditional philosophical schools of thought.

As with the original version, this book is partially intended as a companion piece to Elias and Merriam's *Philosophical Foundations of Adult Education*. That book has also been updated with the inclusion of an extensive bibliographic essay documenting contributions to the philosophy of adult education in the fifteen-year period since its publication. The six philosophical categories that structured that book were preserved in the essay update. Those schools are Liberal Adult Education, Humanistic Adult Education, Behavioristic Adult Education, Progressive Adult Education, Radical Adult Education, and Analytical Philosophy of Adult Education. Critical theory and feminist theory were addressed under the category of radical adult education, and phenomenology can be found within the discussion of humanistic adult education.

While the six philosophical categories from *Philosophical*

Foundations provide a loose framework for reading the selections in this book, these pieces can be read for what they have to offer in and of themselves. They represent some of the most provocative thinking about the purposes and functions of education, and adult education in particular, in contemporary American society. Students of adult education can read these selections for insights into how some of the field's most prominent thinkers conceive of the theory and practice of adult education; they might also be read to stimulate discussions about some of the ethical and social issues facing our field today. Each selection is preceded by a short biography of the author and short introduction to the particular sample of his or her work.

As with any edited collection, hard decisions had to be made about what to include. These decisions were made on the basis of the work's representativeness of a particular philosophical position, the extent to which it addressed or had obvious implications for adult education, and the difficulty of obtaining permission for its use.

I would like to thank Mary Roberts, editor at Krieger Publishing for prodding me into undertaking this much-needed revision of *Selected Writings*. I also want to thank Nancy Carmack and Vivian Mott, two of the most capable doctoral students in our program here at The University of Georgia, for their assistance in all phases of this project. It would not have been completed without their help.

Sharan B. Merriam

About the Editor

Sharan B. Merriam is professor of adult and continuing education at The University of Georgia. She received her B.A. degree from Drew University in English, her M.Ed. degree from Ohio University in English Education, and her Ed.D. degree from Rutgers University in Adult Education. Before coming to The University of Georgia, she served on the faculties of Northern Illinois University and Virginia Polytechnic Institute and State University.

Her research and writing activities have focused on adult learning and development, and qualitative research methods. She was coeditor of *Adult Education Quarterly*, the major journal of research and theory in adult education. She is also coeditor with Phyllis Cunningham of the 1989 *Handbook of Adult and Continuing Education*. This encyclopedic work is commissioned once every ten years by the American Association for Adult and Continuing Education (AAACE) to provide an update overview of the field of adult education.

Dr. Merriam has written or coauthored a number of books including *Philosophical Foundations of Adult Education, Coping with Male Mid-Life, Adult Education: Foundations of Practice*, winner of the 1985 Cyril O. Houle World Award for Literature in Adult Education, *Themes of Adulthood Through Literature, A Guide to Research for Educators and Trainers of Adults*, winner of the 1984 Phillip E. Frandson Memorial Award for Literature in Continuing Education, and *Case Study Research in Education*. Her most recent publications include a textbook titled *Learning in Adulthood: A Comprehensive Guide*, and a popular book on adult development titled *Lifelines: Patterns of Work, Love, and Learning in Adulthood*.

Sir Richard Livingstone (1880-1960) was educated in the classics at Oxford University, England. After several years as vice-chancellor of Queen's University in Belfast, Livingstone spent most of his years at Oxford, first as a fellow at Corpus Christi College and later as vice-chancellor of Oxford University. He traveled extensively throughout the United States and Canada lecturing on the classics and education at prestigious colleges and universities.

Livingstone's interest in the classics is reflected in many posts he held ranging from being a member of the Prime Minister's Committee on Classics, to president of the Classical Association, to being general editor of the Clarendon Series of Greek and Latin Authors. His publications on Greek life and culture (*The Greek Genius and its Meaning to Us, Greek Ideals and Modern Life, Portraits of Socrates, The Legacy of Greece,* etc.) and on education (*The Future in Education, Education for a World Adrift, Education and the Spirit of the Age,* etc.) were translated into many languages and were widely read both in Europe and North America.

The selection presented here is from *On Education,* which was published in the United States in 1945. The chapter deals with the topic of adult education and is representative of the British point of view, both then and now. In Livingstone's view, adult education is liberal education in which the person studies humanities and, perhaps, the history of science for the purpose of developing the mind, body, and character. A clear distinction is drawn between liberal adult education, which aims at producing a complete human being, and technical or vocational education "which aims at earning a living or making money."

SIR RICHARD LIVINGSTONE

1 Cultural Studies in Adult Education

EDUCATION. But what education? The question might have been easier to answer in the age of a restricted curriculum than to-day, when art, folk-dancing, choral-singing, drama, handicrafts, health subjects and much more have taken their place with the older studies. Education is like a restaurant which used to offer a few old-fashioned dishes and now has a menu covering several pages. There are great advantages in this; the enlargement in the scope of education, the sense that it covers the whole of life, is all to the good. But there is a certain risk. For the bill of fare in these restaurants of education is not divided into any categories or courses. Soup, fish, entrées, joints, sweets, dessert are flung together in indiscriminate disorder; the customer selects but there is nothing to guide his selection, nor any suggestion that in education too there are such things as food values and order in a meal. This is a mistake. The days of widespread famine and starving intellectual appetites may still be with us to explain and excuse our indiscriminate feeding; but as famine gives way to a world in which there is food enough for all, it is desirable that we should consider whether adult education should not be more methodical than it is. But what method, and based on what?

Seen in its many manifestations, education seems an infinite number of topics, classes, techniques, standards, examinations—a Many in which no One can be discerned. That is one reason why there is so much waste in it. We enter this maze with high hopes but no clear purpose and the deeper we plunge into it the more we lose any sense of direction, till we end by following our particular alley, blindly conscientious, through an *inextricabilis error* in which we have long ceased to look for a clue. Perhaps this is an unfair description of education, but most people who have taught or learnt will know what I mean by describing it as a maze without a clue. Yet there *are* clues to the maze. One clue is the old conception of a liberal education.

What is a liberal education? Most people would probably reply,

Subjects like history, literature, languages, pure mathematics and science are a liberal education, but subjects like book-keeping, business administration, commercial French, accountancy, cooking and shorthand are not. They are technical or vocational, not liberal.

So far as it goes, that answer would be true. But why are some subjects classed as liberal education and others not? In itself liberal education is an odd phrase. What has the adjective "liberal" to do with education, and why should a "liberal" education be regarded as a good thing? To answer that question, we must go back to the country where the phrase "liberal education" was first used. The word "liberal", "belonging to a free man", comes from a world where slavery existed, and has survived into times when, in the literal sense, it has no meaning because there are no slaves. To understand it, we must imagine ourselves in the Greek world where the great distinction was between free men and slaves, and a liberal education was the education fitted to a free citizen.

That distinction may seem obsolete in a world where slavery has been abolished. But though slavery has gone, the ideal of a free man's education is not antiquated. Here, as so often, the Greeks saw to the heart of the matter and put their fingers on an essential distinction. If we had understood and remembered this idea of a free man's education, our views of education would have been less confused and we should have gone straighter to our goal. Of slaves the Greeks took little account. Their condition prevented them from being men in the full sense of the word. But they held that the free man, the real man, the complete man, must be something more than a mere breadwinner, and must have something besides the knowledge necessary to earn his living. He must have also the education which will give him the chance of developing the gifts and faculties of human nature and becoming a full human being. They saw clearly that men were breadwinners but also that they were, or ought to be, something more: that a man might be a doctor or a lawyer or a shopkeeper or an artisan or a clerk, but that he was also a man, and that education should recognize this and help each individual to become, so far as his capacities allowed, what a man ought to be. That was the meaning of a liberal education, and that is its aim—the making of men; and clearly it is different from a technical education which simply enables us to earn our bread, but does not make us complete human beings.

And what is a complete human being? Again I shall take the Greek answer to this question. Human beings have bodies, minds and characters. Each of these is capable of what the Greeks called "virtue" *(ápetń)* or what we might call "excellence". The virtue or excellence of the body is health and fitness and strength, the firm and sensitive hand, the clear eye; the excellence of the mind is to know and to understand and to think, to have some idea of what the world is and of what man has done and has been and can be; the excellence of the character lies in the great virtues. This trinity of body, mind and character is man: man's aim, besides earning his living, is to make the most of all three, to have as good a mind, body and character as possible; and a liberal education, a free man's education, is to help him to this; not because a sound body, mind and character help to success, or even because they help to happiness, but because they are good things in themselves, and because what is good is worth while, simply because it is good. So we get that clear and important distinction between technical education which aims at earning a living or making money or at some narrowly practical skill, and the free man's education which aims at producing as perfect and complete a human being as may be.

This is not to despise technical education which is essential; everyone has to learn to make a living and to do his job, and he cannot do it without training: technical or vocational education is as much wanted as liberal education. But they are not to be confused. They are both important, both necessary, but they are different. And yet to some extent they overlap. Take French. A man may study it in order to be able to order his meals in a French restaurant, or for business purposes; then it is technical education. He, *as a man*, is no better for being able to talk to a French waiter, or to order goods in the French language. But he may study French to extend his knowledge of the thoughts and history and civilisation of great people; then it is liberal education. He, *as a man*, is more complete for that knowledge. Or take carpentering: its study may be a means to a living or to making furniture or boats or other objects; then it is technical education. But it may also give a clearer eye, a finer sense of touch, a more deft hand, and in so far make a better human being; then carpentering is liberal education. Or take Greek: it may be studied in order to get access to the wisdom and beauty of Greek literature; then it is liberal education. Or its student may have no interest in these things, but simply be taking it in order to get an extra credit in the School Certificate; then it is technical education—if it is anything. In fact as Aristotle remarked, "in education it makes all the difference *why* a man does or learns anything; if he studies it for the sake of his own development or with a view to excellence it is liberal".[1]

[1]*Politics*, viii, 2, 6.

This is the kind of education (without prejudice to others) which we want—that people should study "for the sake of their own development or with a view to excellence", so that they may become human beings in the Greek meaning of the words, and not remain mere business men, mere chemists or physicists, mere clerks, mere artisans or labourers. If so, we have a clue to the maze of education, a guide to choosing dishes from the educational menu. Whatever else we select to meet our personal tastes or needs, the dinner must include the vitamins necessary to human health, so that we achieve that liberal education which makes men fully developed, within the range of their individual capacities, in body, character and mind.

I shall only attempt to deal with a certain aspect of the liberal education of the mind (not that in practice it can be cut off cleanly from the other two). Here we enter an enormous field—that vast complex of related and unrelated subjects which fills the lecture lists of all the universities and the shelves of the libraries of the world. This is the food which the intellect produces and on which in turn it feeds. Yet this bewildering variety can be reduced under two heads—the study of the material universe, and the study of man as a sentient, thinking and spiritual being. The first of these consists in the sciences which study and attempt to explain the material universe through Astronomy, Physics, Chemistry, Botany, Geology, Geography, and those which study man regarded as a physical phenomenon through Anatomy, Biology, and the rest. Only scientists are competent to deal with the difficult problem of teaching these to the ordinary man. The elements of different sciences can be taught—thus biology and chemistry are taught in the Danish People's High Schools—but it is even more desirable to bring home to the student the meaning and importance of science in human life. That perhaps can best be done, historically by a description of the growth of science, and biographically by some account of great men of science, their personalities and their work. This brings us to the second great branch of knowledge, of which it is a part and which is usually called Humanism. Its subject is Man—man, viewed in himself and his proper nature, viewed as literature views him, as a being with feelings and prejudices, virtues and vices, ruled by intellect, or perverted by passion,

inspired by ideals, torn by desires, acting on plan and calcula-
tion or carried away by unreflecting emotion, sacrificing his
life now for gold and now for an idea, an adulterer, a patriot, a
glutton, a dreamer, AEgisthus, OEdipus, Hamlet, Macbeth,
Faust—or man, viewed as a being governed by the laws of a
universe outside him, viewed as philosophy views him, subject to limitations of time and space, of his own origin, nature
and destiny, related to beings and forces outside him, adapting
himself to those relations and modifying his action according
to his conception of them, a creature with moral capacities or
the descendant of an ape, determining his character and his
future according to his wishes, or merely one wheel among
many millions blindly revolving in a great machine: or,
thirdly, man viewed as a political and social being, as history
views him, creating states and overthrowing them, making
laws and refusing to be bound by them, opposing religion to
politics, and freedom to law, binding art and politics, empire
and freedom, public and private life into one harmonious
whole, or crowning one to the exclusion of the rest, fighting,
colonising, making money and spending it, treating his
neighbour as a fellow-being, or using him as a tool for the production of wealth, monarchist, parliamentarian, socialist,
anarchist, Pericles or Augustus, Cromwell or Robespierre.
Before the student of literature, philosophy, and history are
displayed *all* the forces and ideas that have governed man, personal, religious, or political; to see why he has rejected this and
espoused that, why this failed and that was successful, what
are liberty and religion, family affection and personal greed,
and, in a word, to study man. As he reviews them and com-
pares them with the present, he can see, as far as a man can
see, what ideas have come down to his own day, and what new
elements are combining with them, can forecast in some
degree the future, and by virtue of his knowledge guide the
streaming forces, and shape the molten mass, serve his country and use to the best advantage his own powers.

Robert Maynard Hutchins (1899-1977) received the A.B. and LL.B. degrees from Yale University. This academic preparation reflected the type of liberal education that he supported so eloquently throughout his life. After serving as secretary of Yale University and later as dean of the Law School, Robert Hutchins became president of the University of Chicago at the age of thirty. As president from 1929 to 1945, he instituted many innovative ideas such as eliminating course credit and compulsory attendance. Students elected to take comprehensive exams when they determined that they were ready to do so. Through such practices he hoped to develop thoughtful, independent learners. From 1945 to 1951 he was chancellor of the university and, after that, associate director of the Ford Foundation.

The following selection from The *Conflict in Education* (1953) was chosen to represent his many writings because it discusses the need for a liberal education. For Hutchins, a liberal education was the best way for people to "learn to think for themselves about the fundamental issues of human life and organized society." Pragmatism, Marxism, and positivism were inadequate frameworks for developing intellectual, moral, and spiritual beings because they all put too much emphasis on science, thus ignoring the past. There was more to be gained, he felt, from a study of history, philosophy, language, and literature.

In his final work, *The Learning Society* (1968), Hutchins envisioned a society where everyone would begin a liberal education in an educational institution and would continue to develop his or her intellect and character throughout life. In a true learning society, education would be the aim of society's institutions and of the culture itself.

ROBERT M. HUTCHINS

2 The Conflict in Education

Liberal education consists of training in the liberal arts and of understanding the leading ideas that have animated mankind. It aims to help the human being learn to think for himself, to develop his highest human powers. As I have said, it has never been denied that this education was the best for the best. It must still be the best for the best unless modern times, industry, science, and democracy have made it irrelevant. The social, political, and economic changes that have occurred have not required that liberal education be abandoned. How could they? It is still necessary to try to be human; in fact it is more necessary, as well as more difficult, than ever.

Liberal education was the education of rulers. It was the education of those who had leisure. Democracy and industry, far from making liberal education irrelevant, make it indispensable and possible for all the people. Democracy makes every man a ruler, for the heart of democracy is universal suffrage. If liberal education is the education that rulers ought to have, and this I say has never been denied, then every ruler, that is every citizen, should have a liberal education. If industry is to give everybody leisure, and if leisure, as history suggests, tends to be degrading and dangerous unless it is intelligently used, then everybody should have the education that fits him to use his leisure intelligently, that is, liberal education. If leisure makes liberal education possible, and if industry is to give everybody leisure, then industry makes liberal education possible for everybody.

In most countries, even those in which the education of adults is most highly developed, such education is thought of as compensatory: it makes up for the deficiencies in the formal schooling of the individual. Where formal schooling is vocational, adult education is vocational, too. Where schooling is liberal, as it has largely been in the United Kingdom and Scandinavia, adult education is liberal; for it is thought unjust and undesirable that those who because of the accidents of youth could not complete the formal schooling that the average citizen obtained in childhood and youth should remain without it all their lives.

But this surely is too limited a view of the education of adults. That education should be liberal, and it should be interminable. We are led to this conclusion by looking at the nature of man and the nature of knowledge. The man who stops learning is as good as dead, and the conditions of modern industrial society, which put little strain on a man's intelligence in the conduct of his work, place a premium on the premature cessation of thought. It is impossible to say that a man can develop his highest powers once and for all in youth. He has to keep on using them. I am not suggesting that he must go to school all his life. But I am proposing that he should learn all his life; and I think he will find that informal association with others who have the same purpose in view will help him and them to achieve it.

At a time when only the few were governors and only the few had leisure, liberal education was the education of the few. It has never been anything else. I hope I have shown that the experience of the United States does not prove that liberal education for all is impossible. I cannot refer to any experience to show that it is possible. I am sure that it is difficult. Aristotle remarked that learning is accompanied by pain. One reason why the philosophy of John Dewey as distorted by his followers remade American education in forty years is that the education it was thought to propose was relatively painless, both for the pupils and the teachers. The principal reason for the popularity in the United States of what is called Progressive Education, in which Mr. Dewey also had a hand, is that the children have a good time in school. In a child-centered society, like that of the United States, any effort to insist on painful work in school naturally encounters resistance.

I must admit also that where pragmatism and positivism hold sway, as they do in most of the West today, anything that I should regard as liberal education may be almost if not quite impossible. So it is impossible where Marxism is the dominant philosophy, and for many of the same reasons. I do not wish to resort to the doctrine of guilt by association in lumping pragmatism, positivism, and Marxism together. But they have at least these characteristics in common, characteristics that are fatal to liberal education in any definition of it that I can comprehend. They all repudiate the past. They all exaggerate the role of science and the scientific method, and appear to hold that the only way of obtaining valid knowledge is the way of experimental science. This of course reinforces the repudiation of the past, because experimental science is a recent phenomenon. Since the content of liberal education is the greatest ideas that the greatest men have had, regardless of the time at which they lived or the kind of society they lived in, and since the methods of liberal education include the methods of history, philosophy, and language as well as of science, liberal education can hardly arise in the face of pragmatism, positivism, or Marxism. Education is a secondary, dependent subject.

As to pragmatism, positivism, and Marxism, we may hope that they will gradually lose their power and that we may pass on to a coherent view of man as an intellectual, moral, spiritual being. Only if we get our philosophy straight can we think straight about education.

It will be said at once that even with a perfectly straight philosophy there are certain things we cannot do. We cannot make silk purses out of sows' ears, and the more accurately we think about the nature and potentialities of silk, purses, sows, and ears, the more clearly we shall see the impossibility of this task. And we may be told that even if the ears of certain sows are of a texture and consistency that seem to lend themselves to our experiment, the wide variations in the total volume of ears are such that to try to put them all through our silk purse factory on the same machinery will ruin all the ears without giving us any purses.

It is certainly one answer to this to say, as Stringfellow Barr once said, that he was not interested in a silk purse; all he wanted was a good, useful leather wallet. When I urge liberal education for all, I am not suggesting that all the people must become great philosophers, historians, scientists, or artists. I am saying that they should know how to read, write, and figure and that they should understand the great philosophers, historians, scientists, and artists. This does not seem to me an unattainable goal. If it is, unless some better kind of liberal education can be invented than the one that I have described, we shall be forced to abandon universal suffrage; for I do not believe that men can solve the problems raised by their own aggregation unless they can learn to think for themselves about the fundamental issues of human life and organized society. If anybody knows a better way of helping them learn to think for themselves about these issues, I hope he will present it. It seems to me that we must agree at least on this: the alternatives are democracy, with liberal education for all, and aristocracy, with liberal education for the few. If we choose the latter alternative, as Plato did, we may ignore, as Plato did, the education of the masses. All the educational system has to do with them is to find some innocuous way in which they can put in their time until we are ready to have them go to work.

Since education in the West is built very largely on the doctrine of individual differences, so that the study of the individual child and his individual interests is supposed to be the principal preoccupation of his teachers from his earliest days, and premature and excessive specialization is a common characteristic of both the American college and the British public school, it will be argued that a program of liberal education for all ignores the most important thing about men, and that is that they are different. I do not ignore it; I deny it. I do not deny the fact of individual differences; I deny that it is the most important fact about men or the one on which an educational system should be erected.

Men are different. They are also the same. And at least in the present state of civilization the respects in which they are the same are more important than those in which they are different. Politics, the architectonic science, teaches us that we are remorselessly headed toward the unification of the world. The only question is whether that unification will be achieved by conquest or consent. The most pressing task of men everywhere is to see to it that this consummation is achieved by consent. And this can be done only by the unremitting effort to move toward world community and world organization. The liberal arts are the arts of communication. The great productions of the human mind are the common heritage of all mankind. They supply the framework through which we understand one another and without which all factual data and area studies and exchanges of persons among countries are trivial and futile. They are the voices in the Great Conversation that constitutes the civilization of the dialogue.

Now, if ever, we need an education that is designed to bring out our common humanity rather than to indulge our individuality. Our individual differences mean that our individual development must vary. If we all struggle to make the most of our individual human powers, the results will be different, because our powers differ. But the difference is one of degree, and not of kind. In a modern, industrial, scientific democracy every man has the responsibility of a ruler and every man has the leisure to make the most of himself. What the modern, industrial, scientific democracy requires is wisdom. The aim of liberal education is wisdom. Every man has the duty and every man must have the chance to become as wise as he can.

Allan D. Bloom (1930–1992). At the age of nineteen, Allan Bloom received his B.A. in an accelerated Honors program from the University of Chicago in 1949. After receiving an M. A. in 1953, Bloom studied under noted philosopher Leo Strauss, earning his Ph.D. from the University of Chicago in 1955. Following postgraduate work at the University of Heidelberg, Bloom lectured in liberal arts, political science, government and philosophy at the University of Chicago, Yale University, Cornell University and the University of Toronto. Bloom was at Cornell University during the campus conflicts of 1969; he resigned in protest of the administration's failure to protect threatened professors when armed students occupied the administration building. Bloom returned to Chicago in 1979 and continued to distinguish himself with numerous awards, among them the Cornell Society for the Humanities Award in 1969, the Gugenheim Foundation Award in 1976, and the Prix Jean-Jacques Rouseau from the City of Geneva in 1987, for his classic, *The Closing of the American Mind: How Higher Education Has Failed Democracy and Impoverished the Souls of Today's Students* (1987).

Bloom was also translator and contributing author of Jean-Jacques Rousseau's *Politics and the Arts* and *Emile*, and translator and author of an interpretive essay in *The Republic of Plato*.

The book, *The Closing of the American Mind*, began as an article in the *National Review* in which he discussed the failures of American universities. As an impassioned philosopher and educator, Bloom believed that the universities' failure to uphold a traditional respect for liberal education has left us largely without the intellectual foundations necessary for the maintenance of justice, human rights, and other civil liberties. The book prompted a spirited educational and political debate as he argued that privileged college students, "who are most likely . . . to have the greatest moral and intellectual effect on the nation" are largely without the learning and moral judgment necessary to pursue that goal effectively.

ALLAN BLOOM

3 The Student and the University

LIBERAL EDUCATION

What image does a first-rank college or university present today to a teenager leaving home for the first time, off to the adventure of a liberal education? He has four years of freedom to discover himself—a space between the intellectual wasteland he has left behind and the inevitable dreary professional training that awaits him after the baccalaureate. In this short time he must learn that there is a great world beyond the little one he knows, experience the exhilaration of it and digest enough of it to sustain himself in the intellectual deserts he is destined to traverse. He must do this, that is, if he is to have any hope of a higher life. These are the charmed years when he can, if he so chooses, become anything he wishes and when he has the opportunity to survey his alternatives, not merely those current in his time or provided by careers, but those available to him as a human being. The importance of these years for an American cannot be overestimated. They are civilization's only chance to get to him.

In looking at him we are forced to reflect on what he should learn if he is to be called educated; we must speculate on what the human potential to be fulfilled is. In the specialties we can avoid such speculation, and the avoidance of them is one of specialization's charms. But here it is a simple duty. What are we to teach this person? The answer may not be evident, but to attempt to answer the question is already to philosophize and to begin to educate. Such a concern in itself poses the question of the unity of man and the unity of the sciences. It is childishness to say, as some do, that everyone must be allowed to develop freely, that it is authoritarian to impose a point of view on the student. In that case, why have a university? If the response is "to provide an atmosphere for learning," we come back to our original questions at the second remove. Which atmosphere? Choices and reflection on the reasons for those choices are unavoidable. The university has to stand for something. The practical effects of unwillingness to think positively about the contents of a liberal education are, on the one hand, to ensure that all the vulgarities of the world outside the university will flourish within it, and, on the other, to impose a much harsher and more illiberal necessity on the student—the one given by the imperial and imperious demands of the specialized disciplines unfiltered by unifying thought.

The university now offers no distinctive visage to the young person. He finds a democracy of the disciplines—which are there either because they are autochthonous or because they wandered in recently to perform some job that was demanded of the university. This democracy is really all anarchy, because there are no recognized rules for citizenship and no legitimate titles to rule. In short there is no vision, nor is there a set of competing visions, of what an educated human being is. The question has disappeared, for to pose it would be a threat to the peace. There is no organization of the sciences, no tree of knowledge. Out of chaos emerges dispiritedness, because it is impossible to make a reasonable choice. Better to give up on liberal education and get on with a specialty in which there is at least a prescribed curriculum and a prospective career. On the way the student can pick up in elective courses a little of whatever is thought to make one cultured. The student gets no intimation that great mysteries might be revealed to him, that new and higher motives of action might be discovered within him, that a different and more human way of life can be harmoniously constructed by what he is going to learn.

Simply, the university is not distinctive. Equality for us seems to culminate in the unwillingness and incapacity to make claims of superiority, particularly in the domains in which such claims have always been made—art, religion and philosophy. When Weber found that he could not choose between certain high opposites—reason vs. revelation, Buddha vs. Jesus—he did not conclude that all things are equally good, that the distinction between high and low disappears. As a matter of fact he intended to revitalize the consideration of these great alternatives in showing the gravity and danger involved in choosing among them; they were to be heightened in contrast to the trivial considerations of modern life that threatened to overgrow and render indistinguishable the profound problems the confrontation with which makes the bow of the soul taut. The serious intellectual life was for him the battleground of the great decisions, all of which are spiritual or "value" choices. One can no longer present this or that particular view of the educated or civilized man as authoritative; therefore one must say that education consists in knowing, really knowing, the small number of such views in their integrity. This distinction between profound and superficial— which takes the place of good and bad, true and false—provided a focus for serious study, but it hardly held out against the naturally relaxed democratic tendency to say, "Oh, what's the use?" The first university disruptions at Berkeley were explicitly directed against the multiversity smorgasbord and, I must confess, momentarily and partially engaged my sympathies. It may have even been the case that there was some small element of longing for an education in the motivation of those students. But nothing was done to guide or inform their energy, and the result was merely to add multilife-styles to multidisciplines, the diversity of perversity to the diversity of specialization. What we see so often happening in general happened here too; the insistent demand for greater community ended in greater isolation. Old agreements, old habits, old traditions were not so easily replaced.

Thus, when a student arrives at the university, he finds a bewildering variety of departments and a bewildering variety of courses. And there is no official guidance, no university-wide agreement, about what he *should* study. Nor does he usually find readily available examples, either among students or professors, of a unified use of the university's resources. It is easiest simply to make a career choice and go about getting prepared for that career. The programs designed for those having made such a choice render their students immune to charms that might lead them out of the conventionally respectable. The sirens sing *sotto voce* these days, and the young already have enough wax in their ears to pass them by without danger. These specialties can provide enough courses to take up most of their time for four years in preparation for the inevitable graduate study. With the few remaining courses they can do what they please, taking a bit of this and a bit of that. No public career these days—not doctor nor lawyer nor politician nor journalist nor businessman nor entertainer—has much to do with humane learning. An education, other than purely professional or technical, can even seem to be an impediment. That is why a countervailing atmosphere in the university would be necessary for the students to gain a taste for intellectual pleasures and learn that they are viable.

The real problem, is those students who come hoping to find out what career they want to have, or are simply looking for an adventure with themselves. There are plenty of things for them to do—courses and disciplines enough to spend many a lifetime on. Each department or great division of the university makes a pitch for itself, and each offers a course of study that will make the student an initiate. But how to choose among them? How do they relate to one another? The fact is they do not address one another. They are competing and contradictory, without being aware of it. The problem of the whole is urgently indicated by the very existence of the specialties, but it is never systematically posed. The net effect of the student's encounter with the college catalogue is bewilderment and very often demoralization. It is just a matter of chance whether he finds one or two professors who can give him an insight into one of the great visions of education that have been the distinguishing part of every civilized nation. Most professors are specialists, concerned only with their own fields, interested in the advancement of those fields in their own terms, or in their own personal advancement in a world where all the rewards are on the side of professional distinction. They have been entirely emancipated from the old structure of the university, which at least helped to indicate that they are incomplete, only parts of an unexamined and undiscovered whole. So the student must navigate among a collection of carnival barkers, each trying to lure him into a particular sideshow. This undecided student is an embarrassment to most universities, because he seems to be saying, "I am a whole human being. Help me to form myself in my wholeness and let me develop my real potential," and he is the one to whom they have nothing to say.

Cornell was, as in so many other things, in advance of its time on this issue. The six-year Ph.D. program, richly supported by the Ford Foundation, was directed specifically to high school students who had already made "a firm career choice" and was intended to rush them through to the start of those careers. A sop was given to desolate humanists in the form of money to fund seminars that these young careerists could take on their way through the College of Arts and Sciences. For the rest, the educators could devote their energies to arranging and packaging the program without having to provide it with any substance. That kept them busy enough to avoid thinking about the nothingness of their endeavor. This has been the preferred mode of not looking the Beast in the

Jungle in the face—structure, not content. The Cornell plan for dealing with the problem of liberal education was to suppress the students' longing for liberal education by encouraging their professionalism and their avarice, providing money and all the prestige the university had available to make careerism the centerpiece of the university.

The Cornell plan dared not state the radical truth, a well-kept secret: the colleges do not have enough to teach their students, not enough to justify keeping them four years, probably not even three years. If the focus is careers, there is hardly one specialty, outside the hardest of the hard natural sciences, which requires more than two years of preparatory training prior to graduate studies. The rest is just wasted time, or a period of ripening until the students are old enough for graduate studies. For many graduate careers, even less is really necessary. It is amazing how many undergraduates are poking around for courses to take, without any plan or question to ask, just filling up their college years. In fact, with rare exceptions, the courses are parts of specialties and not designed for general cultivation, or to investigate questions important for human beings as such. The so-called knowledge explosion and increasing specialization have not filled up the college years but emptied them. Those years are impediments; one wants to get beyond them. And in general the persons one finds in the professions need not have gone to college, if one is to judge by their tastes, their fund of learning or their interests. They might as well have spent their college years in the Peace Corps or the like. These great universities—which can split the atom, find cures for the most terrible diseases, conduct surveys of whole populations and produce massive dictionaries of lost languages—cannot generate a modest program of general education for undergraduate students. This is a parable for our times.

There are attempts to fill the vacuum painlessly with various kinds of fancy packaging of what is already there—study abroad options, individualized majors, etc. Then there are Black Studies and Women's or Gender Studies, along with Learn Another Culture. Peace Studies are on their way to a similar prevalence. All this is designed to show that the university is with it and has something in addition to its traditional specialties. The latest item is computer literacy, the full cheapness of which is evident only to those who think a bit about what literacy might mean. It would make some sense to promote literacy, inasmuch as most high school graduates nowadays have difficulty reading and writing. And some institutions are quietly undertaking this worthwhile task. But they do not trumpet the fact, because this is merely a high school function that our current sad state of educational affairs has thrust upon them, about which they are not inclined to boast.

Now that the distractions of the sixties are over, and undergraduate education has become more important again (because the graduate departments, aside from the professional schools, are in trouble due to the shortage of academic jobs), university officials have had somehow to deal with the undeniable fact that the students who enter are uncivilized, and that the universities have some responsibility for civilizing them. If one were to give a base interpretation of the schools' motives, one could allege that their concern stems from shame and self-interest. It is becoming all too evident that liberal education—which is what the small band of prestigious institutions are supposed to provide, in contrast to the big state schools, which are thought simply to prepare specialists to meet the practical demands of a complex society—has no content, that a certain kind of fraud is being perpetrated. For a time the great moral consciousness alleged to have been fostered in students by the great universities, especially their vocation as gladiators who fight war and racism, seemed to fulfill the demands of the collective university conscience. They were doing something other than offering preliminary training for doctors and lawyers. Concern and compassion were thought to be the indefinable X that pervaded all the parts of the Arts and Sciences campus. But when that evanescent dissipated during the seventies, and the faculties found themselves face to face with ill-educated young people with no intellectual tastes—unaware that there even are such things, obsessed with getting on with their careers before having looked at life—and the universities offered no counterpoise, no alternative goals, a reaction set in.

Liberal education—since it has for so long been ill-

defined, has none of the crisp clarity or institutionalized prestige of the professions, but nevertheless perseveres and has
money and respectability connected with it—has always been
a battleground for those who are somewhat eccentric in relation to the specialties. It is in something like the condition
of churches as opposed to, say, hospitals. Nobody is quite certain of what the religious institutions are supposed to do anymore, but they do have some kind of role either responding
to a real human need or as the vestige of what was once a
need, and they invite the exploitation of quacks, adventurers,
cranks and fanatics. But they also solicit the warmest and most
valiant efforts of persons of peculiar gravity and depth. In liberal education, too, the worst and the best fight it out, fakers
vs. authentics, sophists vs. philosophers, for the favor of public
opinion and for control over the study of man in our times.
The most conspicuous participants in the struggle are administrators who are formally responsible for presenting some
kind of public image of the education their colleges offer, persons with a political agenda or vulgarizers of what the specialties know, and real teachers of the humane disciplines who
actually see their relation to the whole and urgently wish to
preserve the awareness of it in their students' consciousness.

So, just as in the sixties universities were devoted to re-
moving requirements, in the eighties they are busy with attempts to put tbem back in, a much more difficult task. The
word of the day is "core." It is generally agreed that "we went
a bit far in the sixties," and that a little fine-tuning has now
become clearly necessary.

There are two typical responses to the problem. The easiest and most administratively satisfying solution is to make
use of what is already there in the autonomous departments
and simply force the students to cover the fields, i.e., take one
or more courses in each of the general divisions of the university: natural science, social science and the humanities. The
reigning ideology here is *breadth*, as was *openness* in the age
of laxity. The courses are almost always the already existing
introductory courses, which are of least interest to the major
professors and merely assume the worth and reality of that
which is to be studied. It is general education, in the sense
in which a jack-of-all-trades is a generalist. He knows a bit

of everything and is inferior to the specialist in each area. Students may wish to sample a variety of fields, and it may be good to encourage them to look around and see if there is something that attracts them in one of which they have no experience. But this is not a liberal education and does not satisfy any longing they have for one. It just teaches that there is no high-level generalism, and that what they are doing is preliminary to the real stuff and part of the childhood they are leaving behind. Thus they desire to get it over with and get on with what their professors do seriously. Without recognition of important questions of common concern, there cannot be serious liberal education, and attempts to establish it will be but failed gestures.

It is a more or less precise awareness of the inadequacy of this approach to core curricula that motivates the second approach, which consists of what one might call composite courses. These are constructions developed especially for general-education purposes and usually require collaboration of professors drawn from several departments. These courses have titles like "Man in Nature," "War and Moral Responsibility," "The Arts and Creativity," "Culture and the Individual." Everything, of course, depends upon who plans them and who teaches them. They have the clear advantage of requiring some reflection on the general needs of students and force specialized professors to broaden their perspectives, at least for a moment. The dangers are trendiness, mere popularization and lack of substantive rigor. In general, the natural scientists do not collaborate in such endeavors, and hence these courses tend to be unbalanced. In short, they do not point beyond themselves and do not provide the student with independent means to pursue permanent questions independently, as, for example, the study of Aristotle or Kant as wholes once did. They tend to be bits of this and that. Liberal education should give the student the sense that learning must and can be both synoptic and precise. For this, a very small, detailed problem can be the best way, if it is framed so as to open out on the whole. Unless the course has the specific intention to lead to the permanent questions, to make the student aware of them and give him some competence in the important works that treat of them, it tends to be a pleasant diversion and a dead

end—because it has nothing to do with any program of further
study he can imagine. If such programs engage the best energies of the best people in the university, they can be bene-
ficial and provide some of the missing intellectual excitement
for both professors and students. But they rarely do, and they
are too cut off from the top, from what the various faculties
see as their real business. Where the power is determines the
life of the whole body. And the intellectual problems unre-
solved at the top cannot be resolved administratively below.
The problem is the lack of any unity of the sciences and the
loss of the will or the means even to discuss the issue. The
illness above is the cause of the illness below, to which all
the good-willed efforts of honest liberal educationists can at
best be palliatives.

Of course, the only serious solution is the one that is
almost universally rejected: the good old Great Books approach, in which a liberal education means reading certain
generally recognized classic texts, just reading them, letting
them dictate what the questions are and the method of ap-
proaching them—not forcing them into categories we make
up, not treating them as historical products, but trying to read
them as their authors wished them to be read. I am perfectly
well aware of, and actually agree with, the objections to the
Great Books cult. It is amateurish; it encourages an autodi-
dact's self-assurance without competence; one cannot read all
of the Great Books carefully; if one only reads Great Books,
one can never know what a great, as opposed to an ordinary,
book is; there is no way of determining who is to decide what
a Great Book or what the canon is; books are made the ends
and not the means; the whole movement has a certain coarse
evangelistic tone that is the opposite of good taste; it engenders
a spurious intimacy with greatness; and so forth. But one thing
is certain: wherever the Great Books make up a central part
of the curriculum, the students are excited and satisfied, feel
they are doing something that is independent and fulfilling,
getting something from the university they cannot get elsewhere. The very fact of this special experience, which leads
nowhere beyond itself, provides them with a new alternative
and a respect for study itself. The advantage they get is an
awareness of the classic—particularly important for our inno-

cents; an acquaintance with what big questions were when there were still big questions; models, at the very least, of how to go about answering them; and, perhaps most important of all, a fund of shared experiences and thoughts on which to ground their friendships with one another. Programs based upon judicious use of great texts provide the royal road to students' hearts. Their gratitude at learning of Achilles or the categorical imperative is boundless. Alexandre Koyré, the late historian of science, told me that his appreciation for America was great when—in the first course he taught at the University of Chicago, in 1940 at the beginning of his exile—a student spoke in his paper of Mr. Aristotle, unaware that he was not a contemporary. Koyré said that only an American could have the naive profundity to take Aristotle as living thought, unthinkable for most scholars. A good program of liberal education feeds the student's love of truth and passion to live a good life. It is the easiest thing in the world to devise courses of study, adapted to the particular conditions of each university, which thrill those who take them. The difficulty is in getting them accepted by the faculty.

None of the three great parts of the contemporary university is enthusiastic about the Great Books approach to education. The natural scientists are benevolent toward other fields and toward liberal education, if it does not steal away their students and does not take too much time from their preparatory studies. But they themselves are interested primarily in the solution of the questions now important in their disciplines and are not particularly concerned with discussions of their foundations, inasmuch as they are so evidently successful. They are indifferent to Newton's conception of time or his disputes with Leibniz about calculus; Aristotle's teleology is an absurdity beneath consideration. Scientific progress, they believe, no longer depends on the kind of comprehensive reflection given to the nature of science by men like Bacon, Descartes, Hume, Kant and Marx. This is merely historical study, and for a long time now, even the greatest scientists have given up thinking about Galileo and Newton. Progress is undoubted. The difficulties about the truth of science raised by positivism, and those about the goodness of science raised by Rousseau and Nietzsche, have not really penetrated to the center of scientific consciousness. Hence, no Great Books, but incremental progress, is the theme for them.

Social scientists are in general hostile, because the classic texts tend to deal with the human things the social sciences deal with, and they are very proud of having freed themselves from the shackles of such earlier thought to become truly scientific. And, unlike the natural scientists, they are insecure enough about their achievement to feel threatened by the works of earlier thinkers, perhaps a bit afraid that students will be seduced and fall back into the bad old ways. Moreover, with the possible exception of Weber and Freud, there are no social science books that can be said to be classic. This may be interpreted favorably to the social sciences by comparing them to the natural sciences, which can be said to be a living organism developing by the addition of little cells, a veritable body of knowledge proving itself to be such by the very fact of this almost unconscious growth, with thousands of parts oblivious to the whole, nevertheless contributing to it. This is in opposition to a work of imagination or of philosophy, where a single creator makes and surveys an artificial whole. But whether one interprets the absence of the classic in the social sciences in ways flattering or unflattering to them, the fact causes social scientists discomfort. I remember the professor who taught the introductory graduate courses in social science methodology, a famous historian, responding scornfully and angrily to a question I naively put to him about Thucydides with "Thucydides was a fool!"

More difficult to explain is the tepid reaction of humanists to Great Books education, inasmuch as these books now belong almost exclusively to what are called the humanities. One would think that high esteem for the classic would reinforce the spiritual power of the humanities, at a time when their temporal power is at its lowest. And it is true that the most active proponents of liberal education and the study of classic texts are indeed usually humanists. But there is division among them. Some humanities disciplines are just crusty specialties that, although they depend on the status of classic books for their existence, are not really interested in them in their natural state—much philology, for example, is concerned with the languages but not what is said in them—and will and can do nothing to support their own infrastructure. Some humanities disciplines are eager to join the real sciences and transcend their roots in the now overcome mythic past. Some humanists make the legitimate complaints about lack of competence in the teaching and learning of Great Books, although their criticism is frequently undermined by the fact that they are only defending recent scholarly interpretation of the classics rather than a vital, authentic understanding. In their reaction there is a strong element of specialist's jealousy and narrowness. Finally, a large part of the story is just the general debilitation of the humanities, which is both symptom and cause of our present condition.

To repeat, the crisis of liberal education is a reflection of a crisis at the peaks of learning, an incoherence and incompatibility among the first principles with which we interpret the world, an intellectual crisis of the greatest magnitude, which constitutes the crisis of our civilization. But perhaps it would be true to say that the crisis consists not so much in this incoherence but in our incapacity to discuss or even recognize it. Liberal education flourished when it prepared the way for the discussion of a unified view of nature and man's place in it, which the best minds debated on the highest level. It decayed when what lay beyond it were only specialties, the premises of which do not lead to any such vision. The highest is the partial intellect; there is no synopsis.

Often called the dean of twentieth-century American education, John Dewey (1859–1952) had a profound impact upon education worldwide. After receiving a Ph.D. from The John Hopkins University, he taught philosophy at several universities and headed the Department of Philosophy and Education at the University of Chicago before moving to Columbia University in 1904. He retired from Columbia in 1930 but continued to write and lecture until his death in 1952.

John Dewey wrote voluminously in the areas of philosophy, psychology, and education. He was also actively involved in professional organizations and social reform. He was founder and president of the American Association of University Professors, a charter member of New York City's first teacher's union, and a founder of the New School for Social Research.

As the chief proponent of pragmatism and progressive thought, Dewey's ideas brought about major changes in educational theory and practice. In perhaps his most famous book, *Democracy and Education* (1916), Dewey assigns education a prominent role in bringing about social change. Democracy and education are interdependent and by their nature lead to individual development and social growth. Progressive education also entails focusing upon the learners' needs and interests, incorporating practical as well as liberal subjects into the curriculum, and defining education as the interaction of experience with the environment. In the selection from *Experience and Education* (1938), Dewey discusses the critical role of the learner's experiences. In advocating the use of these experiences as the starting point for instruction, Dewey echoes a major tenet of contemporary adult education. The development of the intellectual content of experiences, which was the goal of progressive education, was best achieved, in his opinion, through the experimental method of science.

JOHN DEWEY

4 Experience and Education

It is hardly necessary to insist upon the first of the two conditions which have been specified. It is a cardinal precept of the newer school of education that the beginning of instruction shall be made with the experience learners already have; that this experience and the capacities that have been developed during its course provide the starting point for all further learning. I am not so sure that the other condition, that of orderly development toward expansion and organization of subject-matter through growth of experience, receives as much attention. Yet the principle of continuity of educative experience requires that equal thought and attention be given to solution of this aspect of the educational problem. Undoubtedly this phase of the problem is more difficult than the other. Those who deal with the pre-school child, with the kindergarten child, and with the boy and girl of the early primary years do not have much difficulty in determining the range of past experience or in finding activities that connect in vital ways with it. With older children both factors of the problem offer increased difficulties to the educator. It is harder to find out the background of the experience of individuals and harder to find out just how the subject-matters already contained in that experience shall be directed so as to lead out to larger and better organized fields . . . .

Unless the problem of intellectual organization can be worked out on the ground of experience, reaction is sure to occur toward externally imposed methods of organization. There are signs of this reaction already in evidence. We are told that our schools, old and new, are failing in the main task. They do not develop, it is said, the capacity for critical discrimination and the ability to reason. The ability to think is smothered, we are told, by accumulation of miscellaneous ill-digested information, and by the attempt to acquire forms of skill which will be immediately useful in the business and commercial world. We are told that these evils spring from the influence of science and from the magnification of present requirements at the expense of the tested cultural heritage from the past. It is argued that science and its method must be subordinated; that we must return to the logic of ultimate first principles expressed in the logic of Aristotle and St. Thomas, in order that the young may have sure anchorage in their intellectual and moral life, and not be at the mercy of every passing breeze that blows.

If the method of science had ever been consistently and continuously applied throughout the day-by-day work of the school in all subjects, I should be more impressed by this emotional appeal than I am. I see at bottom but two alternatives between which education must choose if it is not to drift aimlessly. One of them is expressed by the attempt to induce educators to return to the intellectual methods and ideals that arose centuries before scientific method was developed. The appeal may be temporarily successful in a period when general insecurity, emotional and intellectual as well as economic, is rife. For under these conditions the desire to lean on fixed authority is active. Nevertheless, it is so out of touch with all the conditions of modern life that I believe it is folly to seek salvation in this direction. The other alternative is systematic utilization of scientific method as the pattern and ideal of intelligent exploration and exploitation of the potentialities inherent in experience.

The problem involved comes home with peculiar force to progressive schools. Failure to give constant attention to development of the intellectual content of experiences and to obtain ever-increasing organization of facts and ideas may in the end merely strengthen the tendency toward a reactionary return to intellectual and moral authoritarianism. The present is not the time nor place for a disquisition upon scientific method. But certain features of it are so closely connected with any educational scheme based upon experience that they should be noted.

In the first place, the experimental method of science attaches more importance, not less, to ideas as ideas than do other methods. There is no such thing as experiment in the scientific sense unless action is directed by some leading idea. The fact that the ideas employed are hypotheses, not final truths, is the reason why ideas are more jealously guarded and tested in science than anywhere else. The moment they are taken to be first truths in themselves there ceases to be any reason for scrupulous examination of them. As fixed truths they must be accepted and that is the end of the matter. But as hypotheses, they must be continuously tested and revised, a requirement that demands they be accurately formulated.

In the second place, ideas or hypotheses are tested by the consequences which they produce when they are acted upon. This fact means that the consequences of action must be carefully and discriminatingly observed. Activity that is not checked by observation of what follows from it may be temporarily enjoyed. But intellectually it leads nowhere. It does not provide knowledge about the situations in which action occurs nor does it lead to clarification and expansion of ideas.

In the third place, the method of intelligence manifested in the experimental method demands keeping track of ideas, activities, and observed consequences. Keeping track is a matter of reflective review and summarizing, in which there is both discrimination and record of the significant features of a developing experience. To reflect is to look back over what has been done so as to extract the net meanings which are the capital stock for intelligent dealing with further experiences. It is the heart of intellectual organization and of the disciplined mind.

I have been forced to speak in general and often abstract language. But what has been said is organically connected with the requirement that experiences in order to be educative must lead out into an expanding world of subject-matter, a subject-matter of facts or information and of ideas. This condition is satisfied only as the educator views teaching and learning as a continuous process of reconstruction of experience. This condition in turn can be satisfied only as the educator has a long look ahead, and views every present experience as a moving force in influencing what future experiences will be. I am aware that the emphasis I have placed upon scientific method may be misleading, for it may result only in calling up the special technique of laboratory research as that is conducted by specialists. But the meaning of the emphasis placed upon scientific method has little to do with specialized techniques. It means that scientific method is the only authentic means at our command for getting at the significance of our everyday experiences of the world in which we live. It means that scientific method provides a working pattern of the way in which and the conditions under which experiences are used to lead ever onward and outward. Adaptation of the method to individuals of various degrees of maturity is a problem for the educator, and the constant factors in the problem are the formation of ideas, acting upon ideas, observation of the conditions which result, and organization of facts and ideas for future use. Neither the ideas, nor the activities, nor the observations, nor the organization are the same for a person six years old as they are for one twelve or eighteen years old, to say nothing of the adult scientist. But at every level there is an expanding development of experience if experience is educative in effect. Consequently, whatever the level of experience, we have no choice but either to operate in accord with the pattern it provides or else to neglect the place of intelligence in the development and control of a living and moving experience.

Social philosopher, educator, activist, scholar—these are words that help to define the life of Eduard C. Lindeman (1885–1953). With a B.A. from Michigan Agricultural College, Lindeman spent his early career as a state extension director of 4-H in Michigan and as an instructor of rural sociology at a YMCA college in Illinois. His first book, *Social Discovery: An Approach to the Study of Functional Groups*, which was published in 1924, led to a faculty position in social philosophy at the New York School of Social Work. He held this position until his retirement in 1950.

Lindeman became well known through his teaching, writing, and work with numerous citizens' organizations including the Urban League, the American Civil Liberties Union, Association of American Indian Affairs—and professional associations such as the American Association for Adult Education. In the late 1930s he also served as director of the Department of Community Organization for Leisure in the Works Progress Administration.

A lifelong interest in adult education began with his early work with the YMCA and cooperative extension. Soon after his appointment to the School of Social Work, Lindeman wrote *The Meaning of Adult Education*. Widely read more than half a century after its publication in 1926, this seminal work reflects progressive education's faith in education's ability to develop individual and social intelligence, that is, the practical understanding of the world in which we live. In the chapter presented here, Lindeman discusses the assumptions underlying his view of adult education: (1) adult education is inclusive of all aspects of life; (2) "its purpose is to put meaning into the whole of life"; (3) the approach should be through real life situations, not subjects; and (4) the learner's experiences should be the resources for learning.

EDUARD C. LINDEMAN

5 For Those Who Need To Be Learners

EDUCATION conceived as preparation for life locks the learning process within a vicious circle. Youth educated in terms of adult ideas and taught to think of learning as a process which ends when real life begins will make no better use of intelligence than the elders who prescribe the system. Brief and rebellious moments occur when youth sees this fallacy clearly, but alas, the pressure of adult civilization is too great; in the end young people fit into the pattern, succumb to the tradition of their elders—indeed, become elderly-minded before their time. Education within the vicious circle becomes not a joyous enterprise but rather something to be endured because it leads to a satisfying end. But there can be no genuine joy in the end if means are irritating, painful. Generally therefore those who have "completed" a standardized regimen of education promptly turn their faces in the opposite direction. Humor, but more of pathos lurks in the caricature of the college graduate standing in cap and gown, diploma in hand, shouting: "Educated, b'gosh!" Henceforth, while devoting himself to life, he will think of education as a necessary annoyance for succeeding youths. For him, this life for which he has suffered the affliction of learning will come to be a series of dull, uninteresting, degrading capitulations to the stereotyped pattern of his "set". Within a single decade he will be out of touch with the world of intelligence, or what is worse, he will still be using the intellectual coins of his college days; he will find difficulty in reading serious books; he will have become inured to the jargon of his particular profession and will affect derision for all "highbrows"; he will, in short, have become a typical adult who holds the bag of education—the game of learning having long since slipped by him.

Obviously, extension of the quantity of educational facilities cannot break the circle. Once the belief was current that if only education were free to all intelligence would become the proper tool for managing the affairs of the world. We have gone even further and have made certain levels of education compulsory. But the result has been disappointing; we have succeeded merely in formalizing, mechanizing, educational processes. The spirit and meaning of education cannot be enhanced by addition, by the easy method of giving the same dose to more individuals. If learning is to be revivified, quickened so as to become once more an adventure, we shall have need of new concepts, new motives, new methods; we shall need to experiment with the qualitative aspects of education.

A fresh hope is astir. From many quarters comes the call to a new kind of education with its initial assumption affirming that *education is life*—not a mere preparation for an unknown kind of future living. Consequently all static concepts of education which relegate the learning process to the period of youth are abandoned. The whole of life is learning, therefore education can have no endings. This new venture is called *adult education*—not because it is confined to adults but because adulthood, maturity, defines its limits. The concept is inclusive. The fact that manual workers of Great Britain and farmers of Denmark have conducted the initial experiments which now inspire us does not imply that adult education is designed solely for these classes. No one, probably, needs adult education so much as the college graduate for it is he who makes the most doubtful assumptions concerning the function of learning.

Secondly, education conceived as a process coterminous with life revolves about *non-vocational* ideals. In this world of specialists every one will of necessity learn to do his work, and if education of any variety can assist in this and in the further end of helping the worker to see the meaning of his labor, it will be education of a high order. But adult education more accurately defined begins where vocational education leaves off. Its purpose is to put meaning into the whole of life. Workers, those who perform essential services, will naturally discover more values in continuing education than will those for whom all knowledge is merely decorative or conversational. The possibilities of enriching the activities of labor itself grow less for all workers who manipulate automatic machines. If the good life, the life interfused with meaning and with joy, is to come to these, opportunities for expressing more of the total personality than is called forth by machines will be needed. Their lives will be quickened into creative activities in proportion as they learn to make fruitful use of leisure.

Thirdly, the approach to adult education will be via the route of *situations*, not subjects. Our academic system has grown in reverse order: subjects and teachers constitute the starting-point, students are secondary. In conventional education the student is required to adjust himself to an established curriculum; in adult education the curriculum is built around the student's needs and interests. Every adult person finds himself in specific situations with respect to his work, his recreation, his family-life, his community-life, et cetera—situations which call for adjustments. Adult education begins at this point. Subject-matter is brought into the situation, is put to work, when needed. Texts and teachers play a new and second-

ary role in this type of education; they must give way to the
primary importance of the learner. (Indeed, as we shall see
later, the teacher of adults becomes also a learner.) The
situation-approach to education means that the learning process
is at the outset given a setting of reality. Intelligence performs
its function in relation to actualities, not abstractions.

In the fourth place, the resource of highest value in adult
education is the *learner's experience*. If education is life, then
life is also education. Too much of learning consists of
vicarious substitution of some one else's experience and
knowledge. Psychology is teaching us, however, that we learn
what we do, and that therefore all genuine education will keep
doing and thinking together. Life becomes rational, meaningful as we learn to be intelligent about the things that happen to us. If we lived sensibly, we should all discover that the
attractions of experience increase as we grow older.
Correspondingly, we should find cumulative joys in searching
out the reasonable meaning of the events in which we play
parts. In teaching children it may be necessary to anticipate objective experience by uses of imagination but adult experience
is already there waiting to be appropriated. Experience is the
adult learner's living textbook.

Authoritative teaching, examinations which preclude
original thinking, rigid pedagogical formulae—all of these have
no place in adult education. "Friends educating each other,"
says Yeaxlee,[2] and perhaps Walt Whitman saw accurately with
his fervent democratic vision what the new educational experiment implied when he wrote: "learn from the simple—teach
the wise." Small groups of aspiring adults who desire to keep
their minds fresh and vigorous; who begin to learn by confronting pertinent situations; who dig down into the reservoirs of
their experience before resorting to texts and secondary facts;
who are led in the discussion by teachers who are also searchers
after wisdom and not oracles: this constitutes the setting for
adult education, the modern quest for life's meaning.

But where does one search for life's meaning? If adult
education is not to fall into the pitfalls which have vulgarized
public education, caution must be exercised in striving for
answers to this query. For example, once the assumption is
made that human nature is uniform, common and static—that

[2]B.A. Yeaxlee, *Spiritual Values in Adult Education:* 2 volumes Oxford University
Press, 1925.

all human beings will find meaning in identical goals, ends or aims—the standardizing process begins: teachers are trained according to orthodox and regulated methods; they teach prescribed subjects to large classes of children who must all pass the same examination; in short, if we accept the standard of uniformity, it follows that we expect, e.g., mathematics, to mean as much to one student as to another. Teaching methods which proceed from this assumption must necessarily become autocratic; if we assume that all values and meanings apply equally to all persons, we may then justify ourselves in using a forcing-method of teaching. On the other hand, if we take for granted that human nature is varied, changing and fluid, we will know that life's meanings are conditioned by the individual. We will then entertain a new respect for personality.

Since the individual personality is not before us we are driven to generalization. In what areas do most people appear to find life's meaning? We have only one pragmatic guide: meaning must reside in the things for which people strive, the goals which they set for themselves, their wants, needs, desires and wishes. Even here our criterion is applicable only to those whose lives are already dedicated to aspirations and ambitions which belong to the highest levels of human achievement. The adult able to break the habits of slovenly mentality and willing to devote himself seriously to study when study no longer holds forth the lure of pecuniary gain is, one must admit, a personality in whom many negative aims and desires have already been eliminated. Under examination, and viewed from the standpoint of adult education, and viewed from the standpoint of adult education, such personalities seem to want among other things, intelligence, power, self-expression, freedom, creativity, appreciation, enjoyment, fellowship. Or, stated in terms of the Greek ideal, they are searchers after the good life. They want to count for something; they want their experiences to be vivid and meaningful; they want their talents to be utilized; they want to know beauty and joy; and they want all of these realizations of their total personalities to be shared in communities of fellowship. Briefly they want to improve themselves; this is their realistic and primary aim. But they want also to change the social order so that vital personalities will be creating a new environment in which their aspirations may be properly expressed.

At the time of his death, Paul Bergevin (1906–1993) was professor emeritus of Adult Education at Indiana University, Bloomington, Indiana. His B.S. and M.S. degrees were in economics from Purdue University and he held an Ed.D. in adult education from Indiana University. His career in teaching and writing included being a visiting professor at Cornell University, Florida State University, Helsinki University, and University of Missouri. In addition, he was a consultant in adult education to the Egyptian government, the U.S. Catholic Conference, and the Madison State Hospital in Madison, Indiana.

His interests in the field of adult education centered on how adult learning is affected by physiological and psychological changes through the life span, religious adult education, education of the mentally disturbed adult, and the philosophy of adult education. With colleague John McKinley, he developed a model, referred to as participation training, for training people to participate actively in the learning experience. Their book, *Participation Training for Adult Education*, outlines the processes involved in the model.

In the following selection from another of Bergevin's books, *A Philosophy for Adult Education* (1967), the author discusses the relationship between a democratic society and adult education. Like Lindeman and Dewey, Bergevin saw adult education as having the dual goals of personal development and social progress. In his words, adult education contributes to the "civilizing process" both individually and socially. That is, the civilizing process for an individual involves movement toward being "a responsible member of the social order." For a society, the process is a "corporate, social movement involving the whole of society, as it moves from barbarism toward refinement in behavior, tastes, and thought."

PAUL BERGEVIN

6 The Adult, His Society, and Adult Education: An Overview

Our environment and the way we relate to it have much to do with making us the kind of persons we are. Talking with others, listening to the radio, watching television, reading, attending formal classes and lectures, traveling, even getting bawled out by the boss—all these experiences leave their marks on us and change us in one way or another. It is difficult to think of anything we do that does not either encourage our development toward maturity or thwart it.

The term "maturity" is used here to mean the growth and development of the individual toward wholeness in order to achieve constructive spiritual, vocational, physical, political, and cultural goals. A maturing person is continually advancing toward understanding and constructive action in the movement from mere survival (the state of lower animals) to the discovery of himself both as a person and as a responsible member of the social order.

1. THE CIVILIZING PROCESS

This action of the environment through society on the individual becomes, when positive, what we call the civilizing process. This developmental and evolutionary activity of society continually exposes us to the best of traditional and contemporary social experiences and teaches us how to relate to one another with understanding, dignity, and love. It should promote mature rationality in the lives of each of us and in our institutions.

The civilizing process is a corporate, social movement involving the whole of society, as it moves from barbarism toward refinement in behavior, tastes, and thought. It is also an evolutionary movement, one aimed toward further discovery and implementation of the human capabilities that will help us realize the kind of happiness achieved through "the pursuit of excellence," which Aristotle prescribes for "the good life."

An individual cannot really become a person outside the social order. The civilizing process contributes to the maturing individual and he, in turn, shares with others in making the civilizing process possible. This personal development contributes to the forward thrust of the civilizing process, making it a truly social movement. It also helps realize the corporate, social potential of the maturation process.

If an adult is to contribute to the civilizing process, he must know the direction in which society is moving in specific as well as in broad terms. As far as he is able, he must know what society is, what its general objectives are, and what he can do—culturally, vocationally, physically, politically, or spiritually—to assist in maintaining and furthering social objectives. He must also be aware of the responsibility society has for the individual, and the individual for society. This view is based on the assumption, supported in this book, that the individual is a member of a society that struggles to release him from his external as well as his self-imposed limitations and restrictions. Sometimes individuals do not wait for society to release them from these limitations, but they try to release themselves and others by assuming responsibility for disciplined and intelligent social action. On the other hand, there are always influences that retard the growth and progress of individuals and society. Again, some of these influences may be self-imposed, others may be social. Sometimes it is hard to distinguish one type from another.

Such things as value systems, the corporate nature of society, personal responsibility and privilege, and the nature of the individual and the group must be understood and dealt with by each of us according to his ability. No person can feel free from the responsibility of trying to extract some meaning from these terms. Those who are "educated" or in positions of educational, political, ecclesiastical, or economic authority are not solely responsible for carrying the full load. It would be undesirable if they did. History has many illustrations of people failing to assume responsibility in their role as thoughtful citizens. Such failures usually result in calls for quick action, and the ever-ready demagogue pops up to speed the process of political and social change.

Therefore, we as adults need to know. We need to act intelligently on what we know. We need to learn to discipline ourselves, to accept responsibility for, and to have something to say about some of the forces that shape us.

At the beginning of this chapter, we observed that it is difficult to think of any experience that does not influence our development in some way. Adult education in its broad sense can be said to include all those experiences, and they can be called "educational" because they modify, change, or reinforce our behavior in some way. In this very broad sense adult education can have negative as well as positive influences on us.

In its specific sense, however, adult education is a consciously elaborated program aiding and reinforcing the civilizing process. The over-all aim of the professional or lay adult educator, then, will be to bring each of us into some kind of constructive relationship with the civilizing process, always remembering that this process should represent those positive elements in environment and society that help us develop mature rationality in our lives and institutions.

We can be taught to hate other people and develop a quantitative value system, or we can be taught to love and to contribute to a value system that places quality in a sensible perspective with quantity. The quantitative idea tends to promote a society based on materialism and on a mechanization of thought and action in which the person becomes subordinated to the group and to the mechanical things he possesses and produces. The other idea seeks out and promotes human welfare through continually incorporating "the nature of things" into the civilizing process. Either idea can be promoted through the education of adults. It would be short-sighted, then, to consider adult education good or bad, *per se*.

We are all baffled by the complexities of our nature as well as by the seemingly endless complications of other natural phenomena. A favorite way of trying to escape the reality of complication is to develop some single purpose that can fit our finite concepts. Scarcely any area of study or investigation has escaped this snare. Actually, it's easier if grandpa, or the clergy, or our teachers classify and simplify for us; then all we have to do is remember the information and pass it on to others at appropriate times.

Related to the single-purpose idea is our penchant for placing everything in a good or bad category. Education is good. People ought to get a lot of it—when they are young. After you've been to school, you don't need anymore. Education is like the residual insect sprays, only the effect supposedly lasts longer.

Adult education can be truly "good" in that it can help us to see ourselves, to develop, to relate our particular talents and abilities to the job of living, and to take our rightful places as maturing citizens in the civilizing process. Adult education can be "bad." It can teach us to love ourselves more than we love others; it can teach us to follow the demagogue without question; it can help us develop ideas and learn skills necessary to produce products or situations that can enslave or destroy us.

Adult education must, then, have a purpose greater than that of learning the skills of the craftsman and the physician and the entrepreneur, important as those are. If we are truly engaged in the maturity process, we do not live to work and make money, or have a physician keep us alive merely to be alive. We learn what to do with our lives, how to use our money and our good health to enrich our lives. We use these resources, money and education and health, to help us live. A significant task of adult education is to teach us how to live a full, productive life in which the ability to make a living and stay well is important, but equally important is the knowledge of what to do culturally and spiritually with our lives and talents.

Some of us believe that if everyone were exposed to the "truths" revealed in the view of education or religion or politics we hold, the problems of society would be solved. We often try to press upon others the ideas we know most about, or are able to understand, or believe we understand. But if we were to broaden our knowledge, we might give some credence to the views and customs of other persons.

Vocational educators and those concerned with liberal arts are both disturbed about what each considers the short-sighted views of the other. History is filled with examples of persons in power who display a singleminded devotion to some cult, and who are restless until they convert or "liberate" those who do not understand them or disagree with them. We need to understand the views of others and might possibly use some of this new-found knowledge to enrich our own. Systems developed by human beings inevitably contain some of the deficiencies of their developers.

The vigorous presentation of different ideas gives a vitality to society which is essential to its survival and its advancement as a maturing organism. When we are forced, either subtly or overtly, to follow certain ideas blindly, we lose those helpful values that might exist within the ideas themselves; for we have not been given the freedom we need to come into an understanding relationship with the ideas according to our own abilities.

The subject areas of economics, philosophy, history, psychology, literature, languages, and the sciences are of prime importance in some phases of adult education. It would be of great value if all adults could be offered and would accept the opportunity to participate in well-operated programs involving the best of the past and the present represented in those fields.

Some programs of adult education presently include these vital, broad areas of learning on a basis appropriate to the development of the adult as a maturing, participating member of an evolving society rather than as a part of a separatist movement emphasizing snob-appeal.

Much work must be done in the field of adult education to bring the great stores of information contained in the arts and sciences into intimate relationship with the adult learner. Special programs must be developed to expose adults to other cultures through languages, philosophy, history, geography, ecology, sociology, and so on. These areas must be developed to show a relationship to the adult's own needs and to show what is meant by such ideas as responsibility for one another, freedom, discipline, and a free society.

These subjects certainly encompass funds of knowledge that can be focused on adult living. But they are too often taught to adults as subjects,'' just as we do in college. If you want it, here it is. If you can't get it, that's too bad.'' *Most adults are not scholars and they aren't interested in becoming scholars.* Adult learning programs must take this fact into consideration.

Children have to attend school; adults don't, usually, and most of them won't unless they can see some advantage in it. Our adult educational ideas must be adapted to these facts. Whether we like it or not, everybody needs to be exposed to learning, not for learning's sake but for humanity's sake. The content of the learning must be broad and appropriate to the variety of objectives pursued. Sometimes what we think of as subjects—history, mathematics, art, etc.—are useful. Many times programs of learning should be developed around the particular problems and needs of the participants.

Freedom is necessary to give each of us a chance to find himself, a chance to live a life in keeping with his unique personality. Encumbrances often make it difficult, if not impossible, for us to discover our potential and the degree of happiness that could come from the effective exploitation of it. Many persons believe that freedom is in the nature of things, a human need that must be understood and utilized if we are to mature, to develop, to grow.

It is also in the nature of things for us to be grasping and ego-centered. Our nature makes us compassionate and socio-centered when directed along those lines or revengeful and capable of destruction when trained in that direction. Since reason is a device often used to justify our views and behavior, it is at the mercy of the reasoner. We have the faculty of making almost anything sound right.

Our many-sided nature gives rise to many capabilities and resulting behaviors. We have what we choose to call our better nature. It conforms to a degree and directs its energy to the established social views and patterns; and we have our darker side, which is the antithesis of this view. When we speak of the nature of things, we think of conditions as they actually are—good, bad, and indifferent. Our nature is composed of these qualities. Nature is nature and, of itself, defies categorization into good and bad. It is up to us to select, to discover our potential, and to utilize it within the limits of our particular natures and of the environment in which we find ourselves. We have discovered many interesting and valuable facts about ourselves. We know that we can love and we can hate, that we need freedom and discipline, that we are ambitious and lazy, that we are ego-centered and socio-centered, and that we have many other characteristics that contribute to our ambivalent feelings.

Perhaps the most important thing we have ever discovered in our nature is that we can learn. We can learn to cope with some of the conflicts and ambivalences that seem to be a part of the natural order. We can learn both to care for ourselves and to see to it that those less fortunate are helped to learn to lead a useful life, or made more comfortable if they are unable to be productive. We have learned that we must do something, that our energy and talent must be expended in one direction or another. It is just as natural for this talent and energy to be expended in anti-social acts as it is in deeds that will further desirable patterns of personal and social behavior.

In truth, the continuing education of adults is not a leisure-time activity, nice if one has the time for it. It is the determining factor in the race between building and destroying, between the civilizing process and barbarism. We adults are capable of either and both.

We claim to prefer the civilizing process. While we have many differing views on how this is to be accomplished, most of these views have similar ends: to discover and satisfy human needs, to liberate human kind, to give us an opportunity to become the kind of creatures we ought to become.

When there is a race, there is a winner and a loser. While the race is still going on, the opportunity to make one's support felt on either side still exists. The support the civilizing effort needs can be supplied by tens of millions of adults who are willing to try to learn to carry their share of the social load and to identify and develop the part of their nature that leads toward maturing citizenship.

These goals require continuous effort. The adult who believes that having been to school when he was younger will suffice so far as learning is concerned is a social liability. Of course, schools aren't the only places people can learn. Actually, the schools should teach people how to learn, using subjects as examples and vehicles of learning. Learning can take place anywhere, and one kind or another does. But the kind of learning that helps us become increasingly mature, that helps us identify our personal and corporate problems and handle them intelligently—this is the kind of learning that can improve the chances of the civilizing process being the winner.

To hope that we can get along with what we have learned in school, regardless of how far we went, is about as futile as if we were to place a small sum of money in a bank and expect it to last the rest of our lives. In the case of the money and the bank, it is clear that we would soon be broke and then, if we failed to go to work, we would become public charges.

Many of us are, indeed, social public charges, even though we are making our way financially. We are making injudicious decisions, misleading people, and making choices based on prejudices, misinformation, and half-assimilated facts. We can never have all the information we need; we can not always be right; but we can learn to do a better job than we now do. Only when we begin to show as much enthusiasm for the continuing education of every adult citizen as we do for our children's education can we expect realistic results.

To participate effectively in a free society an adult must learn to do a good job vocationally; he must have some kind of spiritual support; he must know something of the world of which he is a part and his culture; he must know something of himself and his fellow man. All this requires learning, and the learning acquired in school is not sufficient to hold a person for life. Such social concepts as freedom and political equality can become nothing more than platitudes, unless a large portion of the populace in what is called a democracy has the understanding and integrity to interpret these principles intelligently and relate them to responsible citizenship. The nature of a society and its success as a liberating force depend on the ability of its citizens to understand and support social concepts like freedom and equality.

Cyril O. Houle (1913–   ) has had a long and distinguished career in education. He received a Ph.D. from the University of Chicago and honorary degrees from Rutgers University and Florida State University. He has been a senior consultant with the Kellogg Foundation, and was also on the faculty in adult education at the University of Chicago from 1939 until his retirement.

In addition to teaching at the University of Chicago, Houle has been a visiting professor at several other universities, a consultant to UNESCO, a Fulbright Fellow to Great Britain, and an advisor to universities in Liberia and Nigeria. In recognition for his contributions to the field of adult and continuing education, he was awarded the William Pearson Tolley Medal for Distinguished Leadership in Adult Education in 1966, and the Award of Merit by the National Association of Public School Adult Education in 1967. In the early 1980s, the Cyril O. Houle World Award for Literature in Adult Education was established to honor Dr. Houle's contributions to the field. This coveted award is given annually to the author of the book selected by a review committee as making the most outstanding contribution to the literature in the field.

Dr. Houle's several books reflect his career-long interest in adult and higher education. *The Inquiring Mind* (1962) is a study of adults' motivations for participating in learning activities. *The External Degree* (1973) explores the history and the issues related to nontraditional forms of higher education. *Continuing Learning in the Professions* (1980) is the culmination of a comprehensive study of the continuing education of seventeen professional groups. In *Patterns of Learning* (1984), Houle examines the lives of individuals who have engaged in learning through a variety of methods. *Governing Boards: Their Nature and Nurture* (1989) was followed by a comprehensive review of the literature in the field, *The Literature of Adult Education: A Bibliographic Essay* (1992).

The selection presented here is from *The Design of Education* (1972), a book that conceptualizes what Houle sees as the system underlying the practice of adult education. The seven assumptions upon which this system rests reflect Houle's philosophical orientation. For Houle, adult education is a practical, systematic, situation specific, and cooperative endeavor.

CYRIL O. HOULE

7 The Design Of Education

Adult education is the process by which men and women (alone, in groups, or in institutional settings) seek to improve themselves or their society by increasing their skill, knowl-

edge, or sensitiveness; or it is any process by which individuals, groups, or institutions try to help men and women improve in these ways. The fundamental system of practice of
the field, if it has one, must be discerned by probing beneath
many different surface realities to identify a basic unity of
process.

SOME ASSUMPTIONS

The system proposed rests on seven assumptions: *Any
episode of learning occurs in a specific situation and is profoundly influenced by that fact.* Every human being lives in
a complex personal and social milieu which is unique to him,
which constantly changes, and which influences all his experience. Any segment of that experience devoted to learning
occurs in a distinctive and specific situation which can be
separated out for analysis but which is inherently part of his
total milieu. The purposes, pattern, and results of that learning are all profoundly affected by the situation in which it
occurs. Every activity he undertakes is unlike any other; for
example, every class he attends is unique. If he participates
in more than one educational situation such as independent
study, tutorial instruction, group participation, or membership
in a voluntary association, each kind is different from the others.

The uniqueness of situations applies equally to each person who shares in them and to the social settings in which
the instruction occurs. Each learner in a group and each educator who guides its members lives within his own milieu
and is influenced in a distinctive way by the situation in which
he finds himself. If attention is shifted away from individuals
toward the social entities in which they learn—groups, classes,
or institutions—the same distinctiveness of milieu and situation also applies.

*The analysis or planning of educational activities must
be based on the realities of human experience and upon their
constant change.* Since every situation is unique, the effort
to understand or to plan educational activities must be centered as far as possible upon realities, not upon forms or ab-

stractions. An objective is a purpose which guides a learner or an educator, not the formal statement of that purpose. Anyone who designs an educational activity may make as clear and exact a forecast as possible of what he hopes to achieve, but the words of that forecast do not capture all his ideas, nor are those ideas the sole determinants of what will occur after the activity begins. He must constantly reshape his plans and procedures in order to come to terms with changes brought about by the desires and abilities of other people or the specific instructional resources he finds available. The evolving objectives are different from his initial statement of them. The methods he uses are not exactly like those in his lesson plans. And no predetermined method of evaluating the results of instruction can adequately measure the achievement of goals which do not become evident until the episode is completed or which exist only in the private intentions of the teacher or the learner.

Reality is hard to grasp (as the literature of epistemology demonstrates), but that fact does not mean that the effort to discern it should be abandoned. A continuing effort to perceive the reality of an educational activity must be attempted before the learning begins, while it is occurring, and as it is appraised afterward.

Education is a practical art. As is true in such established professions as law or medicine, success in the process of education is always measured by what occurs in the specific instances of its practice. What is the verdict of the jury, how well and how speedily is the patient returned to health, to what degree does the learner master the knowledge he seeks? As a sophisticated practical art, education draws upon many theoretical disciplines in the humanities and the social and biological sciences. It also uses an extensive and complex body of principles which has emerged from analysis of its own previous practice, and it has a history and lore of its own. But if this abstract and applied knowledge is to prove effective, it must be used in a specific situation to bring about a desired end.

To illustrate the point further, it may be said that any learning or teaching design is similar to plans made by an architect. He has a deep knowledge of esthetics, engineering, economics, and other sciences. He is aware of architectural traditions; of the range of building materials available, the methods of putting them together, and their relative values in various settings; and of the ways by which harmony is achieved between a building and its environment. Yet he knows that he must design each particular building in terms of its immediate terrain and surroundings, using the construction materials and labor available, and staying within the allotted budget. The educator's design has similar imperatives. He may know a great deal about the theory and practice of education but in each case he has a specific learner or group of learners to reach; limited resources of money, time, and materials to use; and a given setting in which to work. His success is judged by himself and others not by how much he knows but by his competence in using that knowledge to deal with the situation at hand.

The entire career of the educator is judged by some balancing out of the relative successes and failures of all the programs he designs and conducts. The variation among these programs may be simple. For example, a literacy teacher may simply repeat her courses over and over again for twenty years, making only changes required by different groups of students or by the appearance of new teaching aids. Usually, however, variations are complex. Just as the architect builds many houses, so the educator deals with many different situations, in each of which he applies his talents and his resources of knowledge to the task at hand. Success in each case may be judged separately, but he and others appraise his career in terms of his capacity to deal with the whole range of his endeavors.

The same generalization applies to the learner. He may design a program of independent study for himself or he may fit into an activity designed by a tutor, group leader, teacher, or institutional staff. In each case, his success is judged, by himself and by others, in terms of his mastery of the goals he seeks. His total learning achievement, however, is not measured by the results of any one act or episode but by the fruits of all the endeavors in which he has engaged.

Education is a cooperative rather than an operative art. The distinction between these two terms is an ancient one.

An operative art is one in which the creation of a product or performance is essentially controlled by the person using the art. The painter, sculptor, engineer, actor, shoemaker, and builder are operative artists. A cooperative art, though no less creative than an operative one, works in a facilitative way by guiding and directing a natural entity or process. The farmer, physician, and educator are three classic examples of cooperative artists. The farmer does not create the crops; he helps nature produce them. The physician aids and reinforces the processes by which the patient gets well. ("God heals," said Benjamin Franklin, "but the doctor takes the fee.") The educator does not put ideas into the minds of learners nor does he give them skills or sensitiveness. Instead he helps them learn these things for themselves and, by the use of his art, facilitates the accomplishment of desired goals.

In education the term *cooperative* is used in two major senses. In its profoundest meaning, it signifies action by both learner and educator in accordance with the dictates of nature. The learner must work in terms of his innate individualism as well as in terms of the social stimulation supplied by any learning group of which he may be a part. Also, like all other human beings, he has limitations. Some of them are generic; no hand can span two octaves on the piano. Others are specific; only a relatively few people in any generation can become master pianists. The learner's education is profoundly influenced at every point by his capacities and concerns, and, as they change over time so must his goals and his facility in achieving them. As for the educator, his aims and procedures are always influenced by his abilities and interests. He must work in terms of the opportunities and limitations they make possible.

In its second sense, the term *cooperative* implies voluntary interaction among individuals during learning. Even the solitary student guiding his own program with no fixed instructor seeks the help and encouragement which others can give him. When education occurs in any social setting, those who take part should have some sense of collaboration in both its planning and its conduct. At one extreme, this sharing is so complete that it requires a group to decide everything that it does together. At the other extreme, the sharing may be implicit in the teaching-learning situation, as when many people flock to hear a lecturer. Those who attend vote with their feet, as the saying goes, and one cannot assume from their physical passivity and silence as they sit in the auditorium that they are not cooperating fully in their instruction.

Any individual or group who designs an educational program must take both forms of cooperativeness into account. An educational program must originally be planned in terms of the estimated nature of the learner or learners and of the educator (if there is one) and then revised in the light of the constantly changing reality which appears as the program is put into effect. In some situations, it is possible to involve learners or their representatives in planning and thus foster a collaborative approach. In other situations, the educator must act alone, drawing upon his experience and his knowledge of people to design the program and then being alert to adjust it to meet the realities he encounters when he embarks upon it. Even a lecturer, using what is often thought to be a highly teacher-centered method, can constantly sense his audience's response and shift his approach to deal with it.

The planning or analysis of an educational activity is usually undertaken in terms of some period which the mind abstracts for analytical purposes from complicated reality. Learning can occur in a random fashion or as the unintended byproduct of acts performed for other purposes. Even when knowledge is consciously sought, its pursuits may vary in depth and scope from the simple looking up of a word in a dictionary to the undertaking of a lifelong and intensive inquiry. But the elective planning or analysis of education is aided by the selection of a time dimension which sets boundaries to what is either sought or observed.

Thus an evening college instructor may design a course in introductory chemistry in terms of an eighteen-week semester with two hours of class and four hours of laboratory work per week. He may then plan smaller segments of the course, each built on a unit of content, and may even decide in advance how he will conduct each session. He is aware that his course fits within at least three larger patterns to which thought must be given by himself or by others: the total offering of the evening college, his program of teaching, and the place of his course in the degree sequences taken by his students. All three patterns influence what he does in his own course since they help determine the answer to some important questions. What are the prerequisites for his course? How much time can he devote to it in terms of his other obligations? Is it designed as an introduction for those who plan to specialize in chemistry or as a survey course for those who want to broaden their general education? Or must it fulfill both of these functions because the evening college staff is not able or willing to separate the two groups of students?

Each student in the course also plans in terms of several temporal patterns. He selects the degree program whose successful completion requires that he take chemistry. He has some freedom of choice as to when that subject comes within the sequence of his work. During the semester in which he takes it, he determines what other courses give him as balanced a program as possible. He also plans the use of his time each day in terms of his needs to work, to have time for his family and recreation, to attend classes and laboratory sessions, and to make his preparations for them.

As this example suggests, good program planning or analysis usually requires both educator and learner to have at least four periods in mind, each of which gains meaning by its interaction with the others and all of which are logical abstractions, patterns imposed on reality for the sake of utility. An educational episode is a related series of learning or teaching events making up a coherent whole. It is more than a single exposure to knowledge but less than a long-sustained series of endeavors. Examples are a course, a residential conference, a workshop, a plan of reading based on a list of books, or a series of meetings by a group studying a topic. Of the four periods, the episode is the one most frequently and most intensively chosen for planning and analysis and is therefore the central time focus used in this book. An educational act is a specific and relatively brief learning or teaching event. It may be part of an episode, it may stand alone (as in an isolated lecture to an audience or an educational program on television), or it may be one event in a chain of otherwise unrelated occurrences (as when a discussion group chooses a different topic each time it meets). An educational series is a succession of related episodes, as in a curriculum for a degree, a progression of annual conferences, or a linking of courses of graduated difficulty. An aggregate of simultaneous episodes is a pattern of educational activities occurring in the same span of time in the life of an individual, group, or institution. The episodes may be linked together, may include one or more courses in a series, or may be unrelated except for the common period during which they occur.

Sometimes a learner or an educator does not set any time limitation on his educational planning. Through choice or necessity, he embarks on an activity with no clear idea of how long it will sustain his interest or attention. For example, he joins or accepts the leadership of a group, starts out to visit cultural institutions, or enters into a tutorial relationship which may be broken off at any point. In such a case, his planning occurs one act at a time with only a very general idea of continuity beyond it. Later, in retrospect, the sum of his actions may be seen to have been an episode, a series, or an aggregate, but such was not his original intent.

The planning or analysis of an educational activity may be undertaken by an educator, a learner, an independent analyst, or some combination of the three. In many educational activities, two distinct roles appear: the provider of focus, direction, and content, and the person or persons whose learning is shaped and led. In formal settings, the first of these is usually called a teacher and the second a student or a pupil. But the first may also be called a leader, a counselor, a coordinator, a curator, a supervisor, or any of a number of other terms, and the second may be referred to as a participant, a member, a counselee, a patron, a client, or another similar name. The terms *educator* and *learner* are used generically here to indicate the two roles. A third role sometimes appears when somebody who stands outside the educational activity itself helps to plan or analyze it. An administrator, a curriculum specialist, a consultant, an external examiner, or other people may plan, study, or appraise a program either independently or in collaboration with the educator, the learner, or both. This third role is here designated as that of *analyst*.

While the usual patterns of collaboration among these

three are well understood, it is not always realized each can operate independently of the others. The educator may do the whole job of planning, conducting, and appraising an educative program by himself, as when a public health specialist devises and provides a series of posters to teach the basic principles of nutrition. The learner may work completely on his own, as when he plans, carries out, and appraises a series of visits to Civil War battlefields because he is interested in American history. The analyst can design an activity which never comes to fruition, or he can study the operation of a program for which he has no responsibility and with which he may never come in direct contact.

Any design of education can best be understood as a complex of interacting elements, not as a sequence of events. In theory, the process of education usually goes through the stages of identification and refinement of objectives, selection of means of accomplishing them, conduct of the planned activity, and retrospective evaluation of it. If these various elements are to be identified and understood, they must be recorded in some fashion, and the temporal order is as good as any other for the purpose. But practice usually does not follow this logical pattern. An activity may be initiated because some resource is available or intriguing. For example, the director of an educational television station may begin his planning when a time slot opens up on his schedule, or an experimenter with computerized instruction may develop a course which tests that method. In such cases, the objective is chosen to fit the means, not the reverse.

Even more important, the mind seldom works in a completely logical fashion. The procedure of planning or analyzing an educational program is often very like the process of research. A distinguished group of psychologists once observed:

> [Research] is a rather informal, often illogical, and sometimes messy-looking affair. It includes a great deal of floundering around in the empirical world. . . . Somewhere and somehow in the process of floundering, the research worker will get an idea. In fact, he will get many ideas. On largely intuitive grounds he will reject most of his ideas and will accept others as the basis for extended work. . . . If the idea happens to be a good

one, he may make a significant positive contribution to his science—"may" because between the idea and the contribution lies a lot of persistence, originality, intuition, and hard work.[1]

From beginning to end, the design of an educational activity is usually in a constant state of reformulation. It emerges first in at least an embryo form when the possibility of the activity first appears, and it is reconsidered frequently during the time of planning, the time of action, and the time of retrospection. All the component parts of the design mesh together at every point at which it is considered. Only when they are separated for formal analysis do they appear to be logical and linear.

When stated baldly as propositions, some of these seven assumptions may sound platitudinous since they underlie so much excellent practice. They are presented here, however, chiefly because they are so often violated in other practice. All too often, abstract systems of teaching, such as textbooks, lesson plans, or course outlines, are worked out on the basis of a generalized conception of content, method, evaluation, and the nature of the "typical" student and are then imposed virtually intact upon many different situations. An institution builds up a generic pattern of service, such as a ten-session course meeting one night a week for ten successive weeks, and then seems unable to vary it, implying that all knowledge relevant to its purpose should be conveyed in this fashion. These and similar rigidities deny in practice the situational approach to education expressed in the foregoing assumptions.

Practically speaking, the learner or the educator may use this approach in either of two ways. He may work wholly within the situation in which he finds himself, building up a design of activity which is determined entirely by its dictates. Or he may begin with a generalized program but adapt it, profoundly if necessary, to fit the requirements of the situation. The failure to use this second approach creatively leads to excessive formality of education.

[1]*American Psychological Association, Education and Training Board, "Education for Research in Psychology,"* American Psychologist, *1959,* 14, *169.*

Burrhus Frederic Skinner's (1904–1990) unsuccessful attempt to make a living as a writer led him to redirect his career toward the study of psychology. After receiving advanced degrees from Harvard University, he became a research fellow at Harvard and then a psychology professor at the University of Minnesota from 1936–1945. *Behavior of Organisms*, published in 1938, established his reputation as a behavioral psychologist, and he subsequently became chair of the Department of Psychology at Indiana University. In 1948, he joined the Harvard University faculty where he was professor emeritus until his death in 1990.

Widely known for his views on behavior and society, Skinner consistently maintained that human behavior is shaped and controlled by the environment. To develop a better world, the environmental forces that control behavior need to be identified and changed—it is a futile diversion, he wrote in the following selection, to concentrate efforts on changing human nature itself. This theme permeates all of Skinner's writings. *Walden Two* (1948), for example, presents a fictional account of an urban society based on behavioral engineering. *Beyond Freedom and Dignity* (1972) is a philosophical statement in which Skinner confronts the true nature of human will, freedom, and dignity in a behaviorist society.

Skinner's experimental work with operant conditioning, positive and negative reinforcement, extinction and avoidance behavior, and reinforcement schedules has had a pervasive impact on contemporary education. Behavior modification, behavioral objectives, competency-based programs, and programmed instruction are in use at all levels of instruction, including adult and continuing education, training, and human resource development.

B. F. SKINNER

8 The Steep and Thorny Way to a Science of Behaviour

A critic contends that a recent book of mine does not contain anything new, that much the same thing was said more than four centuries ago in theological terms by John Calvin. You will not be surprised, then, to find me commending to you the steep and thorny way to that heaven promised by a science of behaviour. But I am not one of those ungracious pastors, of whom Ophelia complained, who 'recking not their own rede themselves tread the primrose path of dalliance'. No, I shall rail at dalliance, and in a manner worthy, I hope, of my distinguished predecessor. If I do not thunder or fulminate, it is only because we moderns can more easily portray a truly frightening hell. I shall merely allude to the carcinogenic fallout of a nuclear holocaust. And no Calvin ever had better reason to fear his hell, for I am proceeding on the asumption that nothing less than a vast improvement in our understanding of human behaviour will prevent the destruction of our way of life or of mankind.

Why has it been so difficult to be scientific about human behaviour? Why have methods which have been so prodigiously successful almost everywhere else failed so ignominiously in this one field? Is it because human behaviour presents unusual obstacles to a science? No doubt it does, but I think we are beginning to see how they may be overcome. The problem, I submit, is digression. We have been drawn off the straight and narrow path, and the word *diversion* serves me well by suggesting not only digression but dalliance. In this lecture I shall analyse some of the diversions peculiar to the field of human behaviour which seem to have delayed our advance towards the better understanding we desperately need.

I must begin by saying what I take a science of behaviour to be. It is, I assume, part of biology. The organism that behaves is the organism that breaths, digests, conceives, gestates, and so on. As such, it will eventually be described and explained by the anatomist and physiologist. So far as behaviour is concerned, they will give us an account of the genetic endowment of the species and tell us how that endowment changes during the lifetime of the individual and why, as a result, the individual then responds in a given way upon a given occasion. Despite remarkable progress, we are still a long way from a satisfactory account in such terms. We know something about the chemical and electrical effects of the nervous system and the location of many of its functions, but the events which actually underlie a single instance of behaviour—as a pigeon picks up a stick to build a nest, or a child a block to complete a tower, or a scientist a pen to write a paper—are still far out of reach.

Fortunately, we need not wait for further progress of that sort. We can analyse a given instance of behaviour in its relation to the current setting and to antecedent events in the history of the species and the individual. Thus, we do not need an explicit account of the anatomy and physiology of genetic endowment in order to describe the behaviour, or the behavioural processes, characteristic of a species, or to speculate about the contingencies of survival under which they might have evolved, as the ethologists have convincingly demonstrated. Nor do we need to consider anatomy and physiology in order to see how the behaviour of the individual is changed by his exposure to contingencies of reinforcement during his lifetime and how as a result he behaves in a given way on a given occasion. I must confess to a predilection here for my own specialty, the experimental analysis of behaviour, which is a quite explicit investigation of the effects upon individual organisms of extremely complex and subtle contingencies of reinforcement.

There will be certain temporal gaps in such an analysis. The behaviour and the conditions of which it is a function do not occur in close temporal or spatial proximity, and we must wait for physiology to make the connection. When it does so, it will not invalidate the behavioural account (indeed, its assignment could be said to be specified by that account), nor will it make its terms and principles any the less useful. A science of behaviour will be needed for both theoretical and practical purposes even when the behaving organism is fully understood at another level, just as much of chemistry remains useful even though a detailed account of a single instance may be given at the level of molecular or atomic forces. Such, then, is the science of behaviour from which I suggest we have been diverted—by several kinds of dalliance to which I now turn.

Very little biology is handicapped by the fact that the biologist is himself a specimen of the thing he is studying, but that part of the science with which we are here concerned has not been so fortunate. We seem to have a kind of inside information about our behaviour. It may be true that the environment shapes and controls our behaviour as it shapes and controls the behaviour of other species—but *we* have feelings about it. And what a diversion they have proved to be! Our loves, our fears, our feelings about war, crime, poverty, and God—these are all basic, if not ultimate, concerns. And we are as much concerned about the feelings of others. Many of the great themes of mythology have been about feelings—of the victim on his way to sacrifice or of the warrior going forth to battle. We read what poets tell us about their feelings, and we share the feelings of characters in plays and novels. We follow regimens and take drugs to alter our feelings. We become sophisticated about them in, say, the manner of La Rochefoucauld, noting that jealousy thrives on doubt, or that the clemency of a ruler is a mixture of vanity, laziness, and fear. And with some pyschiatrists we may even try to establish an independent science of feelings in the intrapsychic life of the mind or personality.

And do feelings not have some bearing on our formulation of a science of behaviour? Do we not strike because we are angry and play music because we feel like listening? And if so, are our feelings not be to added to those antecedent events of which behaviour is a function? This is not the place to answer such questions in detail, but I must at least suggest the kind of answer that may be given. William James questioned the causal order: perhaps we do not strike because we are angry but feel angry because we strike. That does not bring us back to the environment, however, although James and others were on the right track. What we feel are conditions of our bodies, most of them closely associated with behaviour and with the circumstances in which we behave. We both strike *and* feel angry for a common reason, and that reason lies in the environment. In short, the bodily conditions we feel are *collateral products* of our genetic and environmental histories. They have no explanatory force; they are simply additional facts to be taken into account.

Feelings enjoy an enormous advantage over genetic and environmental histories. They are warm, salient, and demanding, where facts about the environment are easily overlooked. Moreover, they are *immediately* related to behaviour, being collateral products of the same causes, and have therefore commanded more attention than the causes themselves, which are often rather remote. In doing so, they have proved to be one of the most fascinating attractions along the path of dalliance.

A much more important diversion has for more than 2000 years made any move towards a science of behaviour particularly difficult. The environment acts upon an organism at the surface of its body, but when the body is our own, we seem to observe its progress beyond that point—for example, we seem to see the real world become experience, a physical presentation become a sensation or a percept. Indeed, this second stage may be all we see. Reality may be merely an inference, and according to some authorities a bad one. What is important may not be the physical world on the far side of the skin, but what that world means to us on this side.

Not only do we seem to see the environment on its way in, we seem to see behaviour on its way out. We observe certain early stages—wishes, intentions, ideas, and acts of will—before they have, as we say, found expression in behaviour. And as for our environmental history, that can also be viewed and reviewed inside the skin for we have tucked it all away in the storehouse of our memory. Again this is not the place to present an alternative account, but several points need to be made. The behaviouristic objection is not primarily to the metaphysical nature of mind stuff. I welcome the view, clearly gaining in favour among psychologists and physiologists and by no means a stranger to philosophy, that what we introspectively observe, as well as feel, are states of our bodies. But I am not willing to give introspection much of a toehold even so, for there are two important reasons why we do not discriminate precisely among our feelings and states of mind and hence why there are many different philosophies and psychologies.

In the first place, the world within the skin is private. Only the person whose skin it is can make certain kinds of contact with it. We might expect that the resulting intimacy should make for greater clarity, but there is a difficulty. The privacy interferes with the very process of coming to know. The verbal community which teaches us to make distinctions among things in the world around us lacks the information it needs to teach us to distinguish events in our private world. It cannot teach us the difference between diffidence and embarrassment, for example, as readily or as accurately as that between red and blue or sweet and sour.

Secondly, the self-observation which leads to introspective knowledge is limited by anatomy. It arose very late in the evolution of the species, because it is only when a person begins to be asked about his behaviour and about why he behaves as he does that he becomes conscious of himself in this sense. Self-knowledge depends upon language and in fact upon language of a rather advanced kind, but when questions of this sort first began to be asked, the only nervous systems available in answering them were those which had evolved for entirely different reasons. They had proved useful in the internal economy of the organism, in the co-ordination of movement, and in operating upon the environment, but there was no reason why they should be suitable in supplying information about those very extensive systems which mediate behaviour. To put it crudely, introspection cannot be very relevant or comprehensive because the human organism does not have nerves going to the right places.

One other problem concerns the nature and location of the knower. The organism itself lies, so to speak, between the environment that acts upon it and the environment it acts upon, but what lies between those inner stages—between, for example, experience and will? From what vantage point do we watch stimuli on their way into the storehouse of memory or behaviour on its way out to physical expression? The observing agent, the knower, seems to contract to something very small in the middle of things.

In the formulation of a science with which I began, it is the *organism as a whole* that behaves. It acts in and upon a physical world, and it can be induced by a verbal environment to respond to some of its own activities. The events observed as the life of the mind, like feelings, are *collateral products*, which have been made the basis of many elaborate metaphors. The philosopher at his desk asking himself what he really knows, about himself or the world, will quite naturally begin with his experiences, his acts of will, and his memory, but the effort to understand the mind from that vantage point, beginning with Plato's supposed discovery, has been one of the great diversions which have delayed an analysis of the role of the environment.

It did not, of course, take inside information to induce people to direct their attention to what is going on inside the behaving organism. We almost instinctively look inside a system to see how it works. We do this with clocks, as with living systems. It is standard practice in much of biology. Some early efforts to understand and explain behaviour in this way have been described by Onians in his classis *Origins of European thought*.[1] It must have been the slaughterhouse and the battlefield which gave man his first knowledge of anatomy and physiology. The various functions assigned to parts of the organism were not usually those which had been introspectively observed. If Onians is right, the *phrénes* were the lungs, intimately associated with breathing and hence, so the Greeks said, with thought and, of course, with life and death. The *phrénes* were the seat of *thumós*, a vital principle whose nature is not now clearly understood, and possibly of ideas, in the active sense of Homeric Greek. (By the time an idea had become an object of quiet contemplation, interest seems to have been lost in its location.) Later, the various fluids of the body, the humours, were associated with dispositions, and the eye and the ear with sense data. I like to imagine the consternation of that pioneer who first analysed the optics of the eyeball and realized that the image on the retina was upside down!

Observation of a behaving system from without began in earnest with the discovery of reflexes, but the reflex arc was not only not the seat of mental action, it was taken to be a usurper, the spinal reflexes replacing the *Rückenmarkseele* or soul of the spinal cord, for example. The reflex arc was essentially an anatomical concept, and the physiology remained largely imaginary for a long time. Many years ago I suggested that the letters CNS could be said to stand, not for the central nervous system, but for the conceptual nervous system. I had in mind the great physiologists Sir Charles Sherrington and Ivan Petrovich Pavlov. In his epoch-making *Integrative action*

[1]ONIANS, R.D. (1951). The origins of European thought. *Cambridge University Press.*

of the nervous system[2] Sherrington had analysed the role of the synapse, listing perhaps a dozen characteristic properties. I pointed out that he had never seen a synapse in action and that all the properties assigned to it were inferred from the behaviour of his preparations. Pavlov had offered his researches as evidence of the activities of the cerebral cortex though he had never observed the cortex in action but had merely inferred its processes from the behaviour of his experimental animals. But Sherrington, Pavlov, and many others were moving in the direction of an instrumental approach, and the physiologist is now, of course, studying the nervous system directly.

The conceptual nervous system has been taken over by other disciplines—by information theory, cybernetics, systems analyses, mathematical models, and cognitive psychology. The hypothetical structures they describe do not depend upon confirmation by direct observation of the nervous system for that lies too far in the future to be of interest. They are to be justified by their internal consistency and the successful prediction of selected facts, presumably not the facts from which the constructions were inferred.

These disciplines were concerned with how the brain or the mind must work if the human organism is to behave as it does. They offer a sort of thermodynamics of behaviour without reference to molecular action. The computer with its apparent simulation of Thinking Man supplies the dominant analogy. It is not a question of the physiology of the computer—how it is wired or what type of storage it uses—but of its behavioural characteristics. A computer takes in information as an organism receives stimuli, and processes it according to an inbuilt program as an organism is said to do according to its genetic endowment. It encodes the information, converting it to a form it can handle, as the organism converts visual, auditory, and other stimuli into nerve impulses. Like its human analogue it stores the encoded information in a memory, tagged to facilitate retrieval. It uses what it has stored to process information as received, as a person is said to use prior experience to interpret incoming stimuli, and later to perform variousoperations—in short, to compute. Finally, it makes decisions and behaves: it prints out.

[2]*SHERRINGTON, C.S. (1906).* Integrative action of the nervous system. *Yale University Press, New Haven, Conn., U.S.A.*

There is nothing new about any of this. The same things were done thousands of years ago with clay tiles. The overseer or tax collector kept a record of bags of grain, the number, quality, and kind being appropriately marked. The tiles were stored in lots as marked; additional tiles were grouped appropriately; the records were eventually retrieved and computations made; and a summary account was issued. The machine is much swifter, and it is so constructed that human participation is needed only before and after the operation. The speed is a clear advantage, but the apparent autonomy has caused trouble. It has seemed to mean that the mode of operation of a computer resembles that of a person. People do make physical records which they store and retrieve and use in solving problems, but it does not follow that they do anything of the sort in the mind. If there were some exclusively subjective achievement, the argument for the so-called higher mental processes would be stronger, but, so far as I know, none has been demonstrated. True, we say that the mathematician sometimes intiuitively solves a problem and only later, if at all, reduces it to the steps of a proof, and in doing so he seems to differ greatly from those who proceed step by step, but the differences could well be in the evidence of what has happened, and it would not be very satisfactory to define thought simply as unexplained behaviour.

Again, it would be foolish of me to try to develop an alternative account in the time available. What I have said about the introspectively observed mind applies as well to the mind that is constructed from observations of the behaviour of others. The *accessibility* of stored memories, for example, can be interpreted as the *probability* of acquired behaviours, with no loss in the adequacy of the treatment of the facts, and with very considerable gain in the assimilation of this difficult field with other parts of human behaviour.

I have said that much of biology looks inside a living system for an explanation of how it works. But not all of biology. Sir Charles Bell could write a book on the hand as evidence of design. The hand was evidence; the design lay elsewhere. Darwin found the design, too, but in a different place. He could catalogue the creatures he discovered on the voyage of the *Beagle* in terms of their form or structure, and he could classify barnacles for years in the same way, but he looked beyond structure for the principle of natural selection. It was *the relation of the organism to the environment* that mattered in evolution. And it is the relation to environment which is of primary concern in the analysis of behaviour. Hence, it is not enough to confine oneself to organization or structure, even of the most penetrating kind. That is the mistake of most phenomenology, existentialism, and the structuralism of anthropology and linguistics. When the important thing is a relation to the environment, as in the phylogeny and ontogeny of behaviour, the fascination with an inner system becomes a simple digression.

We have not advanced more rapidly to the methods and instruments needed in the study of behaviour precisely because of the diverting preoccupation with a supposed or real inner life. It is true that the introspective psychologist and the model builder have investigated environments, but they have done so only to throw some light on the internal events in which they are interested. They are no doubt well-intentioned helpmates, but they have often simply misled those who undertake the study of the organism as a behaving system in its own right. Even when helpful, an observed or hypothetical inner determiner is no explanation of behaviour until it has itself been explained, and the fascination with an inner life has allayed curiosity about the further steps to be taken.

I can hear my critics: 'Do you really mean to say that all those who have inquired into the human mind, from Plato and Aristotle through the Romans and scholastics, to Bacon and Hobbes, to Locke and the other British empiricists, to John Stuart Mill, and to all those who began to call themselves psychologists—that they have all been wasting their time?'' Well, not all their time, fortunately. Forget their purely psychological speculations, and they were still remarkable people. They would have been more remarkable, in my opinion, if they could have forgotten that speculation themselves. They were careful observers of human behaviour, but the intuitive wisdom they acquired from their contact with real people was flawed by their theories.

It is easier to make the point in the field of medicine. Until the present century very little was known about bodily processes in health and disease from which useful therapeutic practices could be derived. Yet it should have been worthwhile to call in a physician. Physicians saw many ill people and should have acquired a kind of wisdom—unanalysed perhaps, but still of value in prescribing simple treatments. The history of medicine, however, is largely the history of barbaric practices—blood-lettings, cuppings, poultices, purgations, violent emetics—which much of the time must have been harmful. My point is that these measures were not suggested by the intuitive wisdom acquired from familiarity with illness; they were suggested by *theories*, theories about what was going on inside an ill person. Theories of the mind have had a similar effect—less dramatic, perhaps, but quite possibly far more damaging. The men I have mentioned made important contributions in government, religion, ethics, economics, and many other fields. They could do so with an intuitive wisdom acquired from experience. But philosophy and psychology have had their bleedings, cuppings, and purgations too, and they have obscured simple wisdom. They have diverted wise people from a path which would have led more directly to an eventual science of behaviour. Plato would have made far more progress towards the good life if he could have forgotten those shadows on the wall of his cave.

Still another kind of concern for the self distracts us from the programme I have outlined. It has to do with the individual, not as an object of self-knowledge, but an an agent, an initiator, a creator. I have developed this theme in *Beyond freedom and dignity.*[3] We are more likely to give a person credit for what he does if it is not obvious that it can be attributed to his physical or social environment, and we are likely to feel that truly great achievements must be inexplicable. The more derivative a work of art, the less creative; the more conspicuous the personal gain, the less heroic an act of sacrifice. To obey a well-enforced law is not to show civic virtue. We see a concern for the aggrandizement of the individual, for the maximizing of credit due him, in the self-actualization of so-called humanistic psychology, in some versions of existentialism, in Eastern mysticism and certain forms of Christian mysticism in which a person is taught to reject the world in order to free

[3]*SKINNER, B.F. (1972). Beyond freedom and dignity. Jonathan Cape, London.*

himself for union with a divine principle or with God, as well as in the simple structuralism which looks to the organization of behaviour rather than to the antecedent events responsible for that organization. The difficulty is that, if the credit due a person is infringed by evidences of the conditions of which his behaviour is a function, then a scientific analysis appears to be an attack on human worth or dignity. Its task is to explain the hitherto inexplicable and hence to reduce any supposed inner contribution which has served in lieu of explanation. Freud moved in this direction in explaining creative art, and it is no longer just the cynic who traces heroism and martyrdom to powerful indoctrination. The culminating achievement of the human species has been said to be the evolution of man as a moral animal, but a simpler view is that it has been the evolution of cultures in which people behave morally although they have undergone no inner change of character.

Even more traumatic has been the supposed attack on freedom. Historically, the struggle for freedom has been an escape from physical restraint and from behavioural restraints exerted through punishment and exploitative measures of other kinds. The individual has been freed from features of his environment arranged by governmental and religious agencies and by those who possess great wealth. The success of that struggle, though it is not yet complete, is one of man's great achievements, and no sensible person would challenge it. Unfortunately, one of its by-products has been the slogan that 'all control of human behaviour is wrong and must be resisted'. Nothing in the circumstances under which man has struggled for freedom justifies this extension of the attack on controlling measures, and we should have to abandon all the advantages of a well-developed culture if we were to relinquish all practices involving the control of human behaviour. Yet new techniques in education, psychotherapy, incentive systems, penology, and the design of daily life are currently subject to attack because they are said to threaten personal freedom, and I can testify that the attack can be fairly violent.

The extent to which a person is free or responsible for his achievements is not an issue to be decided by rigorous proof, but I submit that what we call the behaviour of the human organism is no more free than its digestion, gestation, immunization, or any other physiological process. Because it involves the environment in many subtle ways it is much more complex, and its lawfulness is, therefore, much harder to demonstrate. But a scientific analysis moves in that direction, and we can already throw some light on traditional topics, such as free will or creativity, which is more helpful than traditional accounts, and I believe that further progress is imminent.

The issue is, of course, determinism. Slightly more than a hundred years ago in a famous paper Claude Bernard raised with respect to physiology the issue which now stands before us in the behavioural sciences. The almost insurmountable obstacle to the application of scientific method in biology was, he said, the belief in 'vital spontaneity'. His contemporary, Louis Pasteur, was responsible for a dramatic test of the theory of spontaneous generation, and I suggest that the spontaneous generation of behaviour in the guise of ideas and acts of will is now at the stage of the spontaneous generation of life in the form of maggots and micro-organisms a hundred years ago.

The practical problem in continuing the struggle for freedom and dignity is not to destroy controlling forces but to change them, to create a world in which people will achieve far more than they have ever achieved before in art, music, literature, science, technology, and above all the enjoyment of life. It could be a world in which people feel freer than they have ever felt before, because they will not be under aversive control. In building such a world, we shall need all the help a science of behaviour can give us. To misread the theme of the struggle for freedom and dignity and to relinquish all efforts to control would be a tragic mistake.

But it is a mistake that may very well be made. Our concern for the individual as a creative agent is not dalliance; it is clearly an obstacle rather than a diversion. For ancient fears are not easily allayed. A shift in emphasis from the individual to the environment, particularly to the social environment, is reminiscent of various forms of totalitarian statism. It is easy to turn from what may seem like an inevitable movement in that direction and to take one's chances with libertarianism. But much remains to be analysed in that position. For example, we may distinguish between liberty and license by holding to the right to do as we please provided we do not infringe similar rights in others, but in doing so we conceal or disguise the public sanctions represented by private rights. Rights and duties, like a moral or ethical sense, are examples of hypothetical internalized environmental sanctions.

In the long run, the aggrandizement of the individual jeopardizes the future of the species and the culture. In effect it infringes the so-called rights of billions of people still to be born, in whose interests only the weakest of sanctions are now maintained. We are beginning to realize the magnitude of the problem of bringing human behaviour under the control of a projected future, and we are already suffering from the fact that we have come very late to recognize that mankind will have a future only if he designs a *viable* way of life. I wish I could share the optimism of both Darwin and Herbert Spencer that the course of evolution is necessarily towards perfection. It appears, on the contrary, that that course must be corrected from time to time. But, of course, if the intelligent behaviour that corrects it is also a product of evolution, then perhaps they were right after all. But it could be a near thing.

Perhaps it is now clear what I mean by diversions and obstacles. The science I am discussing is the investigation of the relation between behaviour and the environment—on the one hand, the environment in which the species evolved and which is responsible for the facts investigated by the ethologists and, on the other hand, the environment in which the individual lives and in response to which at any moment he behaves. We have been diverted from, and blocked in, our inquiries into the relations between behaviour and those environments by an absorbing interest in the organism itself. We have been misled by the almost instinctive tendency to look inside any system to see how it works, a tendency doubly powerful in the case of behaviour because of the apparent inside information supplied by feelings and introspectively observed states. Our only recourse is to leave that subject to the physiologist, who has, or will have, the only appropriate instruments and methods. We have also been encouraged to move in a centripetal direction because the discovery of controlling forces in the environment has seemed to reduce the credit due us for our achievements and to suggest that the struggle for freedom has not been as fully successful as we had imagined. We are not yet ready to accept the fact that the task is to change, not people, but rather the world in which they live.

We shall be less reluctant to abandon these diversions and to attack these obstacles, as we come to understand the possibility of a different approach. The role of the environment in human affairs has not, of course, gone unnoticed. Historians and biographers have acknowledged influences on human conduct, and literature has made the same point again and again. The Enlightenment advanced the cause of the individual by improving the world in which he lived—the Encyclopedia of Diderot and D'Alembert was designed to further changes of that sort—and by the nineteenth century, the controlling force of the environment was clearly recognized. Bentham and Marx have been called behaviourists, although for them the environment determined behaviour only after first determining consciousness, and this was an unfortunate qualification because the assumption of a mediating state clouded the relation between the terminal events.

The role of the environment has become clearer in the present century. Its selective action in evolution has been examined by the ethologists, and a similar selective action during the life of the individual is the subject of the experimental analysis of behaviour. In the current laboratory, very complex environments are constructed and their effects on behaviour studied. I believe this work offers consoling reassurance to those who are reluctant to abandon traditional formulations. Unfortunately, it is not well known outside the field. Its practical uses are however, beginning to attract attention. Techniques derived from the analysis have proved useful in other parts of biology—for example, physiology and psychopharmacology—and have already led to the improved design of cultural practices, in programmed instructional materials, contingency management in the classroom, behavioural modification in psychotherapy and penology, and many other fields.

Much remains to be done, and it will be done more rapidly when the role of the environment takes its proper place in competition with the apparent evidences of an inner life. As Diderot put it, nearly two hundred years ago, 'Unfortunately it is easier and shorter to consult oneself than it is to consult nature. Thus the reason is inclined to dwell within itself.' But the problems we face are not to be found in men and women but in the world in which they live, especially in those social environments we call cultures. It is an important and promising shift in emphasis because, unlike the remote fastness of the so-called human spirit, the environment is within reach and we are learning how to change it.

And so I return to the role that has been assigned to me as a kind of twentieth-century Calvin, calling upon you to forsake the primrose path of total individualism, of self-actualization, self-adoration, and self-love, and to turn instead to the construction of that heaven on earth which is, I believe, within reach of the methods of science. I wish to testify that, once you are used to it, the way is not so steep or thorny after all.

Preparation of this paper has been supported by a Career Award from the National Institute of Mental Health (Grant K6-MH-21,775-01).

Leonard (1922–   ) and Zeace Nadler (1925–   ) are partners in Nadler Associates, a human resource development consulting practice. Leonard Nadler received his B.B.A. degree in 1948 in accounting from the City College of New York, his M.A. degree in business education from City College, and his Ed.D. degree in educational administration from Teachers College, Columbia University. Zeace Nadler has a B.A. degree in English literature from Brooklyn College.

Dr. Nadler is professor emeritus of the School of Education and Human Development, The George Washington University, where he developed the graduate program in human resource development (HRD). Zeace Nadler has also taught in the HRD program at George Washington University, and has been involved in consulting with her husband in the United States and abroad. Dr. Nadler has been instrumental in developing the theoretical base for the field of human resource development. He was awarded an honorary Doctor of Human Letters from the National College of Education, and the first Distinguished Contribution to HRD Award from the American Society for Training and Development (ASTD). In addition, he has been chosen as one of the ten outstanding trainers by the readers of *Training Magazine*, and been elected to the HRD Hall of Fame. He has published widely in the field of human resource development, including editing *The Handbook of Human Resource Development* (1984).

In addition to *Developing Human Resources* (1991, 3rd ed.) from which the following selection is taken, Leonard and Zeace Nadler have coauthored numerous articles and two books, *The Comprehensive Guide to Successful Meetings and Conferences* (1967) and *The Conference Book* (1977). In the chapter on "Employee Training" from *Developing Human Resources*, the Nadlers present a performance-based systems model of training, centering on input, performance and output. The emphasis on training, changing behavior, and measurable outcomes reflects an underlying behaviorist philosophy.

LEONARD AND ZEACE NADLER

9 Employee Training

This chapter focuses on training—learning, provided by employers to employees, that is related to their present jobs. The other two types of learning activities (education and development) in the HRD model are discussed in the next two chapters. Each activity area of the HRD program makes specific contributions to the organization and to the individual.

Training, as defined and discussed here, is the most prevalent form of learning provided by employers.

In most organizations, the job any individual does is fairly well defined. If there is a classification system, as in the government and in some other large organizations, each job has a definite designation such as a number, letter, or combination of those two, with a detailed description of what the individual in that job classification is expected to do. This is not always the same as a job description, which is written for functional purposes or to assist in recruitment and selection. When there is a lack of agreement on what a job is, the result is a great degree of confusion in an organization. Providing appropriate training is only one way of reducing that confusion, but it is the one that is the concern of this book. As will be discussed in Chapter Ten on the learning specialist, training is not the only way to approach clarifying what job is to be done. But once there is agreement, training can be utilized to improve performance.

WHY TRAIN?

A frequently asked question is, To what extent do employers provide training and why? There have been sporadic attempts to find some answers. Statistics are not easily obtainable due to the lack of agreement on terminology and the lack of a mechanism for collecting such data. Despite these limitations, there have been some attempts at data collection worth noting. A study by the Bureau of Labor Statistics of the United States Department of Labor found that "since obtaining their current jobs, 35 percent of all workers had taken training to improve their job skills" (Carey and Eck, 1985).

There are many reasons why an employer should provide training. King (1964) listed the following reasons:

- shortage of labor
- high turnover
- expanding production
- diversification of products
- automation

- redundancy (layoffs)
- improvement of quality
- reduction of scrap
- raising the caliber of the staff
- establishing new factories

It is interesting to note that most of these reasons are still relevant today and will probably be the core reasons for training for many years to come. Of course, as can be expected, the importance of any of these items will continue to shift under the impact of newer technologies and a changing work force. To that list could be added a few other items, some of which may overlap slightly:

- deterioration of performance
- change in the work process or materials
- job redesign
- new employees

These reasons are applicable to almost any work situation, and the list grows longer when one looks at organizations and individuals. Rather than discuss each one of the fourteen items separately, we have grouped them into general areas for discussion below.

This essence of any job is performance, which can be depicted as a continual cycle of:

input > performance > output > input > performance > output

This constant chaining is the essence of how work gets done in organizations, as one person's output becomes another person's input. The output-input is of various kinds. In the case of manufacturing, it will consist of specific physical elements, such as parts of a machine, or a finished product, such as an automobile. It can also be an internal report, a phone call, or some other action that constitutes part of the performance required of a particular job. At some point, the output may be to an individual or to a group or organization outside of the employing organization—to a consumer or customer.

When the system is functioning at its planned level, this flow proceeds undisturbed. But what happens when the performance results in an output that is not up to standard? The

performance of the next person who is expecting the standard
input is affected adversely, because the input is different from
the one anticipated. Internally, this can result in a loss of production, lowered productivity, and subsequent cost increases
or profit losses. When unsatisfactory performance produces
output that is sent outside the organization, it results in customer dissatisfaction. Inadequate performance, in the form of
substandard output, is one of the major reasons why organizations must provide training.

Assuming all other factors remain unchanged, why
should performance move from adequate to unsatisfactory?
There are many reasons and some are fairly easy to identify.
Let us look at what is typically a nonjob performance behavior
for most of us. Think of your last experience of driving your
car, when you observed other drivers changing lanes without
signaling, going through caution (yellow) lights and stop (red)
lights, not coming to a complete stop at a stop sign, or tail-
gating. (Notice, it is always easier to see somebody else's performance failures than it is to see one's own.) You probably
wondered how those other drivers could ever have obtained
driver's licenses when they did not seem to know the basic
rules of driver performance. One answer is that they did know
what to do, but poor driver performance is too rarely punished
and good performance is never overtly rewarded. This is similar to what happens in many work situations.

At work, employees can be expected to change the ways
they work because they are not machines that can be programmed and expected to continue performing in an unchanged fashion until they break down. Returning to our
previous example, notice what happens in some jurisdictions
when a driver receives a certain number of moving violations
as notification of poor performance. The substandard driver,
as evidenced by citations from law enforcement officers, is assigned to a driver refresher (training) program. This assignment is based on the assumption that the driver has forgotten
how to perform and that the training will remedy the situation. If, indeed, forgetting is the cause, the training is certainly
appropriate. Unfortunately, as in many work situations, the
lack of adequate performance may not be caused by a lack of
skill or knowledge about how to perform, but by people's in-

ability to see why any other performance is desirable. In such cases, training will not alter performance.

It is possible, however, that the performers have forgotten the desirable behaviors. That happens in many situations where the performance is repetitive. The performer develops shortcuts or engages in practices that do not seem to be wrong—practices that are more comfortable for the performer than those previously learned. This behavior is frequently seen in technical workers who develop their own ways of performing some tasks. If their variations nevertheless produce the desired output, it is best to maintain the status quo. If the variations produce a different or lower level of output, or if they conflict with the performance of others, it may be necessary to provide training.

The introduction of new technology has always been a factor in the workplace, but since the early 1960s, the proliferation has been astounding. Until recently, the introduction of new technology took place slowly and over a long period of time. Previously, employees who had achieved journeyman status, or had other indicators that they had mastered a craft or trade, could be fairly certain that the skills and knowledge acquired would be useful throughout an entire work life. This is no longer the case for most of those in the work force. Some new technology creates new jobs, but here the concern is with new technology that an employee is required to use on the existing job. The job is the same, but now the employee is expected to perform differently.

In the early 1950s, one of the authors was in graduate school at Columbia University where studies were being conducted on a new technology for the office—the electric typewriter. At first, it was assumed that it would be easy for a good typist to move from the manual typewriter to the electric typewriter. Since the keyboards were the same, the new technology merely presented the possibility that the typist could now perform more rapidly; but it did not work out that way. Instead, the research discovered that a new typist could learn to use the electric typewriter much more rapidly and efficiently than could a highly efficient experienced manual typist. When the manual machine typists were given appropriate training, it was found that they had to unlearn their old performance before they were able to learn the new performance required by the new technology.

Ultimately, the manual typist performed on the electric typewriter at the same level as the new electric typist, but it required training. And when organizations did not provide such training, and compared the output, the manual typist was inadequate on the electric machine. Generalizations were made such as, those old manual typists cannot cope with the new technology, and the manual typists were purposely working slowly to sabotage the introduction of the new office technology. Does this sound familiar? Those comments seem to accompany the introduction of almost any new technology when previous performers are compared with new performers. Those who make such comments overlook the need to provide appropriate training for those who are expected to use the new technology on their present jobs.

More recently, the same situation has been observed with the introduction of computer-based word processing, which required clerk-typists to learn to use the new computer technology. It was possible to hire new workers who had the requisite skills, and in some situations this was done. One result, however, was a decline in the morale of other workers, who could see themselves being replaced by new technology. An organization that provided the requisite training benefited from lower turnover and improved morale as well as from improved performance.

There are innumerable similar situations, but perhaps the clerk-typist to word processor movement has been more visible than most. Other technological changes requiring training are not always so observable, but it is important that any time management decides to introduce a new technology, the training implications should be explored with the HRD people. In too many situations, the HRD people have not adequately communicated to management the need for training to accompany technological change.

It is unfortunate that too many line managers do not appreciate the need to couple new technology with appropriate training. Toffler has pointed out that "if the company is going to re-tool, it has a responsibility to help its people re-tool also" (1983, p. 54). That concept is certainly not yet generally accepted among managers and executives. Toffler goes on to emphasize that "for every dollar we put into new machines, several dollars will have to be invested in human capital—in training, education, relocation, social rehabilitation, in cultural adaptation" (1983, p. 54). Perhaps this is too radical an idea for many managers, but when the new equipment fails, or critical accidents take place, the need for training and education becomes woefully apparent.

In recent years, there have been several dramatic incidents that highlight the need for appropriate training. In March 1979, the United States experienced the first major nuclear disaster, at Three Mile Island (TMI) nuclear facility in Pennsylvania. It would not be helpful to dwell on the effects; rather, we want to emphasize the training deficiencies that were uncovered during the investigation. On April 11, 1979, President Carter issued an executive order creating the President's Commission on the Accident at Three Mile Island. Their report is known as the Kemeny Report, named after the Chairman John G. Kemeny, President of Dartmouth College. One of the findings of the Kemeny Commission was that the equipment was good enough, and that, except for human failures, the major accident would have been a minor incident. The Kemeny Commission made four major recommendations concerning training. They saw the inadequacy in that area as crucial to the whole incident, and among their recommendations can be found statements such as: the training must be continuously integrated with operating experience, there should be continuous training of the operators to respond to emergencies, supervisors of operators should have at the minimum at least the same training as the operators, and the situation required a high level of realism in the operator training.

The Nuclear Regulatory Commission, Special Inquiry Group, in its report *Three Mile Island: A Report to the Commissioners and the Public*, emphasized that "the operators on duty had not received training adequate to ensure that they would be able to recognize and respond to a serious accident during the first hour or two after it occurred" (1979, p. 103). They further noted that "the largest portion of operator training is reading and classroom training," and "that operators are trained primarily for normal power operations and for startup and shutdown of the plan, not for accidents" (1979, p. 103). These statements, and those of the Kemeny Commission, highlight the need for training to be related to performance.

In August 1987, the United States experienced one of its most horrendous air crashes when Northwest Airlines flight number 522 failed to gain altitude on takeoff and crashed to the ground killing all but one of the passengers. On one hand, it was pointed out that the pilot had over thirty years of flying experience. At the same time, many statements were made by leading officials and investigators about the tendency of flight crews, in general, to become so accustomed to what they do that they neglect to follow standard procedures. One government spokesman noted that there was no question that the cockpit crew was proficient, but that work can become routine, and routine becomes a risk. Many commentators, at the time, pointed out the need for continual training as one way of overcoming the risk from routine. This obviously applies to many more jobs than just those done by the cockpit crew of an airplane.

Increasing references to *retraining* have confused the field because the use of the prefix *re* communicates the assumption that there has been some prior training, and that is not always the case. Some people use retraining to refer to learning required because of the introduction of new technology, while others use the term to mean training needed when performance is not up to standard. Still others use it to mean the learning needed when employers are displaced by technology and are forced to seek work in different fields. Given this diverse use of the word *retraining*, it should probably be avoided. But since it does not appear that its use will be abandoned, caution should be exercised when using the word.

Not as dramatic as new technology, but still requiring some training, is a change in the process of doing a job. This may be the result of a substitution of materials, such as plastic for metal. Or a new machine incorporating existing technology may change how a process is performed. This kind of change sometimes occurs when several separate steps in a process are combined through the use of a new device. Though it is possible to allow for learning through trial and error, that approach can be costly. By contrast, allocating funds for training can reduce the time necessary to achieve the desired level of quality and quantity and can result in a cost saving.

A process change may involve nonmechanical changes in how people are expected to do their jobs. The executives of an organization may decide to move into project management, matrix, or some other pattern of organizational relationships that is different from the one currently in use. When training is provided, the possibility of a successful change is enhanced, but if training is not provided, such a change may not be successfully accomplished (Lippitt, Langseth, and Mossop, 1985). When change is not readily accepted within an organization, management may react by noting that there is always resistance to change when the root cause is a lack of training to provide learning in the different skills, knowledge, and attitude required by the process of change.

An organization may redesign jobs even though little or no new technology is involved and even though the employees are working up to standard on the existing job. Hackman and Oldham (1980) see the need for redesign from both the individual and the organizational viewpoints, but they believe that one way of improving performance is to change the context in which work is performed through alternative work schedules or alternative work sites. Such changes can be implemented successfully if appropriate training is provided.

Training for new employees is a constant necessity. Theoretically, if the human resource management group performed successfully, jobs would be filled by employees who were recruited and selected because they could do the job and could meet the required quantity and quality standards without further training. Still, at the very least, new employees should participate in an orientation program deigned to enhance their identification with the new employer (Shea, 1981). Such training programs usually consist of information about the organization, employee responsibilities, and employee benefits. All of those are important, but it is often necessary to provide job-related training, though that can be left for later when the new employee actually starts performing. At that point, it may become necessary for the supervisor to provide OJT to bridge the gap between the knowledge the new employee already has and the knowledge that must be learned to apply that previous experience to the present job.

Orientation training should also include components related to job shock that, in some cases, is very much like culture shock. When employees are being trained to work in foreign environments, there is general agreement that they should receive appropriate cross-cultural training (Martin, 1986). Too few HRD people realize that many new employees experience similar cultural shock when they move from one organization to another. It is not as dramatic as packing one's bags and going to another country, but cultural differences from one organization to another can be almost as significant (Nadler, 1985).

There is another need, not as well known, but still essential, and that is the need for legal requirements. Although this is a need that must be met by the individual, it is also in the best interests of the organization that it be met. Without the training, the individual could lose certification or licensure and therefore no longer be able to work in the designated capacity in the organization. In 1986, the *Chronicle of Higher Education* published a chart listing some professional fields and the states that required continuing education (training).

Table 2. Some Professional Fields and
State Requirements for Training.

Profession	Number of States
Architects	1
Certified Public Accountants	47
Engineers	2
Lawyers	20
Nurses	11
Nursing Home Administrators	42
Psychologists	13
Real Estate Personnel	29
Social Workers	19

Source: Adapted from "State Requirements for Continuing Education . . . ," May 21, 1986, p. 16.

Table 2 provides a listing of ten fields and the number of states that require training.

These requirements are established by statute or by regulation and therefore are always subject to change. The term *continuing education* conveys that these are not requirements to enter the field or for the first licensing, but that the individual must engage in a certain number of hours of instruction to retain the licensure. Of course, there is little in this process that relates to identified learning needs, and that perceived deficiency has raised opposition from some who protest against this form of mandatory training. Despite that, the trend to require training in some fields in order to retain a license seems to be growing.

POLICY CONSIDERATIONS

The general level of responsibility for training within the organization is at the level of the immediate supervisor, the person who appraises performance or who is directly concerned with the output of the performance. Such supervisors exist at many levels of the organization, the most common being at the first level where somebody gets work done through the efforts of others. The term *supervisor*, in this sense, applies to all levels of the organization, for the manager who supervises others, at any level, is the supervisor responsible for providing training. The reason for this assignment of responsibility becomes obvious when one considers the definition and earlier discussion of the purposes of training. Supervisors at all levels are concerned primarily with the performance of individuals on their present jobs, so supervisors should be sensitive to the purposes of training as discussed earlier.

An important part of that responsibility is selecting learners. There are times when the selection is obvious, such as when the need is due to below-standard performance. Obviously, those who are performing below the standard are the ones to be trained. It may also be desirable, however, to include others who could benefit from a refresher type of training, though it should be clear to the learner why the training is being provided.

Where performance is quantifiable, such as in the production of a certain number of units, below-standard performance is readily discernible. Service and knowledge jobs, in which substandard performance may not be so apparent, generally involve qualitative performance. In those situations, the selection of learners is not automatic and must be approached with a sensitivity to perceptions. That is, if the learner does not perceive the need for the training, the learner may attribute other reasons for the selection rather than those actually driving the supervisor. The supervisor is responsible for seeing to it that expectations are mutual and clear.

It is possible for a supervisor to select learners to attend training even though that supervisor does not expect any performance improvement. This may be the result of exasperation or because of a vague belief on the part of the supervisor that training is the cure, even though the cause has not been determined. In that case, the supervisor may make a statement to an employee such as, "You have not been performing well, and maybe going to training will wake you up." The result is usually dissatisfaction on the part of the supervisor because performance does not change, irritation on the part of the employee who does not see the need for training, and confusion in the HRD unit where the need for the training has not been determined.

Some learners are selected to attend a training program as a form of reward. The supervisor considers leaving the job site to be a perquisite and selects employees to attend training as a reward for good performance—or to demonstrate the power of the supervisor to dole out those rewards. Nobody expects any different job performance to take place, but, as a supervisor might put it, "It will make the employee feel better." This is usually the case if the training site is a plush conference center, or some other desirable place.

Learners can also be self-selected. That frequently happens when the HRD unit publishes a list of courses, and supervisors are told to encourage their employees to sign up. Each supervisor might even be given a quota of slots available to each supervisor for a particular training program. But, actually, it is not training, for it is not related to any of the purposes previously described. The employee may feel a need to learn, but that need may have nothing to do with the present job. There is a time for learners to volunteer for learning, but that time is generally not appropriate for training. This point will become more apparent in the next chapters dealing with education and development.

For training, learners should be selected by the supervisor and assigned to the training program just as they would be to any other job assignment, because training should be considered a part of normal job activity. The supervisor should consider the implications of the assignment, particularly when the training is off site and could disrupt the employee's family life or previous commitments.

Training requires a budget which may be the responsibility of the supervisor, depending upon the form of financial center that exists, as discussed in Chapter Three. In the case of a budget item center, the budget may be in the HRD unit and, therefore, the supervisor would have no responsibility for it. This is the least desirable situation since the training would not cost the supervisor anything from the operating budget. This arrangement encourages voluntary self-selection by the learners and can generally be expected to result in minimal performance improvement on the present job. The cost and profit financial centers for HRD are more appropriate for training, since, in those configurations, the supervisor has budgetary responsibility. Accordingly, the supervisor will seek the training that will improve job performance and will select those learners who are most appropriate for the particular training program.

EVALUATION

Evaluation is always a critical element in any HRD program. For training there are two elements that can be evaluated: learning and performance. Learning takes place during the training program and should be evaluated during the experience (formative evaluation) and at the end of the experience (summative evaluation). This kind of evaluation should not be confused with the application evaluation of performance, which is concerned with the application of the learning to the job situation. The HRD unit should assume primary responsibility for evaluating the learning, and most training designs include provision for such evaluation, usually through some form of testing. In the case of airline pilots, this may be accomplished by using a sophisticated simulator that enables the HRD people to determine whether the pilot has learned and has achieved the objectives of that particular training experience. The mistake that is frequently made is to confuse that evaluation of learning with performance evaluation, for the latter can only be determined when the pilot is placed in the actual work situation.

Recall the definition of HRD that includes "the possibility of performance improvement." The significance of the word *possibility* is sometimes seen in safety training programs. The learner is trained and, at the end of the program, is able to identify the different pieces of safety equipment and knows when they should be used. On returning to the job, however, the supervisor might say, "O. K., you had your fun at that training session. Now, let's get back to work. Forget about the safety goggles and safety shoes. It takes too much time to put them on and that takes time away from the job. After all, why not be macho and show that you don't need that sissy stuff." Obviously, the supervisor has decreased the possibility that performance will improve—that safety clothing will be worn or safety procedures followed. One way to enhance the possibility that the learner will apply the learning and improve performance is to include the supervisor in the design of the program and in the design of the evaluation of performance that will take place when the employee returns to the job. Without the cooperation of the supervisor, performance evaluation is difficult, if not impossible.

The concept of *possibility* has been of some concern to a few HRD practitioners, and, although it is not a major item, it cannot be summarily dismissed. By no means is the term meant to suggest that HRD cannot be effective. Rather, it is a question of not promising more than HRD can deliver. The goal should always be for the total effectiveness of the HRD effort, not anything less. There can be a difference, however, between the change goal designed into the HRD program, and actual performance back on the job.

The HRD practitioner does not direct or control performance in the operating unit where the learner works. The line managers have to recognize and accept the hands-off position of the HRD unit, with its inherent limitation of only offering the possibility of change that must be reinforced and brought about through the efforts of the line managers.

This chapter has dealt with training for employees, while training for nonemployees is discussed in Chapter Seven. There is another type of HRD program for employees, and while this chapter has dealt with learning related to the present job (training), the next chapter will deal with learning related to a different job (education).

Carl R. Rogers (1902–1987), humanistic psychologist and leader of non-directive client-centered therapy, received M.A. (1928) and Ph.D. (1931) degrees in psychology from Teachers College, Columbia University. He held several clinical positions, such as director of the Rochester Guidance Center, director of counseling services of the United Service Organizations, fellow at the Center for Advanced Study in the Behavioral Sciences, and resident fellow for ten years at the Center for Studies of the Person in California. In addition, he was a professor of psychology at several universities—Ohio State University (1940–44), University of Chicago (1947–57), and University of Wisconsin (1957–63).

Rogers's publications reflect his faith in the human potential for solving one's own problems and for developing into fully functioning persons. Among his better-known books are *Psychotherapy and Personality Change* (1954), *On Becoming a Person* (1961), *Carl Rogers on Encounter Groups* (1970), *Freedom to Learn* (1969), and *Freedom to Learn for the 80's* (1983).

Carl Rogers articulated many of the practical applications of a humanistic philosophy to education. His emphasis upon self-initiated learning that is relevant to the learner, student participation in planning and evaluation, the teacher as facilitator, and group methods has served as a model for adult educators. The following selection is from an address Rogers gave to the 1967 annual conference of the Association for Supervision and Curriculum Development. In it he rejects the traditional conception of teaching as unsuited to the needs of a changing world. Rather, he asserts, the goal of education should be the "facilitation of learning." To bring about significant learning, a personal relationship must exist between facilitator and learner, a relationship that is similar to that between therapist and client.

CARL R. ROGERS

10 The Interpersonal Relationship in the Facilitation of Learning

. . . It is in fact nothing short of a miracle that the modern methods of instruction have not yet entirely strangled the holy curiosity of inquiry; for this delicate little plant, aside from stimulation, stands mainly in need of freedom; without this it goes to wrack and ruin without fail—ALBERT EINSTEIN

I wish to begin this paper with a statement which may seem surprising to some and perhaps offensive to others. It is simply this: Teaching, in my estimation, is a vastly overrated function.

Having made such a statement, I scurry to the dictionary to see if I really mean what I say. Teaching means "to instruct." Personally I am not much interested in instructing another. "To impart knowledge or skill." My reaction is, why not be more efficient, using a book or programmed learning? "To make to know." Here my hackles rise. I have no wish to *make* anyone know something. "To show, guide, direct." As I see it, too many people have been shown, guided, directed. So I come to the conclusion that I *do* mean what I said. Teaching is, for me, a relatively unimportant and vastly overvalued activity.

But there is more in my attitude than this. I have a negative reaction to teaching. Why? I think it is because it raises all the wrong questions. As soon as we focus on teaching, the question arises, what shall we teach? What, from our superior vantage point, does the other person need to know? This raises the ridiculous question of coverage. What shall the course cover? (Here I am acutely aware of the fact that "to cover" means both "to take in" and "to conceal from view," and I believe that most courses admirably achieve both these aims.) This notion of coverage is based on the assumption that what is taught is what is learned; what is presented is what is assimilated. I know of no assumption so obviously untrue. One does not need research to provide evidence that this is false. One needs only to talk with a few students.

But I ask myself, "Am I so prejudiced against teaching that I find no situation in which it is worthwhile?" I immediately think of my experience in Australia only a few months ago. I became much interested in the Australian aborigine. Here is a group which for more than 20,000 years has managed to live and exist in a desolate environment in which a modern man would perish within a few days. The secret of his survival has been teaching. He has passed on to the young every shred of knowledge about how to find water, about how to track game, about how to kill the kangaroo, about how to find his way through the trackless desert. Such knowledge is conveyed to the young as being *the* way to behave, and any innovation is frowned upon. It is clear that teaching has provided him the way to survive in a hostile and relatively unchanging environment.

Now I am closer to the nub of the question which excites me. Teaching and the imparting of knowledge make sense in an unchanging environment. This is why it has been an unquestioned function for centuries. But if there is one truth about modern man, it is that he lives in an environment which is *continually changing*. The one thing I can be sure of is that the physics which is taught to the present day student will be outdated in a decade. The teaching in psychology will certainly be out of date in 20 years. The so-called "facts of history" depend very largely upon the current mood and temper of the culture. Chemistry, biology, genetics, sociology, are in such flux that a firm statement made today will almost certainly be modified by the time the student gets around to using the knowledge.

We are, in my view, faced with an entirely new situation in education where the goal of education, if we are to survive, is the *facilitation of change and learning*. The only man who is educated is the man who has learned how to learn; the man who has learned how to adapt and change; the man who has realized that no knowledge is secure, that only the process of *seeking* knowledge gives a basis for security. Changingness, a reliance on *process* rather than upon static knowledge, is the only thing that makes any sense as a goal for education in the modern world.

So now with some relief I turn to an activity, a purpose, which really warms me—the *facilitation of learning*. When I have been able to transform a group—and here I mean all the members of a group, myself included—into a community of *learners*, then the excitement has been almost beyond belief. To free curiosity; to permit individuals to go charging off in new directions dictated by their own interests; to unleash curiosity; to open everything to questioning and exploration; to recognize that everything is in process of change—here is an experience I can never forget. I cannot always achieve it in groups with which I am associated but when it is partially or largely achieved then it becomes a never-to-be-forgotten group experience. Out of such a context arise true students, real learners, creative scientists and scholars and practitioners, the kind of individuals who can live in a delicate but ever-changing balance between what is presently known and the flowing, moving, altering, problems and facts of the future.

Here then is a goal to which I can give myself whole-heartedly. I see the facilitation of learning as the aim of education, the way in which we might develop the learning man, the way in which we can learn to live as individuals in process. I see the facilitation of learning as the function which may hold constructive, tentative, changing, process answers to some of the deepest perplexities which beset man today.

But do we know how to achieve this new goal in education, or is it a will-of-the-wisp which sometimes occurs, sometimes fails to occur, and thus offers little real hope? My answer is that we possess a very considerable knowledge of the conditions which encourage self-initiated, significant, experiential, "gut-level" learning by the whole person. We do not frequently see these conditions put into effect because they mean a real revolution in our approach to education and revolutions are not for the timid. But we do find examples of this revolution in action.

We know—and I will briefly describe some of the evidence—that the initiation of such learning rests not upon the teaching skills of the leader, not upon his scholarly knowledge of the field, not upon his curricular planning, not upon his use of audio-visual aids, not upon the programmed learning he utilizes, not upon his lectures and presentations, not upon an abundance of books, though each of these might at one time or another be utilized as an important resource. No, the facilitation of significant learning rests upon certain attitudinal qualities which exist in the personal *relationship* between the facilitator and the learner.

We came upon such findings first in the field of psychotherapy, but increasingly there is evidence which shows that these findings apply in the classroom as well. We find it easier to think that the intensive relationship between therapist and client might possess these qualities, but we are also finding that they may exist in the countless interpersonal interactions (as many as 1,000 per day, as Jackson [1966] has shown) between the teacher and his pupils.

Leon McKenzie (1932–   ) majored in philosophy as an undergraduate and pursued the study of philosophy, religion, and adult education at the graduate level, receiving an M.A. from Fordham University and an Ed.D. from Indiana Universtiy. He has been on the faculty of Indiana University in adult education since 1973. In addition to university teaching, McKenzie is director of human resource development at Indiana University Hospitals.

A wide range of interests in adult eduation is reflected in his publications on evaluation, nursing education, simulation gaming, participation, philosophy, and training. His 1978 book, *Adult Education and the Burden of the Future*, made a major contribution to the philosophy of adult education. Strongly influenced by existential philosophy, McKenzie views the central work of being human as the creation of an authentically human future through the exercise of enlightened choice. The primary "givens" of human existence are freedom, albeit a limited freedom, and a sense of responsibility which calls people to collaborate in the construction of the future. *Adult Education and the Burden of the Future* was followed by *The Religious Education of Adults* (1982) which cast the concept of adult religious education into an educational framework rather than a theological one.

The following exerpt is from McKenzie's latest book, *Adult Education and Worldview Construction* (1991). McKenzie presents worldview construction as a goal for adult education. The author critiques two competing ideologies within adult education—the ideology of the far Right and the ideology of the Left. He sees these ideologies as the extreme ends of a continuum that represents the theoretical positions in adult education practice. Although neutrality in matters of social concern is impossible, facilitators must strive to remain impartial and avoid these ideological extremes if learners are to construct their own worldview without interference from the facilitator.

LEON McKENZIE

11 Adult Education and Worldview Construction

Adults will construct interpretive understandings of the world without educational interventions just as they can learn outside of a formal educational setting. Worldview construction takes place in the home, in the marketplace, on the playing field, and in association with others in hundreds of nonschool or nonprogram contexts. This is not to say, however, that education has not been used instrumentally to serve the purpose of worldview construction. Worldview construction may not be explicitly and formally stated as a goal of education in general, and adult education in particular, but insofar as any educational experience contributes to a person's interpretive understanding of the world, education is involved in worldview construction.

Adult education theorists have recognized the association between education and worldview construction without expressly using the words "worldview construction." Many of the goals they identify as proper to the work of adult education are related to the process of worldview construction. The ideas of several of these theorists are noted here to support this claim.

N. F. S. Grundtvig was a nineteenth century Danish philosopher-theologian-educationist-legislator whose ideas made an important impact on the thinking of Eduard Lindeman, a leading founder of American adult education.[1] Grundtvig proposed the idea of folk high school for those over eighteen years of age, a school without a rigidly fixed curriculum. The school was not to impart technical or vocational skills; cotter's schools, trade schools, agricultural schools were already established in Denmark in the 1830s for these purposes. The school was not to be subject centered but rather focused to a large extent on the interests of the learners.[2]

The purposes served by the school were: 1) the establishment of a clearer view of human and civic relationships and 2) the development of a livelier appreciation of the national fellowship from which issued everything great and good in the learner's heritage. Grundtvig was a nationalist in the sense he valued, and believed other Danes should appreciate, the heritage and tradition that grounded their existence as members of a national community. Learners were to be awakened and enlightened, and this was to be accomplished by means of the interchange of ideas via "free talk," what Grundtvig called the living word. Obviously the purposes of the school served also the process of what is described in these pages as worldview construction. Through the interchange of ideas, by means of open discussions, the adult learners were to examine their ideals and outlooks, their history and heritage.

Eduard Lindeman transported much of Grundtvig's philosophy to America. Much of this philosophy was highlighted in 1926 in *The Meaning of Adult Education*, a benchmark publication in the history of adult education in America. Education, according to Lindeman, was not a preparation for life but was coextensive with life. Adult education revolves around nonvocational ideals. " . . . adult education more accurately defined begins where vocational education leaves off. Its purpose is to put meaning into the whole of life."[3] Adult education was not to be identified with the systematic study of subjects but rather with the analysis of situations. The best resource for adult education was the experience of the learner.

Worldview construction, as described previously, concerns the putting of meaning into life. This is accomplished principally through the analysis and interpretation of life situations. This analytic and interpretive process is ongoing; personal experience is foundational for the process. It does not distort Lindeman's meaning to interpret adult education as having a supereminent goal relating to the facilitation of worldview construction.

Paul Bergevin was influenced by Grundtvig, Lindeman, and to a large extent, by Aristotle. Bergevin maintained that adult education functions to achieve purposes transcendent to whatever topic adults happen to be studying. The teacher who helps adults learn how to make chairs, for example, must also in some way help them to better themselves as human beings. Adult education has several general goals among which are: 1) helping adults achieve a degree of happiness and meaning in life, 2) helping adults understand themselves, their talents, their limitations, and their relationships with others, 3) helping adults understand the need for lifelong learning, 4) providing opportunities to help adults grow spiritually, culturally, physically, politically, and vocationally, and 5) providing education for survival, i.e., literacy education, health education, and vocational skills training.[4]

Bergevin's emphasis on the acquisition of happiness and meaning, and the attainment of understanding through adult education stands forth as central to his philosophy. These ends were to be sought, he stated, even when the content of an educational program concerned everyday, mundane, or tech-

nical matters. A transcendent goal and the possibilities of profound understanding come into being whenever adults gather
in a purposeful way. He once remarked to me that the twenty
minute break in his three-hour graduate seminar in adult education philosophy was the most important part of the after-
noon. "Just look at them," he directed. "Real learning is taking
place in so many ways."[5] Bergevin would not argue with the
proposition that the facilitation of worldview construction was
an important aim of adult education. I was privileged to participate in sometimes lengthy discussions with Bergevin that
addressed the needs of adults to order their lives, to find co-
herence and meaning in life, before they could achieve anything resembling happiness.

Jerold Apps expressed some of his philosophical beliefs
anent adult education after reviewing the various competing
philosophies of education. Apps stated his belief that human
beings were more than mere animals and that they had minds
and souls. He indicated that people are constantly searching
to understand themselves, their relationships with the natural
and social environments, and how they relate to a Higher Being. For Apps learning is a process by which we seek these
and various other understandings.[6]

Again, Apps' views reflect an orientation to what has
been described here as worldview construction. Adults are constantly striving for understanding. They seek interpretations
that bring understanding and meaning to their lives. This
quest is ongoing throughout life.

More recently Stephen Brookfield envisioned adult education as involving the identification of external sources and
internalized assumptions framing human conduct. He called
for the critical assessment of these sources and assumptions.
"Such critical awareness will involve a realization of the con-
textual, provisional, and relative nature of supposed 'truth,'
public knowledge and personal belief." Once assumptions are
perceived as irrelevant and inauthentic, there will follow a
transformation of individual and collective circumstances.
This transformation becomes apparent in the renegotiation of
personal relationships, the bestowal of significance to the conditions of work, and an engagement in the alteration of social
forms.[7]

What each of these theorists postulates as goals of adult education, speaking out of different interpretive understandings of the world, is that adult education is not simply training nor is it the transmission of subject matter. Adult education, to use my language, is and can be a major factor in helping adults construct the network of ideas, values, feelings, beliefs, opinions, intuitions, judgments, choices, and actions that constitute a worldview. Historically adult education has been recognized as a force for individual and societal growth; it has also been concerned with worldview construction, albeit these precise words have not been used by adult education theorists explicitly. I suggest there is a common vision shared by the theorists mentioned above and that this vision is directly relevant to what I have called worldview construction.

It may be objected that worldview construction has been defined so broadly as to include almost any philosophical statement of the ideal goals of adult education. I cannot argue with this objection. Worldview construction is, *de facto*, a surpassingly inclusive process. If relationships can be found between worldview construction and many of the ideals enunciated by adult education theorists, it is because worldview construction is a complex concept that serves as a focus of confluence for these ideals. Worldview construction is such a fundamental human activity—such a primary concern of *Dasein*—that most goals stated as proper to adult education will find correspondence with the concept of worldview construction.

WORLDVIEW CONSTRUCTION: TWO IDEOLOGIES

There are many ways of thinking of adult education, many schools of thought vis-á-vis the practice of adult education, many philosophies of adult education. Various schools of thought were categorized by John Elias and Sharan Merriam in their influential work on the philosophical foundations of adult education. Liberal Adult Education has its origins in classical Greek philosophers; emphasis is placed on the development of intellectual powers and the mastery of specific knowledge. Progressive Adult Education originated in the progressive movement in politics and concerns for social progress. The progressive movement envisioned social change as taking place through the instrumentality of education. Behaviorist Adult Education is rooted in modern philosophical and scientific movements, and fosters behavior modification and learning through reinforcement. Humanistic Adult Education is related to existentialism and humanistic psychology; key concepts are freedom and autonomy. Radical Adult Education springs from the same soil that nurtured Marxism, socialism and left-wing Freudianism. Finally, Analytic Adult Education originated in logical positivism and British analytic philosophy.[8]

Which of these philosophies can function most effectively as a basis for the facilitation of worldview construction? The Elias-Merriam classification scheme is helpful for sorting out the tendencies of various theorists and arranging these tendencies in some kind of order. I wish to employ a different arrangement, however, for understanding adult education philosophies. I prefer to view competing schools of thought in terms of points on a continuum. The extreme ends of the continuum are represented by two theoretical positions regarding adult education practice: the ideology of the Right and the ideology of the Left.

What distinguishes these ideologies fundamentally is their orientation toward time. Ideologues of the far Right fix their gaze lovingly on the past. Nostalgia is a foremost governing emotion. The past represents, and must always represent, the standard for thinking, willing, and doing; the past sets out ideals and values that must never be violated. Looking to the past the ideologue of the far Right sees a pristine Garden of Eden that is forever normative for human affairs.

On the other hand, the ideologue of the far Left despises the past and has fallen in love with an idealized and often romanticized future, a utopia. Utopia is normative for present action: Whatever is in tune with the desired future is correct and even required. Hope in the future is the inspiring virtue: the Garden of Eden is located in the future. The past is no more; the heritage of the past must be criticized and, finally, destroyed for the sake of the future.

The question, then, is this: What kind of educational intervention or program, as an expression of an underlying ideology, is most promising for the facilitation of worldview construction among adults? The question cannot be avoided. Educational programs are designed and implemented by human beings. Human beings have prejudices, assumptions, and beliefs that eventually find instantiation in what they do. Everyone has an ideology, even the person who claims freedom from ideology. Not to choose is to choose; not to have an ideology is to have an ideology that maintains it is possible to be perfectly "objective" in viewing the world. Where should the adult educator strive to take a position on the continuum of philosophies?

The Ideology of the Right

By ideology I mean quite plainly a distinctive manner of thinking characteristic of a group of persons. Let it be given that the various points on the continuum of philosophical thinking about adult education represent definite theoretical positions if not full-blown theories. Both ends of the continuum are extreme. Any description of either end of the continuum will approach caricature. Caricature, however, is sometimes helpful for delineating the salient features of any speculative position.

Thinkers located on the far Right, if not completely antiquarian, are enamored of the past. They prize tradition (defined in a narrow sense), continuity, and authority. Through the instrumentality of adult education, it is thought, learners are furnished with obediential potencies, habits of mind, and particular ways of addressing controversial issues. If there is to be change, change must come through evolutionary processes and not through revolution. The principal attribute of correct evolutionary processes is gradualism, a gradualism that is fearful and cautious of any kind of change. The primacy of order is assumed. There can be no authentic advance unless it is orderly. Ideally education forms adults for useful lives within an established order in which social, economic, political, and ethical norms are prescribed. The adult educator is the authority figure who decides what must be learned. Paternalism is the central feature of far Right thinking about adult education.

Ideologies of the Right are not currently in vogue. Liberal Adult Education is the school of thought most likely to tilt toward the Right end of the continuum. Liberal Adult Education, in the classical sense of liberal which indicates the kind of education identified as appropriate for the leisure classes, has relatively few supporters today. Egalitarian dogmas have leveled differences between intellectual elites and academic underachievers, between the well-educated and the hardly educated. Nonetheless educational programs for adults that tend toward the Right of the continuum still exist today.

The Right: A Scenario

Assume an adult educator responsible for library-based adult education programs wishes to conduct a discussion program that deals directly with worldview construction. The educator is concerned that most adults today lack familiarity with the great classical texts of antiquity. A discussion program is developed employing an approach similar to the Great Books model. The program is organized on several assumptions. First, adults need to read some of the classics of Western civilization. Whether they recognize this need is not really relevant; the need for cultural literacy is never recognized by the masses. Second, adults need a leader who selects the classics that will be read and discussed. Unaware of their need for cultural literacy the prospective participants in the program will also be unable to choose the correct books. Third, adults need someone to sequence, direct, and monitor learning activities. The adult educator serves a police function while professing to be the keeper of the truth.

The adult educator, in this scenario, is an authority or expert. Adults are dependent, ill-informed, and unable to determine what is necessary for them to discuss their worldviews intelligently. Further, they are incapable of taking control over the content of the discussions. What is central to the program, of course, is the agenda of the adult educator and not the concerns of the participants relating to worldview construction. The adult educator, in effect, wishes to promote his or her own worldview as normative.

The Ideology of the Left

Thinkers on the Left of the continuum are utopian; they are principally interested in using education as a tool of social engineering for the creation of utopian societies that are described almost exclusively in political and economic terms. They reject traditional ways of thinking and take pride in being members of the *avant garde*. Education is to be used to liberate adults from false consciousness. Learners must critique their assumptions about themselves and others. Evidence that such criticism is effective is adduced when learners experience a transformation of their perspectives and confess their former sins of wrong thinking. Education is primarily emancipatory. The adult educator is a change agent. If the adult educator of the far Right is paternalistic, the adult educator of the far Left is messianic.

Ideologies of the Left are predominant in the literature of adult education today. Neo-Marxist doctrines, particularly the doctrine that views the process of history as determined by class struggle and oppression, are favored in not a few academic centers by professors and the perfervid graduate students who come under their influence. The element of Progressive Adult Education that stresses social change together with Radical Adult Education constitute a major force in the theoretical foundations of adult education today, on many campuses if not elsewhere. One is hardly a member of the club in good standing, in many circles, if he or she does not frequently talk about liberation and emancipation with great earnestness.

A Scenario: The Left

Suppose an adult educator desires to arrange a discussion program that addresses worldview construction. An approach not unlike Jack Mezirow's perspective transformation model is used.[9] The adult learners are assumed, to some degree, to be victims of oppression. Whatever evil happens in their lives, it is further assumed, is attributable solely to the machinations of oppressors, the perversity of society, or unfair economic conditions. Oppressors cannot be trusted to be other than oppressors; they can never change oppressive patterns. The dialectical struggle between bourgeois oppressors and exploited masses is inevitable and ongoing.

The adult educator takes the role of emancipator. Under the guidance of the adult educator learners will put aside their false consciousness or distorted ways of thinking and experiencing the world. The adult educator, of course, defines the nature of false consciousness and determines when the learner's critique of false consciousness has been adequate, i.e., when a change of heart or conversion has taken place. The political agenda of the adult educator controls the discussion process. The adult educator serves a police function while professing to be a liberator. In effect the adult educator holds forth his or her worldview as normative.

A CRITIQUE OF THE RIGHT AND LEFT

It is a peculiar truth that as extremes of the continuum are approached, both Right and Left thinking become similar in many aspects. The ideologue of the Right wishes to assure the correct thinking that has been sanctioned by tradition and so exerts control over the structure and topics of discussion by prescribing canonical texts. The ideologue of the Left desires to eradicate the false thinking inherited from the past, thereby assuring movement toward the blessed Utopia, and so exerts control by pronouncing learners victims and by defining the contents of authentic consciousness. The ideologues of both the Right and the Left claim to serve adult learners by empowering them: with time-tested knowledge (in the case of the Right) or with insight into their oppression (in the case of the Left).

This is not to argue that programs such as the Great Books program are *per se* nefarious or otherwise inappropriate as frameworks for discussion and learning. Nor is it to argue that programs such as Mezirow's perspective transformation are useless. Familiarity with important texts, even when they are prescribed and selected by the adult educator, can further the growth of adult learners since the reactions of adult participants to these texts cannot be easily controlled in any event. Participation in a program that helps learners identify and examine their hidden assumptions can result in greater self-understanding among the learners, and can provoke positive changes in the learner's behavior. It is a fact that too many adults are unfamiliar with classic texts; it is also a fact that many adults are, and have been, victims of oppression.

Ideologies of both the Right and the Left thrive because each of these ideologies has taken hold of a truth. But the truth that we must pay honor to the past has been so heavily emphasized by the extreme Right that it suffers distortion; the truth that we must seek justice for the oppressed, and help them attain justice, has been so fanatically argued by the extreme Left that it has become misshapen. What remains attractive about far Right and far Left ideologies is that they yet retain the sparkling glimmer of truths that have been abused by excessive enthusiasm.

What is argued here, and with insistence, is that the direct facilitation of worldview construction should be balanced ideologically and should make no suppositions about any adult learners who are able to function normally in a learning situation. We must be wary, I strongly urge, of adult educators who attempt to change the worldviews of adults by reliance on subtle mechanisms inspired by the educator's commitment to a particular ideology. Adult educators, in this regard, must be facilitators and not preachers, politicians, salespersons or others who fulfill legitimate roles in contexts other than the setting of education. Adult educators, in respect to worldview construction programs, must refrain from dominating the educational process or insinuating their personal views into that process. If educators want to influence social policy or exercise political influence in specific matters that are publicly disputed they should run for public office.

Impartiality

Is it possible for any adult education program directly concerned with worldview construction to be open in respect to its structure and unbiased as to the management of discussion content? The format for this kind of program exists under the name of Participation Training. This system for adult learning was explained in some detail in a previous chapter.

Is it possible for any adult educator to be an impartial facilitator of adult discussion and dialogue? I respond to this question with an unequivocal "yes." If the word professional means anything at all in relation to the practice of adult education it should imply that facilitators of adult learning are able to restrain their speech acts, moderate their enthusiasms, and refrain from exerting influence on learners to accomplish personal agendas.

Not only is such impartiality possible but it seems that ethical considerations require moderation. To use the office of teacher and all of the legitimacy that surrounds the office to attempt to change a person's worldview is a betrayal of the office. Thomas Singarella and Thomas Sork raise the ethical question of whether adult educators should aspire to change social systems through their influence on changing individuals. "If the goal of the transactor is to produce individual change, then the adult educator is accountable to the individual learner. But if the goal is change in social systems, then to whom is the adult educator accountable?"[10] Clearly the adult educator as citizen is entitled to the full exercise of free speech. The adult educator as teacher or professor should be unhampered in expressing even the most unenlightened opinion in the ordinary classroom setting. But when it comes to efforts, whether overt or subtle, to adjust the adult learner's values, beliefs, feelings, and life practices in a context specifically designed for the sharing and evaluation of learner worldviews, the responsibility of the adult educator to be impartial outweighs his or her right to engage in persuasive behaviors. Granted, adults are ordinarily not as susceptible as children to the influence of authority figures. Nonetheless adults have the right to a context as free of educator influence as possible when they come together to share and examine their existing worldviews. We would be repelled by the idea of a Presbyterian adult educator who tries to influence, either openly or covertly, the members of a discussion group in a

Jewish retirement home to convert to the Presbyterian church. We should also be concerned when an adult educator attempts to insinuate his or her political beliefs into the thinking of adult learners.

Not all adult educators, it seems, agree with the above judgment. Phyllis Cunningham states that adult educators who claim to be apolitical are making a political statement because what one says while declaring neutrality (her word) is "that one is quite satisfied with the present organization of social relationships and the distribution of resources in society." It can be argued, Cunningham declares, that adult educators invent such ideas as scientific objectivity "to sanitize our basic desires to maintain inequality, racism, sexism, and classism since we are satisfied, on balance, with our 'share of the pie.' "[11]

If Cunningham is suggesting that adult educators must oppose in principle any form of injustice or discrimination based on racial, gender, or class biases, I have no argument with her. It is not my position that the adult educator should be impartial when it comes to general ethical norms and the general principles that govern a society espousing equality of opportunity. Every adult educator should teach, by example if not by word, that every person deserves just treatment, that civility is better than boorishness, and that moderation is a virtue. Unfortunately, some teachers, in the course of their teaching, have been known to endorse particular political parties and political candidates. The accusation of racism, sexism, and classism to impugn the motives of those who may honestly disagree with a theoretical position is not unheard of in the field of adult education. At times it seems as if the terms racism, sexism, and classism have become code words used to suppress dissent.

Self-appointed defenders of ideological purity occasionally become extremely prescriptive in support of their views. A case in point: the oral presentation guidelines for the Midwest Research-to-Practice Conference in Adult, Continuing and Community Education caution that careful attention must be taken to avoid the use of sexist language or language which *could be* (emphasis mine) construed as ethnically biased. Just about any language could be construed as ethnically biased by anyone wishing to attack the motives of a speaker. Language police are to be feared because thought police usually follow in their wake.

To practice impartiality as a facilitator of an educative process could mean, as Cunningham notes, that one is content with the *status quo*, but it does not necessarily mean this. Perhaps no one can remain neutral, but the question is one of impartiality and not neutrality. Impartiality can also mean that an adult educator, despite strong feelings and a definite position on sociopolitical issues, does not wish to co-opt any learner's right to define problems anent social relationships and resource distribution in our society. To opt for impartiality may mean that the adult educator judges it is ethically wrong to perpetrate an invasion of another's mind. In other words, the adult educator does not wish to adopt a messianic or paternalistic posture; the impartial adult educator does not equate critical thinking with his or her thinking.

REFERENCES

1. For an excellent review of the connection between the philosophy of N. F. S. Grundtvig and the ideas of Eduard Lindeman, see Clay Warren's "Andragogy and N. F. D. Grundtvig: A Critical Link" in *The Adult Education Quarterly*, Vol. 39, No. 4, 1989, pp. 211–23.

2. The best source for information about Grundvig's philosophy is Hal Koch's *Grundtvig*. Translated by Lewellyn Jones, the book as published New York by the Antioch Press in 1952.

3. Lindeman, Eduard. *The Meaning of Adult Education.* Montreal: Harvest House, 1961, p. 5. For a brief yet thorough analysis of Lindeman's influence on the development of American adult education see Stephen Brookfield's "The Contribution of Eduard Lindeman to the Development of Theory and Philosophy in Adult Education," *Adult Education Quarterly*, Vol. 34, No. 4, 1984, pp. 185–96.

4. Bergevin, Paul. *A Philosophy for Adult Education.* New York: The Seabury Press, 1967, pp. 31–40. Bergevin's reliance on Aristotle is not completely clear from the text of *A Philosophy for Adult Education.* Bergevin's classroom lectures, however, dwelled extensively on the value of Aristotle's ideas, particularly the notion of the golden mean and the avoidance of extreme positions on various continua of opinion. "Steer to the middle path," Bergevin encouraged.

5. This is a close paraphrase. I did not write out Bergevin's exact words.

6. Apps, Jerold. *Toward A Working Philosophy of Adult Education.* Syracuse: Syracuse University Publications in continuing Education, 1973, pp. 58–59.

7. Brookfield, Stephen. "A Critical Definition of Adult Education," *Adult Education Quarterly.* Vol. 36, No. 1, 1985, p. 46. Brookfield believes that "received assumptions" can be jettisoned thereby signifying the adult has become autonomous. Also, he seems to believe that everything received from one's past has been received uncritically. I agree with his emphasis on the need for ongoing assessment of assumptions but argue that we never completely transcend the traditions we have received nor must we in order to be critical thinkers.

8. Elias, John & Merriam, Sharan. *Philosophical Foundations of Adult Education.* New York: Krieger Publishing Company, 1980, pp. 9–11.

9. Mezirow defines perspective transformation as "the emancipatory process of becoming critically aware of how and why the structure of psycho-cultural assumptions has come to constrain the way we see ourselves and our relationships, reconstituting this structure to permit a more inclusive and discriminating integration of experience and acting upon these new understandings." Cf. Mezirow's "A Critical Theory of Adult Learning and Education," *Adult Education,* Vol. 32, No. 1, p. 6. I cite Mezirow's work as

exemplifying the Left not because of the radicalness of
his thinking but because his work represents the most
thoughtful expression of a Left-leaning theory in the
United States, and a theoretical position with which many
adult educators are familiar. Also, it seems to me, perspective transformation is obviously open to abuse at the
hands of self-styled saviors of the adult masses and for
this reason lends easily to the exemplification of far Left
ideology. For an analysis of Mezirow's thinking see the
article by Susan Collard and Michael Law "The Limits
of Perspective Transformation: A Critique of Mezirow's
Theory," *Adult Education Quarterly*, Vol. 39, No. 2, 1989,
pp. 99–107. See also Jack Mezirow's reply in "Transformation Theory and Social Action: A Response to Collard
and Law," in *Adult Education Quarterly*, Vol. 39, No. 3,
1989, pp. 169–75.

10. Singarella, Thomas & Sork, Thomas. "Questions of Values and Conduct: Ethical Issues for Adult Education."
Adult Education Quarterly, Vol. 33, No. 4, 1983, p. 249.

11. Cunningham, Phyllis. "The Adult Educator and Social Re-
sponsibility," in Ralph Brockett (ed.) *Ethical Issues in
Adult Education*. New York: Teachers College, Columbia
University, 1988, p. 136.

Peter Jarvis (1937–   ) is head of the Department of Educational Studies at the University of Surrey, U.K. He is also adjunct professor at the University of Georgia. He received his B.D. degree (1963) from The University of London, his B.A. (1969) in sociology from the University of Sheffield, his M.Sc. (1972) in sociology of education from the University of Birmingham, and his Ph.D. in sociology of the professions in 1977 from the University of Aston.

Jarvis's work has focused primarily on sociological and philosophical studies of adult education and adult learning. He has taught both teacher and adult and continuing education and has also been involved in a variety of research projects. In 1988, he was awarded the Cyril O. Houle World Award for Literature in Adult Education for his book *Adult Learning in the Social Context* (1987). His other publications include *Professional Education* (1983), *Adult and Continuing Education: Theory and Practice* (1983), *The Sociology of Adult and Continuing Education* (1985), *The Teacher-Practitioner in Nursing, Midwifery, and Health Visiting* (1985, with S. Gibson), *An International Dictionary of Adult and Continuing Education* (1990), and *Paradoxes of Learning* (1992). In addition, he has edited *Twentieth Century Thinkers in Adult Education* (1987), *Britain: Policy and Practice in Continuing Education* (1988), *Training Adult Educators in Western Europe* (1991, with A. Chadwick), and *Adult Education: Evolution and Achievements in a Developing Field of Study* (1991, with J. M. Peters & Associates). Jarvis is founding editor of the *International Journal for Lifelong Education*, editor of two book series on adult education, and a frequent speaker and lecturer on adult and continuing education throughout the world.

In the following selection, "Learning and Change" from *Paradoxes of Learning* (1992), Jarvis observes that while learning is a natural response to change, several factors such as risk, ritualized behavior, and social structures often serve to inhibit learning. He concludes that "Learning both produces change and occurs as a result of it."

PETER JARVIS

12 Learning and Change

Change is found in every area of life. There is, for instance, developmental change in people as they age, status change, geographical change, and a multitude of other forms of change. Indeed, change is endemic to social living, and any form of stasis is a rarity, if not an impossible occurrence, since societies and people exist in time. Nevertheless, people habitualize their actions and often appear to treat their external world as if it were static and unchanging. Since there is an indissoluble link between people and their sociocultural milieu, change in either the people or their surroundings is bound to upset any apparent harmony that has been established between them. Hence, disjuncture between people's biographies and their external sociocultural world is not an exception, but a rule.

But change is rarely revolutionary in character; it is most often evolutionary and gradual. The disjuncture between biography and experience is not likely to be anomic, so that potential conditions for learning are a common occurrence throughout life. Paradoxically, however, once people have learned, they have become more experienced and have therefore changed, so that learning is itself one of the social processes that helps create the conditions for yet more learning. Lifelong learning, then, is itself both a symbol and a reality of modern society. But if the change is too swift, individuals may have difficulty in adjusting to the new social conditions, and then they enter situations of nonaction and perhaps nonlearning. They may suffer some form of anomic response or feel that they are prevented from responding because they are too busy, and then the disjuncture experienced is stressful.

The focus of this chapter is on the relationship between learning and change. Paradoxes are inherent in this relationship: learning is a response to change, but it also creates it; learning is a mechanism of adaptation, but it also has the capacity to evoke it; people learn to be safe, but learning is also a risk-taking activity.

The chapter begins with an examination of the ways the social structures inhibit learning. Next it considers some of the possible outcomes of learning. It then addresses the issue of whether education produces change agents. Finally, it focuses on learning and risk.

THE INHIBITING FEATURES OF
THE SOCIAL STRUCTURES

Like culture, social structures do not exist. They cannot be handled or produced for inspection, so that they are not external to the people who experience them, although the different roles people play and the varying degrees of influence they exercise on others are self-evident and beyond dispute. Hence, the differentiation of society is clear, and the structures of a social system are apparent only through the systems of interaction that occur between the members of a social group. Behavioral patterns are self-evident, since the process of interaction is habitualized in ways discussed earlier. Therefore people who form longstanding relationships create expected patterns of behavior that, in turn, create obligations for continuity and even reproduction. People who exercise power over others have certain expectations of how others with less power or influence will act in their presence, and those with less power might act in keeping with their understanding of the expectations of the power-holders. Analysis of this form of social interaction has been conducted most incisively in a number of studies by Goffman (for instance, 1959, 1968a, 1968b, 1971, 1972). Goffman's often brilliant analyses reveal that people ritualize their behavior; they create for themselves forms and patterns to which they expect to conform and that they expect others to understand and adhere to when appropriate. People tend to take for granted the patterns of behavior that they have evolved, so that they are often unaware of the ritual involved. This is a paradoxical situation, inasmuch as people know that they are free to act otherwise but feel constrained to conform, often by relationships that are of their own making.

It was argued earlier that ritualized behavior provides little opportunity to learn. As in the harmonious situation in the Garden of Eden, there may be no disjuncture between the external world and the inner biography. But patterned behavior is essential to the smooth functioning of diverse and diffuse modern society. Many institutions, such as bureaucratic organizations, have evolved so as to ensure that regardless of who the office-holders are, their functions will still be performed in the same manner. Many people appear to have both their public and private lives surrounded by such obligations, so that they have little freedom to do other than conform, even though they still feel that they could act otherwise. Society's structures, including structures of people's own making—norms and folkways that manifest themselves in social action and relationships—guarantee that people's actions are repetitive and ritualized. They may feel disjuncture between their biography and their world but because of their own expectations or those of others, they reject opportunities to do things differently and learn. There are other times when disjuncture turns into dissonance and people do feel compelled to resolve the dilemma in which they find themselves. Obviously, they may not be able to do so if they are subject to the authority of others. The instruments of the state are often used repressively, in some cases to convince people that it is in their best interest to conform and in others, to force them to do so. Some people are brave or foolhardy and risk the consequences of not conforming—they may be authentic persons, but they suffer for being so.

We can now see why existentialists view power as so problematic. Those who exercise power over others often create situations where inauthenticity is manifest, for inauthenticity occurs, according to the different existentialist positions discussed earlier, wherever people cannot be true to themselves or to their situation. The Polonians seek to be true to their biography, the Dadaists to the situation, and those who follow Buber's (1959) understanding of relationships seek to be true to the people involved in the situation with them. At the same time, it has to be recognized that those who hold power do not always employ it in a negative manner; some actually use it constructively to enable others to act in certain ways that may be in their best interest.

For whatever reasons, people frequently find themselves in situations that provide potential learning opportunities and they do experience disjuncture, but they sometimes still feel unable to act otherwise. They feel that the social structures inhibit their potential, and they become dispirited. By contrast, others appear to strive against the odds and transform their situations. This process frequently means that old obligations have been fulfilled and new opportunities occur. To some extent, this might depend on people's social skills or on their holding fast to their Polonian principles.

But change is endemic to modern society, so that social situations change. People grow older, change their status and their occupation, move from one neighborhood or city to another, and so on. In the same way, managers change, governments change, and dictators are removed, so that the power relationships change. Suddenly, some of these inhibiting relationships disappear. People are free to act or speak in a less inhibited fashion. Again, however, they do not always do so. Some people follow their habitualized patterns; Riesman (1950) calls them "tradition-directed" people. Fromm (1984) suggests that the lack of freedom provides a sense of security from which some people do not wish to be free, but rather they seek only to submerge themselves in the outside world. Some others are able to respond to their newfound freedom and act differently and learn from their new primary experiences. Perhaps the best-known research in adult education that documents this is by Aslanian and Brickell (1980), who have shown how life transitions increase adult learning.

In these situations, the disjuncture they experience often causes people to plan experimental or creative behavior, monitoring it and then reflecting and learning from it. They acquire practical knowledge; they may have observed the experimental behavioral pattern in another's actions and copied or avoided it, and they may occasionally have even experimented without any observed precedent. Heller (1984) discusses many of the behavioral patterns of everyday life in detail; these patterns become the basis for learning from experience. However, the same pattern may be observed for secondary experiences: some people seek to hold on to what they already accept, almost afraid of being presented with new information in case it contradicts the information they already possess, while others are quite happy to be presented with new ideas to consider and discuss.

People may not respond to the same changes in the social conditions in the same way. Very rapid social change may mean that the disjuncture between some individuals' biographies and their sociocultural milieu is greater than they can bear. They know that they need to reestablish the equilibrium but are unable to do so, and this results in feelings of stress. Stress is another facet of modernity; it causes some people to opt out of the "rat race" of modern life and others to seek therapy or find other solutions. Consequently, the number of people undergoing therapy has increased, and many more educational or therapeutic courses are being offered.

Learning, then, can be disturbing for some but exciting for others—it is part of the paradox of the human condition. Even so, the human condition is one of human relationships, and in an apparently unstable world, those relationships may be threatened. This is the subject of the following section.

THE EFFECTS OF LEARNING ON THE LEARNERS

Perhaps one of the best-documented changes in society since industrialization has been the change that has accompanied the emergence of the division of labor. Durkheim (1964) calls it a change from mechanical to organic solidarity; Tönnies (1963) regards it as one from community to association. Society has become more differentiated and more organizationally oriented. Paradoxically, as society has become more organizational, people have become more individuated. The tendency for people to regularly meet together and form close-knit communities sharing common interests has diminished. People are certainly born into families, but even the stable relationship of parents is no longer as common as it used to be. Yet the ideals of friendship and marriage still exist.

Throughout this book, it has been pointed out that learning occurs throughout the life span, but obviously some people have more opportunities to learn than others. The more people learn, the more experienced they become and the more that they grow and change. However, this does pose problems for people who initially have close relationships, unless they each have similar opportunities to learn and develop. Consider the mutual interdependence of a dyadic relationship, for example; whether it is friendship or marriage is irrelevant. One member of the dyad is given the opportunity to experiment at work and to undertake new forms of action and learn from them, and also has a chance to meet new people and acquire new knowledge through secondary experience. In contrast, the other member of the dyad has a steady, satisfying job and does not do a great deal that is new. But the lack of new opportunities to learn from either primary or secondary experience means that the growth and development of that person is slower than that of the first member of the dyad. One member is learning all the time and changing rapidly, while the other is exposed to fewer opportunities to learn and so changes at a slower pace. One of the features of dyadic relationship can be its intensity; another might be the shared interests of the partners. But as a result of learning, people's interests change and they envision fresh horizons and determine new goals. The dyadic relationship might be stretched and even broken.

It is not only unequal opportunity to grow that is a problem; some members of dyads like their partners the way that they are and object to any change in them. A partner changes and develops new interests, and the original partnership is threatened by the process, even terminated. People returning to education often encounter these difficulties, because acquiring new knowledge changes their perspectives, and if their friends and partners are not supportive and aware, they may experience tension in their relationships. Many adult educators are aware that returning women students often face this problem. Thompson (1983) provides numerous examples; what amounts to liberation for the women represents a threat to some of the men in the partnerships.

Here, then, is a profound paradox about learning. People live in relationships; indeed, this book has emphasized that mind and the self are formed in relationships. Human relationships are fundamental to society's existence. It is only in these relationships that fundamental values such as love, truth, and justice can become manifest between people. Hence, Buber (1959, 1961) and others urge that wherever possible, relationships should be created and maintained, even though the process is sometimes painful, for it is only in encounter that community can develop and only in relationships that the fullness of humanity can be realized. Yet here again is a paradox of learning, since it is regarded as something that is life enriching but it is also individuating, threatening to some relationships, and can create its own unhappiness and destruction.

People become more experienced as a result of learning; learning is both individual and individuating, and it changes people. Unless relationships are strong enough to endure change, they are threatened—another feature of modern society. Not everyone grows; some prefer the stasis of nonlearning. But as a result of learning, others seek to become change agents within the social group.

CHANGE AGENTS AND
THE PROBLEMS OF STRUCTURE

People learn to adapt to change, but another aspect of the paradox of social living is that learning also helps people evoke change. Freire (1972b, p. 41) discusses the concept of praxis—that is, where "true reflection . . . leads to action." For him, reflection should result in action. The results of reflection need to be in harmony, and the action is part of the process of humanizing the world. It is a symbol of liberation, and the creative process becomes the responsibility of liberated people. They are change agents in the social and political world, in the same way that educators often believe that they are producing change agents to return to organizations and change them. Learning does produce change in people, but the question is whether those people automatically put their learning into practice and change the organizations within which they function. Adherents of behaviorist theories of learning imply that the resulting action is automatic, but Argyris and Schön (1974) suggest that practitioners have espoused-theories and theories-in-use, and they suggest that harmony does not always exist between the two. We have seen that actions are often creative and experimental and that they are planned, considered, and monitored, but we have also emphasized that the structures, obligations, and power relationships sometimes inhibit behavioral change despite the fact that learning has occurred.

Throughout this study, the tension between learning that individuates and social relationships has been implicit. It has also been clear that learning does produce changed people whose relationships, however, are not automatically changed as a result of the changes they experience. Negotiation of change in the relationship may be easier in a dyad or small group than it is in a large bureaucratic organization or a town.

If change in the relationship in a dyad or small group is not possible, those relationships can be terminated, even though this is sometimes painful. But in larger organizations, communities, and societies, it is less easy for individuals to terminate their relationships; they may be employed in an organization or live within a community or a society, so that they have to either accept the current situation and experience dissatisfaction or try to change the situation.

Hence, the community educator frequently works for change, and the change agent also seeks to alter the structures and procedures of the bureaucratic organization. Community educators are often regarded as radical or political because they adopt strategies aimed at changing society. Lovett, Clarke, and Kilmurray (1983, pp. 36–40) propose four models of action in the community:

1. A community organization/education model in which individuals are encouraged to engage in education and develop personally so that they can "better" themselves and leave their community—hence, terminate their relationships and seek new ones

2. A community development/education model in which educators act as resource persons helping people in the community learn so that they can develop richer communities for themselves

3. A community action/education model in which adult educators commit themselves to deprived communities and work with them to change the situation

4. A model in which educators align themselves with people in deprived areas and provide education to illuminate the problems of an area

In the second and third models, the emphasis is on people who have learned remaining in the community and trying to change it as a result of their learning. This is not as a result of automatic action, but through carefully planned action that does not necessarily affect personal relationships but wider social ones. Through political and community action, individuals try to influence others, especially those who exercise power, to change certain aspects of social living, usually through a redistribution of resources. Their communication is at a level of secondary experience, so that direct relationships are not threatened; they try to communicate information to others to persuade them to change their actions. Collective action is often encouraged, rather than individual action, since it is sometimes dangerous for individuals to expose themselves as change agents, because people do not always welcome change. Hence, the structures of society appear to resist the pressures that the change agents exert, and those who hold the reins of power continue to use the social institutions to ensure that no change occurs.

Thus it is clear that the ability to effect change is related to the position people occupy in the social structures. Leaders and managers are obviously in the best position to produce organizational change, and many of the people London (1988) cites as change agents occupy such positions. Enlightened management can create change, although bureaucratic management with too many levels of hierarchy inhibits change and efficiency in a rapidly changing world. A bigger problem exists when the people who have learned and have been changed as a result of their learning experiences are not in positions of power or influence in organizations. This is often true of those who have been sent by their organizations to continuing professional education courses. Employees may return to their employing organizations full of new ideas and changes as a result of their learning experiences, only to be confronted with a management that does not want to change or even to learn. Organizational structures and procedures appear inflexible because the management does not want to initiate change. In these situations, employees either have to become activists to try to get management to change, often being seen as "troublemakers" as a result, or else their two alternatives are to quit their job or conform—the latter often resulting in declining job satisfaction.

It is therefore easy for educators to believe, without ever seeking to understand the impact of new learning on both the learner and the organization, that their courses are producing change agents. It is not uncommon to hear educators or educational policy makers claim that their courses are producing change agents, though in fact the employing organizations often do not want change and fail to change with the advent of new employees. Indeed, it is here that the practitioners on the shop floor often deride the theoretical perspectives of the training school, and talk of the "real world" is to be found in the practice setting. One element, but by no means a major one, in the distinction between theory and practice is located at this point: people prefer habitualized action, but learning often involves change.

People, then, grow and change as a result of learning; this is a continuous process throughout life; organizations, though, have a tendency toward inertia. People prefer harmony rather than the tension of change and new ideas, so that some managers prefer to train employees to "fit in" rather than enabling them to grow and perhaps become change agents. Here, then, the paradox of learning is revealed yet again—reflective learning can produce change and growth and good management often tries to see to it that staff have this opportunity, but stability or even apparent stasis is comfortable, and change can be frightening. Training is often regarded not as an opportunity to learn reflectively and grow, but to learn unreflectively and conform.

However, organizations are not impersonal structures. They consist of people in patterned relationships performing specified roles, so that change becomes possible when those relationships are restructured as a result of learning. Argyris and Schön (1978, p. 29) maintain that "organizational learning occurs when members of the organization act as learning agents for the organization, responding to changes in the internal and external environments of the organization by detecting errors in organizational theory-in-use, and embedding the results of their inquiry in private images and shared maps of the organization." This is possible if the agents are in powerful positions in the organization or if those who exercise power favor change. But even then, if "private images" and "shared maps" are to be changed, the change agents themselves have a major teaching role to play, which is only possible when the organizational climate is conducive to change. If such a climate does not exist, the agent is as political as the radical community educator is.

LEARNING AND RISK

People live in an organizational world: it is a world of bureaucracies. Not only are all the organizations bureaucratic, but so is the state. Bureaucracies have their procedures and expect conformity, so that it is safe for individuals, having learned how to function in a bureaucracy, to follow the established customs and to conform. It becomes a nonlearning situation, where people live in harmony with their sociocultural world and act ritualistically. However, to initiate change, or even to be proactive in learning, individuals have to choose to be different. Proactive learning demands that people be prepared to act contrary to the expected procedures and create new situations and new experiences from which they can learn. Underlying proactivity, therefore, is an element of risk. This is the risk of just breaking away from the established procedures and consequently of being less certain of the outcome of the action than would normally be the case in bureaucratic society. It is also the risk, paradoxically, of offending those with whom relationships have already been established.

Open society, society that seeks to break the inertia of bureaucracy, is inevitably a risk society, and proactive learning is one of the features of this form of society. Indeed, it could be argued that if the learning society emphasizes response to externally imposed change, it is an adaptive society, with people merely learning nonreflectively to discover the harmony of nonlearning, ritualistic activity. However, if the learning society is reflective and oriented toward change, then the society is—almost by definition—a risk society.

CONCLUSION

Learning both produces change and occurs as a result of it; learning can be for the purpose of conformity or for change, it can be nonreflective or reflective. People in contemporary society live in patterned and organized relationships, and any change in one person will mean that the relationships are affected in some way or other. Consequently, some relationships do not survive the effects of learning, and yet it is in those very relationships that the highest values of humanity are manifest. Time does not stand still, and learning occurs throughout the human life span. Wherever action cannot be taken for granted, there is the possibility of new learning and new growth, but if that is always sought individually and in an individuating manner, the richness of human relationship can be lost. This, then, is the paradox of the human condition. In contrast, the survival of organizations, even of the state, may in part depend on nonlearning, or at least on learning that does not produce change.

Before his retirement in 1993, Jack Mezirow (1927–   ) was professor of adult and continuing education at Teachers College, Columbia University, where he directed an experimental, nontraditional doctoral program called Adult Education Guided Independent Study (AEGIS).

Mezirow received his Ed.D. in adult education from the University of California, Los Angeles, in 1955. He was formerly associate dean, University of California Extension, director of human resource development in the Latin American Bureau of AID, senior training adviser to the government of Pakistan, and director of university extension at the University of California, Riverside.

His interests and research in adult education span adult basic education, women's re-entry programs, and adult learning and development. His books include *Last Gamble on Education* (1975, with G. G. Darkenwald and A. B. Knox), *Evaluating Women's Re-entry Programs* (1978, with A. Rose), *Education for Perspective Transformation: College Re-entry Programs for Women* (1978), *Dynamics of Community Development* (1963), *Fostering Critical Reflection in Adulthood: A Guide to Transformative and Emancipatory Learning* (Editor, 1990), and *Transformative Dimensions of Adult Learning* (1991).

In the following selection from *Fostering Critical Reflection in Adulthood,* Mezirow reviews the material from previous chapters in which critical self-reflection and perspective transformation are presented as central to adult learning and development. In adulthood, development is synonomous with perspective transformations. These are effected as we learn to become critically reflective of the cultural and psychological assumptions upon which our meaning schemes and perspectives are based, and as we take action based on our new learning. Also discussed in this chapter are the ethical implications inherent in "challenging and transforming [learners'] meaning perspectives, especially when collective social action is a logical outcome."

JACK MEZIROW

13 Conclusion: Toward Transformative Learning and Emancipatory Education

Transformative learning for emancipatory education is the business of all adult educators. We know that we must respond to initial learner interests and self-defined needs, but we do so with the intent to move the learner to an awareness of the *reasons* for these needs and how the learners' meaning perspectives may have limited the way they customarily perceive, think, feel, and act in defining and attempting to satisfy their needs. This is what being a professional adult educator means, a quite different role from that of a group process technician or a subject matter specialist. Of course, these educators may also be educators of adults, and many professional adult educators may also be subject matter or group process specialists.

It should be clear, then, that every adult educator has a central responsibility for fostering critical reflection and transformative learning. Transformative learning includes learners making informed decisions of how and when to act upon their new perspectives. We have an obligation to assist them to learn how to take the action found necessary by the new perspective. As we have seen, this may involve new ways of understanding and using knowledge or new ways of understanding oneself and acting in interpersonal relationships. It may also involve taking individual social action (writing your congressman, financially supporting a cause, changing your vote, changing relationships within a family or a workplace) or group political action.

While not every adult educator is able to leave the classroom, workshop, or other educational setting to accompany every learner who decides to join a group to take collective political action, we do all have a professional obligation to become skilled in the strategies and tactics of social action education and to share this expertise where we can with those with whom we have a sense of solidarity. We do share a rich body of experience and a proud professional legacy from community development and social action education. These are areas of specialization within adult education, and we have much to learn from social action educators like Heaney and Horton, who devote themselves to working within oppressed groups throughout the entire process of transformation, including taking collective political action themselves.

The authors in this volume raise many other provocative points. Kitchener and King remind us that ill-defined problems require a different learning dynamic and that learners who must overcome distortions in epistemic assumptions are limited by age and education. Reflective judgment may be found in mature adults but is much less likely to be encountered in children, youth, or even young adults. It appears that there is great variation in meaning perspective among adults (and among children as well) who are at different stages of development. Recognition of these individual differences is crucial for educators. Each stage in the development of reflective judgment (or any other dimension of adult development—moral, ethical, ego, and others) involves a developmentally advanced and progressively more functional meaning perspective. The axiom in adult education to "begin where the learner is" takes on a whole new dimension from these findings. The learners may be functioning at several different developmental stages. Educators may have to group learners at one stage with those at the next-higher so that they may better learn from each other. This diversity in ways of knowing also complicates but does not preclude learners arriving at a validating consensus through critical discourse.

It is not that some adults are inherently incapable of thinking abstractly, becoming critically reflective, or making reflective judgments. It is only that they have not learned how to think in these ways. Many are socialized in subcultures—including those of schools—that place little or no value on such ways of knowing. The dependency role of the child inherent in the primary socialization process militates against critical reflection. While it may be true that children have to learn the rules before they can become critically reflective of them, Bowers (1984) argues that schooling can be reconceptualized to foster communicative competence. Reclaiming this stunted function of critical reflection for transformative learning is what emancipatory adult education is all about.

Many of the contributors to this book have noted the threat to psychological security that transformative learning imposes: the challenge to comfortably established beliefs and values—including those that may be central to self-concept—and the changes in long-established and cherished relationships. Recurring themes included role modeling; uncritical group support and solidarity; helping learners to link self-insights with internalized social norms and to understand that others share their dilemma; and providing a secure environment that fosters the trust necessary for critical self-examination and the expression of feelings. In these and other ways, adult educators provide the needed emotional support to help learners over the difficult terrain of transformative learning. . . .

To be an educator in this context means to be an empathic provocateur; it also means to serve as a role model for critical reflection and the ethical idea of caring and to serve as a committed co-learner and occasional guide in the exciting journey of transformative learning. Our tasks as educators are to encourage the multiple readings of "texts," to make a wider range of symbol systems or meaning perspectives available to learners, and to create reflective dialogic communities in which learners are free to challenge assumptions and premises, thereby breaking through the one-dimensionality of uncritically assimilated learning. Our function is to help learners to critically examine the sources and consequences of their own meaning perspectives and the interpretations they have made of their own lives. We must develop skill and sensitivity in the role of 'teacher as stranger" (Greene, 1973), the outsider who helps learners to question why things must be as presented by others and to learn about the sources of these assumptions and their consequences in the lives of those whom they affect.

ETHICAL ISSUES

Educators are understandably concerned with the ethical implications of efforts to assist learners in challenging and transforming their meaning perspectives, especially when collective social action is a logical outcome. Here the risk of indoctrination becomes apparent. There is an obvious dilemma in that even the "neutral" educator, who deliberately avoids the potential for controversy inherent in alternative perspectives, is taking a stand that favors maintenance of the status quo. Moreover, the essence of adult education consists of helping adults construe experience in a way in which they will more clearly understand the reasons for their problems and the options open to them, so that they may assume responsibility for decision making.

Perhaps the most significant kind of adult learning invokes bringing psychocultural assumptions into critical consciousness to help learners understand how they have come into possession of conceptual categories, rules, tactics, and criteria for judging that are implicit in their habits of perception, thought, and behavior. Such transformative learning enhances our crucial sense of agency over ourselves and our lives.

Emancipatory education, which helps learners become aware and critical of the presuppositions that shape their beliefs, is not the same thing as prescribing a preferred action to be taken. Nor does the transformed meaning perspective itself prescribe the action to be taken; instead, it presents a set of rules, tactics, and criteria for judging. The decision to act upon a new perspective is an essential part of the transformative learning process, but even when this leads to a decision to take collective social action, doing so will depend upon situational factors, the knowledge and skills for taking this kind of action, and the personality variables discussed earlier.

Education becomes indoctrination only when educators try to influence specific actions as extensions of their will, or perhaps when they blindly help learners to blindly follow the dictates of an unexamined set of culturally assimilated assumptions that determine how learners perceive, think, and feel about themselves, their relationships, and their world. To show learners a new set of rules, tactics, and criteria that allows them to judge situations in which they must act is significantly different from trying to engineer learner consent to take the action favored by the educator.

This argument does not mean to imply that educators are value free. It is only natural to assume that educators' own meaning perspectives will be included among the alternative perspectives opened up for learners. But no educators who take themselves seriously as educators would permit their own perspectives to be either the only ones made available to learners or would attempt to "sell" their own beliefs or to consciously foster dependency upon themselves. Adults, at least in our own culture, are apt to be educated to think for themselves. The educator can be influential, but the adult learner is often quite appropriately skeptical of authority and

able to differentiate between education and efforts to indoc-
trinate.

Even educators working in collective social action, like
Heaney and Horton, limit their role to fostering critical awareness; to helping learners understand the dynamics of their dependency upon an oppressive system; to helping them discover
action options and to anticipate their consequences, drawing
upon prior experience by others in taking action; to helping
learners develop the ability to take collective action; to helping
them learn how to interpret the feedback on their own efforts;
to helping them learn how to deal with adversity or setbacks;
and to helping them learn direct-action tactics for dealing with
the system.

The social action educator *never* "takes charge" or
becomes a formal leader or spokesperson for learners. The educator's function is to foster leadership and effective participation in others, not to usurp the leadership role. Of course,
social action educators would not choose to assist groups with
whom they did not feel a strong sense of solidarity. Other
emancipatory educators do not have this option. Like all other
educators, social action educators succeed to the degree that
they become less and less necessary to the self-directed learning process. Social action educators in Scandinavia and England inspired pioneers in the United States who established
adult education as a professional field. Today it is a seriously
neglected but highly respected field of practice among professional adult educators.

OTHER THEMES AND ISSUES

Adult educators have differing views on whether individual or social transformations are the ultimate goals of adult
education. What emerges as common ground is that we must
begin with individual perspective transformations before social transformations can succeed. It is also clear that the individual perspective transformation process includes taking
action, which often means some form of social action—which
in turn can sometimes mean collective political action. Few
adult educators may be able to follow up every learner's ex-

perience with collective political action. Those who can, do make such commitments to groups of learners with whom they have feelings of solidarity.

A related question pertains to whether an adult educator should be understood as a professional or nonprofessional role. References made above to professionalism in adult education refer to a higher order of understanding, skills, and competence pertaining to fostering transformative learning, as distinct from the implied exclusivity of a specialized education, degrees, credentials, or peer responsibility for quality assurance. However, adult educators do share two things: a distinctive meaning perspective in which the importance of learner-centeredness, critical discourse, and self-directedness are central theoretical assumptions; and a body of knowledge and skills pertaining to facilitating adult learning in individuals, groups, and communities. There is also a clear trend toward practitioners learning these things in the context of graduate programs in adult education. . . .

Another theme concerns the timing and nature of intervention by educators in the process of transformative learning. When learners are going through the transformative learning process, they often do so without fully recognizing that they are engaged in such a process. Their equilibrium has been upset by the advent of a dilemma, and they are in a state of readiness to learn anything that will ease their distress. They are looking for help, and the help that educators give may include assisting them to learn more about their own meaning perspectives and alternative meaning perspectives for interpreting their situation; providing emotional support for such an inquiry; giving information about alternatives, such as other careers or life-styles or ways to take social action; or giving the emotional support for taking such action. Here the role of the educator in meeting expressed learner needs is self-evident.

The adult educator actively *precipitates* transformative learning when, in the process of helping learners address their expressed needs, he or she seeks to move the learners' interest beyond their articulated needs to understanding the reasons for them and the way that psychocultural forces have shaped the learners' interpretation of the worlds of others, and of themselves. Here, the role of the educator calls for a higher degree of creative effort, to conceptualize ways of drawing learners into critical self-reflection about their own ideas and assumptions. As this process of transformative learning begins, its initiative and control reside in the learner; increasingly, the role of the educator is to provide a sounding board for testing new learner realities.

Individuals who encounter dilemmas that force them to challenge established ways of seeing and thinking and are able to move developmentally toward more inclusive, discriminating, and integrative meaning perspectives may do so as self-directed learners. Although they may need some help in the course of this developmental process, other learners have not begun to feel the need for transformative development. . . .

THE EMANCIPATORY EDUCATOR

In this section, I would like to review the experience of a few other educators who have attempted to facilitate emancipatory education, that is, to encourage critical reflection in order to precipitate or facilitate transformative learning by adults.

Boud, Keogh, and Walker (1985) have suggested that reflective learning has three stages. First is return to the experience to recapture as much detail as possible. They have found it helpful for learners to share this in writing or with others. The educator's role in this stage is to prompt the learner to describe as objectively as possible what has happened without interpreting or analyzing. The second stage is to attend to feelings attached to the experience and to review them. Again, these are frequently written and shared. The third stage is to reevaluate the experience. This often parallels the first two stages. Components include association, integration, validation, and appropriation. *Association* refers to connecting the ideas and feelings about the original experience and those that occurred during reflection with existing knowledge and attitudes. Free association, brainstorming, and other techniques by which the group collects ideas without evaluating them are useful. *Integration* involves an examination of the meaning and utility of the associations by grouping them, drawing simple maps of linkages, and relating the ideas of others. *Validation* involves examining ideas and feelings that are in process of being between new appreciations and existing knowledge and beliefs. It can also involve integrating these and parallel data from others or trying out new perceptions in new situations. Role play may be most useful here. *Appropriation* refers to making the new knowledge a part of how we act and feel.

Shor and Freire (1987) describe a "dialogic method of teaching" for fostering critical reflection and transformation in classroom settings. The educational experience begins with an identification of the learners' real-life problems as they define them in their own idiom. The educator helps them place these and the subject matter of the course in a historical and cultural context through an examination of how social norms and cultural codes affect learners' perception and judgment. For Shor and Freire, transformation means social transformation and the transformation of sociocultural perspectives. I have suggested in Chapter One that learning may include epistemic and psychic transformations as well.

The dialogic method approximates the ideal conditions of critical discourse of free, full participation by all. The situation separates learners from their assumptions. The classroom or counselor's consulting room is a reality separate in time and space from other dimensions of knowing. It allows adults a temporary respite from the pressures of action and convention to experiment with reflection on all aspects of their lives. The time involved has been allocated to new ways of thinking: The learner and educator have a contract to help the learner become a better learner. The learner's expectations are a crucially important condition for an effective educational or therapeutic intervention. With careful attention to fostering a supportive and democratic social climate, the classroom can become the place to experiment with long-held values and beliefs without penalty or humiliation for exposing one's ignorance or taking risks and making mistakes. This separation from mass culture is highly desirable for fostering transformative change. Of course, its implementation means an often stressful return engagement with the outside world. Even groups involved in collective social action need time to regroup, assess action efforts, and reinforce their commitments.

The educator may know more than the learners about the subject of instruction at the outset, but he or she relearns what is known in the context of the learners' efforts to interpret these insights in terms of their own lives. This is what adult educators mean when they write of collaborative learning.

Shor and Freire suggest that educators must begin by building confidence in the learner and being sensitive to established meaning perspectives. As collaborative learners, educators communicate that they respect what students know and look for ways to enable them to show what they know: "I must be clear that I need to reknow what I think I know, to the extent that the educatees know with me and among themselves. I have also to be clear that the starting point for them to experience some knowable object which I propose cannot be my understanding of the object and the reality" (Shor and Freire, 1987, p. 180).

The educator actively seeks to know learners' expectations and aspirations to enable the educator to understand learners' levels of perception, their language, and the difficulties they may have understanding the academic language or the nature of instruction. For Shor and Freire, the educator must be critical of how society works to be able to understand the social functions that education fulfills. He or she must reinvent the abstract academic idiom to permit easy communication with the uninitiated. The authors urge the reading of texts with different perspectives from the learners' as another way of assisting them to "read the world." The teacher's function is to diminish the distance between the learner reading words and the learner reading the world (Shor and Freire, 1987, p. 182).

"Transsituational learning" is identified by Cell (1984) as any change in our ability to interpret a situation. Its most important form is "the development of our capacity to examine an interpretation—especially one of our own—and to develop alternatives to it" (p. 204). The key to transsituational learning is contrast. "The more we learn to think in terms of contrasts, to direct our attention to them as they occur and to generate them for ourselves, the more creative we can be in working with the meaning of a situation" (p. 204). Cell identifies the skills involved in transsituational learning as including evaluation (developing new criteria for assessing situations) and divergence (developing new perspectives on a situation) and the ability to find alternatives in a given situation—new ways of seeing, new questions to ask, new ways to use things. "When we search for the meaning of an event rather than reacting concretely to the event itself, when we treat a problem-statement as if it were a symptom rather than a basic ill, when we inquire into the meaning of our differences with someone else, we use these thought processes" (Samuel Culbert, quoted in Cell, p. 204).

Opening ourselves up to the ideas of others, especially when these provide a new angle of vision, can improve skill in divergence. Talking or reading about viewpoints in other academic disciplines or fields of activity can generate contrasting ideas as can contact with another culture. Any contrasting idea can result in what Cell refers to as a "productive tension" with the original idea. Practice in taking the perspective of the Other can enhance the skill of divergence significantly. Cell refers to the development of these skills as *transcendent learning*, learning through which we change the concepts we use to interpret a situation. Transcendent learning is learning through critical reflection. . . .

Brookfield (1987) describes other effective strategies for facilitating critical thinking. Educators can create a supportive social climate; listen attentively to verbal and nonverbal cues so as to be able to frame critical questions in terms learners understand; sensitively balance the provision of unqualified support with a challenge to old modes of thinking; mirror the learners' attitudes, rationalizations, and habitual ways of thinking and acting to enable them to see themselves from a different perspective; encourage learners to believe that the realization of emancipatory ideas is possible and to act upon these ideas based on a realistic assessment of risk; provide opportunity for reflective evaluation or taking stock of the process of critical thinking; help learners form networks and support groups of fellow learners; and help learners become aware of their preferred learning styles.

Brookfield synthesizes the roles of the teacher of critical thinking proposed in the literature, placing emphasis on assumptions, focusing upon learners' perceptions of their own experiences, encouraging group analysis of relevant issues, and presenting alternative meaning perspectives. "Teachers function sometimes as catalysts of discussion and inquiry, sometimes as contributory group members. They perform such diverse roles as being advocates for missing perspectives, adversaries to propaganda, recorders of sessions, mediators of divisive tendencies and resource persons" (p. 80).

Critical questioning—questioning designed to elicit assumptions rather than to elicit information—involves a set of facilitator skills that usually requires training. One must be able to frame evocative questions that are readily understood by learners, that explore highly personal matters with sensitivity, and that raise intimidating issues in a nonthreatening way. These are skills more familiar to therapists and ethnographic and other qualitative researchers than to adult educators. Brookfield's guidelines include *be specific* (avoid general questions, focus on specific events or particular people, ask about qualities needed for specific roles and accomplishments, and ask how the learner knows he or she has done well); *work from the particular to the general* (ground responses addressing general themes in a specific activity or occurrence); and *be conversational* (avoid appearing to follow a standard, formal, and therefore threatening, interview protocol) (pp. 93–97).

In addition to critical incident exercises as described in this book in Chapter Nine for helping others examine their assumptions, Brookfield recommends criteria analysis (analysis of one's standards for attributing worth and merit), role play and critical debate (defending a position you oppose), and crisis decision simulations (deciding among distasteful choices, such as Whom do you save from drowning, a mother or her infant, if only one can be saved?). Techniques for imagining alternatives include brainstorming, envisioning alternative futures, developing preferred scenarios, inventing futures, and esthetic triggers (poetry, fantasy, art, songwriting, drama).

CLOSING NOTE

As adult educators, we are committed to encourage the opening of public spheres of discourse and to actively oppose social and cultural constraints that impede free, full participation in discursive learning. Such constraints include impediments to freedom, equality, justice, democratic participation, civil and human rights, education, health, safety, shelter, and rewarding employment. A society in which free, full participation in discursive learning is assured every adult learner is an educator's guiding, utopian social vision. Learners and educators become justifiably radicalized when societies preclude the redress of grievances, enforce unjust laws, or become oppressive in response to efforts to make institutions more responsive to the fundamental needs of learners.

While it is appropriate and important for educators to attempt to infer a philosophical orientation of how things should be from a theory that describes the nature of learning, the two should not be confused. Learning is not a desirable outcome or a goal; it is the activity of making an interpretation that subsequently guides decision and action. Learning is grounded in the very nature of human communication. Becoming reflective of the content, process, and especially the premises of one's prior learning is central to cognition for survival in modern societies. It is the way we control our experiences rather than be controlled by them, and it is an indispensable prerequisite to individual, group, and collective transformations, both perspective and social. Especially in modern societies where authority is relative and adults increasingly tend to transform themselves through critical self-reflection, educators seek ways to understand and enhance this vital, natural learning function.

REFERENCES

Argyris, C., Putnam, R., and Smith, D. M. *Action Science: Concepts, Methods, and Skills for Research and Intervention.* San Francisco: Jossey-Bass, 1985.

Boud, D., and Griffin, V. (eds.). *Appreciating Adults Learning: From the Learners' Perspective*. London: Kogan Page, 1987.

Boud, D., Keogh, R., and Walker, D. (eds.). *Reflection: Turning Experience into Learning*. London: Kogan Page, 1985.

Bowers, C. A. *The Promise of Theory: Education and the Politics of Cultural Change*. New York: Longman, Green, 1984.

Brookfield, S. D. *Developing Critical Thinkers: Challenging Adults to Explore Alternative Ways of Thinking and Acting*. San Francisco: Jossey-Bass, 1987.

Cell, E. *Learning to Learn from Experience*. Albany: State University of New York Press, 1984.

Greene, M. *The Teacher as Stranger*. Belmont, Calif.: Wadsworth, 1973.

Habermas, J. *The Theory of Communicative Action*. Vol. 1: *Lifeworld and System: A Critique of Functionalist Reason*. (T. McCarthy, trans.) Boston: Beacon Press, 1978.

Pedler, M. (ed.). *Action Learning in Practice*. Aldershot, England: Gower, 1985.

Schön, D. A. *The Reflective Practitioner: How Professionals Think in Action*. New York: Bask Books, 1983.

Schön, D. A. *Educating the Reflective Practitioner: Toward a New Design for Teaching and Learning in the Professions*. San Francisco: Jossey-Bass, 1987.

Shor, I., and Freire, P. *A Pedagogy for Liberation: Dialogues on Transforming Education*. South Hadley, Mass.: Bergin & Garvey, 1987.

Born in Brazil, Paulo Freire (1921–   ) studied at Recife University to be a teacher of Portuguese. In 1959 he submitted a doctoral thesis on adult literacy and shortly afterwards became a faculty member in philosophy and history of education. Soon he began to experiment with new methods of teaching literacy skills in Recife. It was through this work that he developed a methodology that proved effective in literacy campaigns throughout northeast Brazil. These literacy accomplishments threatened the established social order and led to Freire's imprisonment and exile after a military coup in 1964. While in Chile where he was again involved in literacy work, Freire wrote about his Brazilian experiences. This work appeared in English in 1973 as the first part of *Education for Critical Consciousness.*

In 1969 Freire left Chile to become a visiting professor at Harvard University where he wrote and lectured on adult literacy and "conscientization." In 1970 he left for Geneva and a position as a special consultant to the World Council of Churches. In this role Freire participated in literacy programs throughout the world. After amnesty was granted to over five thousand Brazilian exiles, Freire returned to his homeland in 1980 where he taught at the public university UNICAMP in Sao Paulo. In 1990 the newly elected Marxist mayor of San Paulo invited Freire to become the secretary of education. In this capacity he worked to overhaul the curriculum, repair damaged school buildings, and find ways to increase teachers' salaries and empower teachers, children and parents. His recent books include *The Politics of Education: Culture, Power and Liberation* (1984), *Reading the Word and the World* (1987, with D. Macedo), *Learning to Question: A Pedagogy of Liberation* (1989, with A. Faundez), *Pedagogy of the City* (1993), and *Pedagogy of Hope: Reliving "Pedagogy of the Oppressed"* (1994).

Pedagogy Of the Oppressed, written in 1968 and appearing in English in 1970, is Freire's most important philosophical work. In it he examines the relationships between knowledge, action, and power; the essentially political nature of education; and the need for praxis—critical reflection and action. The following selection from Chapter 2 of this work presents Freire's famous argument against the "banking" concept of education. In its place, he advocates problem-posing education where students and teachers "dialogue" as "co-investigators."

PAULO FREIRE

14 Pedagogy of the Oppressed

A careful analysis of the teacher-student relationship at any level, inside or outside the school, reveals its fundamentally *narrative* character. This relationship involves a narrating Subject (the teacher) and patient, listening objects (the students). The contents, whether values or empirical dimensions of reality, tend in the process of being narrated to become lifeless and petrified. Education is suffering from narration sickness.

The teacher talks about reality as if it were motionless, static, compartmentalized, and predictable. Or else he expounds on a topic completely alien to the existential experience of the students. His task is to "fill" the students with the contents of his narration—contents which are detached from reality, disconnected from the totality that engendered them and could give them significance. Words are emptied of their concreteness and become a hollow, alienated, and alienating verbosity.

The outstanding characteristic of this narrative education, then, is the sonority of words, not their transforming power. "Four times four is sixteen; the capital of Para is Belem." The student records, memorizes, and repeats these phrases without perceiving what four times four really means, or realizing the true significance of "capital" in the affirmation "the capital of Para is Belem," that is, what Belem means for Pam and what Para means for Brazil.

Narration (with the teacher as narrator) leads the students to memorize mechanically the narrated content. Worse yet, it turns them into "containers," into "receptacles" to be "filled" by the teacher. The more completely he fills the receptacles, the better a teacher he is. The more meekly the receptacles permit themselves to be filled, the better students they are.

Education thus becomes an act of depositing, in which the students are the depositories and the teacher is the depositor. Instead of communicating, the teacher issues communiqués and maker deposits which the students patiently receive, memorize, and repeat. This is the "banking" concept of education, in which the scope of action allowed to the students extends only as far as receiving, filing, and storing the deposits. They do, it is true, have the opportunity to become collectors or cataloguers of the things they store. But in the last analysis, it is men themselves who are filed away through the lack of creativity, transformation, and knowledge in this (at best) misguided system. For apart from inquiry, apart from the praxis, men cannot be truly human. Knowledge emerges only through invention and re-invention, through the restless, impatient, continuing, hopeful inquiry men pursue in the world, with the world, and with each other.

In the banking concept of education, knowledge is a gift bestowed by those who consider themselves knowledgeable upon those whom they consider to know nothing. Projecting an absolute ignorance onto others, a characteristic of the ideology of oppression, negates education and knowledge as processes of inquiry. The teacher presents himself to his students as their necessary opposite; by considering their ignorance absolute, he justifies his own existence. The students, alienated like the slave in the Hegelian dialectic, accept their ignorance as justifying the teacher's existence—but, unlike the slave, they never discover that they educate the teacher.

The *raison d'être* of libertarian education, on the other hand, lies in its drive towards reconciliation. Education must begin with the solution of the teacher-student contradiction, by reconciling the poles of the contradiction so that both are simultaneously teachers *and* students.

This solution is not (nor can it be) found in the banking concept. On the contrary, banking education maintains and even stimulates the contradiction through the following attitudes and practices, which mirror oppressive society as a whole:

(a) the teacher teaches and the students are taught;
(b) the teacher knows everything and the students know nothing;
(c) the teacher thinks and the students are thought about;
(d) the teacher talks and the students listen—meekly;
(e) the teacher disciplines and the students are disciplined;
(f) the teacher chooses and enforces his choice, and the students comply;
(g) the teacher acts and the students have the illusion of acting through the action of the teacher;
(h) the teacher chooses the program content, and the students (who were not consulted) adapt to it;

(i) the teacher confuses the authority of knowledge with his own professional authority, which he sets in opposition to the freedom of the students;

(j) the teacher is the Subject of the learning process, while the pupils are mere objects.

It is not surprising that the banking concept of education regards men as adaptable, manageable beings. The more students work at storing the deposits entrusted to them, the less they develop the critical consciousness which would result from their intervention in the world as transformers of that world. The more completely they accept the passive role imposed on them, the more they tend simply to adapt to the world as it is and to the fragmented view of reality deposited in them.

The capability of banking education to minimize or annul the students' creative power and to stimulate their credulity serves the interests of the oppressors, who care neither to have the world revealed nor to see it transformed. The oppressors use their "humanitarianism" to preserve a profitable situation. Thus they react almost instinctively against any experiment in education which stimulates the critical faculties and is not content with a partial view of reality but always seeks out the ties which link one point to another and one problem to another.

Indeed, the interests of the oppressors lie in "changing the consciousness of the oppressed, not the situation which oppresses them",[1] for the more the oppressed can be led to adapt to that situation, the more easily they can be dominated. To achieve this end, the oppressors use the banking concept of education in conjunction with a paternalistic social action apparatus, within which the oppressed receive the euphemistic title of "welfare recipients." They are treated as individual cages, as marginal men who deviate from the general configuration of a "good, organized, and just" society. The oppressed are regarded as the pathology of the healthy society, which must therefore adjust these "incompetent and lazy" folk to its own patterns by changing their mentality. These marginals

[1] *Simone de Beauvoir,* La Pensee de Droite, Aujord'hui *(Paris); ST,* El Pensamiento politico de la Derecha *(Buenos Aires, 1963), p. 34.*

need to be "integrated," "incorporated" into the healthy society that they have "forsaken."

The truth is, however, that the oppressed are not "marginals," are not men living "outside" society. They have always been "inside"—inside the structure which made them "beings for others." The solution is not to "integrate" them into the structure of oppression, but to transform that structure so that they can become "beings for themselves." Such transformation, of course, would undermine the oppressors' purposes; hence their utilization of the banking concept of education to avoid the threat of student *conscientização*.

The banking approach to adult education, for example, will never propose to students that they critically consider reality. It will deal instead with such vital questions as whether Roger gave green grass to the goat, and insist upon the importance of learning that, on the contrary, Roger gave green grass to the rabbit. The "humanism" of the banking approach masks the effort to turn men into automatons—the very negation of their ontological vocation to be more fully human.

Those who use the banking approach, knowingly or unknowingly (for there are innumerable well-intentioned bank-clerk teachers who do not realize that they are serving only to dehumanize), fail to perceive that the deposits themselves contain contradictions about reality. But, sooner or later, these contradictions may lead formerly passive students to turn against their domestication and the attempt to domesticate reality. They may discover through existential experience that their present way of life is irreconcilable with their vocation to become fully human. They may perceive through their relations with reality that reality is really a *process*, undergoing constant transformation. If men are searchers and their ontological vocation is humanization, sooner or later they may perceive the contradiction in which banking education seeks to maintain them, and then engage themselves in the struggle for their liberation.

But the humanist, revolutionary educator cannot wait for this possibility to materialize. From the outset, his efforts must coincide with those of the students to engage in critical thinking and the quest for mutual humanization. His efforts must be imbued with a profound trust in men and their creative power. To achieve this, he must be a partner of the students in his relations with them.

The banking concept does not admit to such partnership—and necessarily so. To resolve the teacher-student contradiction, to exchange the role of depositor, prescriber, domesticator, for the role of student among students would be to undermine the power of oppression and serve the cause of liberation.

Implicit in the banking concept is the assumption of a dichotomy between man and the world: man is merely *in* the world, not *with* the world or with others; man is spectator, not re-creator. In this view, man is not a conscious being *(corpo consciente)*; he is rather the possessor of a consciousness: an empty "mind" passively open to the reception of deposits of reality from the world outside. For example, my desk, my books, my coffee cup, all the objects before me—as bits of the world which surrounds me—would be "inside" me, exactly as I am inside my study right now. This view makes no distinction between being accessible to consciousness and entering consciousness. The distinction, however, is essential: the objects which surround me are simply accessible to my consciousness, not located within it. I am aware of them, but they are not inside me.

It follows logically from the banking notion of consciousness that the educator's role is to regulate the way the world "enters into" the students. His task is to organize a process which already occurs spontaneously, to "fill" the students by making deposits of information which he considers to constitute true knowledge.[2] And since men "receive" the world as passive entities, education should make them more passive still, and adapt them to the world. The educated man is the adapted man, because he is better "fit" for the world. Translated into practice, this concept is well suited to the purposes of the oppressors, whose tranquility rests on how well men fit the world the oppressors have created, and how little they question it. . . .

[2]*This concept corresponds to what Sartre calls the "digestive" or "nutritive" concept of education, in which knowledge is "fed" by the teacher to the students to "fill them out." See Jean-Paul Sartre, "Une idee fundamentale de la phenomenologie de Husserl: L'intentionalite," Situations I (Paris, 1947).*

Those truly committed to liberation must reject the banking concept in its entirety, adopting instead a concept of men as conscious beings, and consciousness as consciousness intent upon the world. They must abandon the educational goal of deposit-making and replace it with the posing of the problems of men in their relations with the world. "Problem-posing" education, responding to the essence of consciousness —*intentionality*—rejects communiqués and embodies communication. It epitomizes the special characteristic of consciousness: being *conscious of*, not only as intent on objects but as turned in upon itself in a Jasperian "split"—consciousness as consciousness of consciousness.

Liberating education consists in acts of cognition, not transferrals of information. It is a learning situation in which the cognizable object (far from being the end of the cognitive act) intermediates the cognitive actors—teacher on the one hand and students on the other. Accordingly, the practice of problem-posing education entails at the outset that the teacher-student contradiction be resolved. Dialogical relations —indispensable to the capacity of cognitive actors to cooperate in perceiving the same cognizable object—are otherwise impossible.

Indeed, problem-posing education, which breaks with the vertical patterns characteristic of banking education, can fulfill its function as the practice of freedom only if it can overcome the above contradiction. Through dialogue, the teacher-of-the-students and the students-of-the-teacher cease to exist and a new term emerges: teacher-student with students-teachers. The teacher is no longer merely the-one-who-teaches, but one who is himself taught in dialogue with the students, who in turn while being taught also teach. They become jointly responsible for a process in which all grow. In this process, arguments based on "authority" are no longer valid; in order to function, authority must be *on the side of* freedom, not *against* it. Here, no one teaches another, nor is anyone self-taught. Men teach each other, mediated by the world, by the cognizable objects which in banking education are "owned" by the teacher.

The banking concept (with its tendency to dichotomize everything) distinguishes two stages in the action of the educator. During the first, he cognizes a cognizable object while he prepares his lessons in his study or his laboratory; during the second, he expounds to his students about that object. The students are not called upon to know, but to memorize the contents narrated by the teacher. Nor do the students practice any act of cognition, since the object towards which that act should be directed is the property of the teacher rather than a medium evoking the cricial reflection of both teacher and students. Hence in the name of the "preservation of culture and knowledge" we have a system which achieves neither true knowledge nor true culture.

The problem-posing method does not dichotomize the activity of the teacher-student: he is not "cognitive" at one point and "narrative" at another. He is always "cognitive," whether preparing a project or engaging in dialogue with the students. He does not regard cognizable objects as his private property, but as the object of reflection by himself and the students. In this way, the problem-posing educator constantly re-forms his reflections in the reflection of the students. The students—no longer docile listeners—are now critical co-investigators in dialogue with the teacher. The teacher presents the material to the students for their consideration, and re-considers his earlier considerations as the students express their own. The role of the problem-posing educator is to create, together with the students, the conditions under which knowledge at the level of the *doxa* is superseded by true knowledge, at the level of the *logos*.

Whereas banking education anesthetizes and inhibits creative power, problem-posing education involves a constant unveiling of reality. The former attempts to maintain the *submersion* of consciousness; the latter strives for the *emergence* of consciousness and *critical intervention* in reality.

Students, as they are increasingly posed with problems relating to themselves in the world and with the world, will feel increasingly challenged and obliged to respond to that challenge. Because they apprehend the challenge as interrelated to other problems within a total context, not as a theoretical question, the resulting comprehension tends to be increasingly critical and thus constantly less alienated. Their response to the challenge evokes new challenges, followed by new understandings; and gradually the students come to regard themselves as committed. . . .

Whereas the banking method directly or indirectly reinforces men's fatalistic perception of their situation, the problem-posing method presents this very situation to them as a problem. As the situation becomes the object of their cognition, the naive or magical perception which produced their fatalism gives way to perception which is able to perceive itself even as it perceives reality, and can thus be critically objective about that reality.

A deepened consciousness of their situation leads men to apprehend that situation as an historical reality susceptible of transformation. Resignation gives way to the drive for transformation and inquiry, over which men feel themselves to be in control. If men, as historical beings necessarily engaged with other men in a movement of inquiry, did not control that movement, it would be (and is) a violation of men's humanity. Any situation in which some men prevent others from engaging in the process of inquiry is one of violence. The means used are not important; to alienate men from their own decision-making is to change them into objects.

This movement of inquiry must be directed towards humanization—man's historical vocation. The pursuit of full humanity, however, cannot be carried out in isolation or individualism, but only in fellowship and solidarity; therefore it cannot unfold in the antagonistic relations between oppressors and oppressed. No one can be authentically human while he prevents others from being so. Attempting to be *more* human, individualistically, leads to *having more*, egotistically: a form of dehumanization. Not that it is not fundamental to *have* in order *to be* human. Precisely because it *is* necessary, some men's *having* must not be allowed to constitute an obstacle to others; *having*, must not consolidate the power of the former to crush the latter.

Problem-posing education, as a humanist and liberating praxis, posits as fundamental that men subjected to domination must fight for their emancipation. To that end, it enables teachers and students to become Subjects of the educational process by overcoming authoritarianism and an alienating intellectualism; it also enables men to overcome their false perception of reality. The world—no longer something to be described with deceptive words—becomes the object of that transforming action by men which results in their humanization.

Problem-posing education does not and cannot serve the interests of the oppressor. No oppressive order could permit the oppressed to begin to question: Why? While only a revolutionary society can carry out this education in systematic terms, the revolutionary leaders need not take full power before they can employ the method. In the revolutionary process, the leaders cannot utilize the banking method as an interim measure, justified on grounds of expediency, with the intention of *later* behaving in a genuinely revolutionary fashion. They must be revolutionary—that is to say, dialogical—from the outset.

Arthur L. Wilson (1950–   ) is on the adult and community education faculty in the Department of Educational Leadership at Ball State University. He received his Ed.D. in adult education from The University of Georgia in 1991. Prior to his graduate work, he worked as an adult literacy and GED instructor, a staff developer, and a professional association educator. He is coauthor, along with Ronald M. Cervero, of *Planning Responsibly for Adult Education: A Guide to Negotiating Power and Interests* (1994).

In addition to his interest in program planning, Wilson has written several articles on history and philosophy in American adult education. This work has focused on the field's 20th century intellectual and philosophical foundations. Working from a critical theory perspective, he believes that certain selective traditions privilege particular intellectual and institutional frameworks to the exclusion of others. In an article in *International Journal of Lifelong Education* (1993), he examined the philosophically pragmatic orientation of much of adult education, revealing how pragmatism and praxis serve certain interests to the exclusion of others. The following article demonstrates how the professionalization process of American adult education represents a selective tradition of privileging a natural science model of empirical investigation as the central framework for improving the practice of adult education. The author suggests that this tradition is responsible not only for the generally acknowledged theory-practice gap, but also the marginalization of such historically prominent adult education traditions as social activism.

ARTHUR L. WILSON

15 The Common Concern: Controlling the Professionalization of Adult Education

ABSTRACT

Using the findings from a study of the adult education handbooks, the purpose of this paper is to present an argument that university researchers in the field of adult education have relied upon a natural science model of empirical analysis to develop the knowledge base of adult education in order to control the development of

ADULT EDUCATION QUARTERLY
Volume 44, Number 1, Fall, 1993, 1–16

the field as a profession. This professionalization process depends upon using scientifically-derived knowledge to standardize professional practice and the training of practitioners in order to develop a market share in a service economy.

There are different perspectives on what constitutes professionalization (Cervero, 1988; Houle, 1980). As early as 1916, Flexner maintained that occupations either were or were not professions. In Houle's (1980) study of learning in the professions, he depicted a dynamic rather than static notion of professionalization. Many occupations are in the process of becoming professional, of trying "to elevate and dignify" their work in order to "become accepted by society as a profession" (p. 27). While Houle provides a more pliable understanding of professionalization, Schön's (1983) depiction of "technical rationality" makes clear that professionalizing occupations have to develop by means of the natural science model of empirical investigation: "professional activity consists in instrumental problem solving made rigorous by the application of scientific theory and technique" (p. 21). This conception of professionalization depends fundamentally upon the putative value and utilitarianism of the natural science model of empirical inquiry and its relevance to professional practice. In other words, if an occupation is to professionalize successfully and be recognized as such, it must develop rigorous (i.e., "scientific") knowledge and systematic practice applications (i.e., "principles of") that only its adherents have access to.

While Schön intimates the purpose of this dependence on science, Larson (1979) states it bluntly: Professions use scientific knowledge and systematic training of practitioners to control a market share of a service economy. In Larson's view, any professionalizing occupation has to develop standardized forms of knowledge which practitioners use to transact their services (their "product") in the professional marketplace. Without a body of knowledge and training in its use, an occupation cannot control a share of the market for its services and thus will not professionalize successfully. Therefore, controlling knowledge production and practitioner training become central issues in the professionalization process. Since the emergence of the modern research university in the late

19th century, the conventional manner of achieving this goal of professional "exclusivity" (Larson, 1979) is to centralize in the modern university researchers who construct the knowledge base of a profession and also train its practitioners. Houle, Schön, and Larson are all in agreement on this point.

I believe that the best way to understand the modern period of adult education in the United States (from the 1920s on) is to understand it in this professionalization context. The thesis of this paper is that the field of adult education has deliberately, but largely uncritically, sought the same path to professionalization as nearly any other professionalizing occupation has in the 20th century: Leaders of the field have intentionally sought to study practice in order to legitimate it scientifically (recall the subtitle to the "black book": Outlines of an Emerging Field of University Study). Certainly this is not a new claim, for a number of commentators have readily referenced it (Brookfield, 1989a; Cunningham, 1989; Law, 1988; Taylor, Rockhill, Fieldhouse, 1985; Welton, 1987). But the major points of the paper are to demonstrate the common set of understandings that have engendered this movement and to argue that the underlying issue of depending on science to professionalize the field was really an issue of who was going to control the field of adult education. The title of the paper is meant to encapsulate the thesis. By using the adult education handbooks (the first edition of which appeared in 1934) as representative and illustrative evidence, I want to demonstrate the repeatedly-stated "common concern" for professionalizing the field by improving its practice scientifically. In order to understand this movement, though, an interpretation of this professionalization concern is needed. In this context, Larson's economic analysis is used to understand why the handbooks so consistently represent the appeal to science for legitimation in order to deal with the central problem of professionalization: market control.

METHODOLOGY: ANALYSIS OF DISCOURSE

To examine the common meanings and shared assumptions characteristic of the historical period represented in the adult education handbooks, I need to explain how to ask the question and how to interpret the answer. To do that, I draw upon Foucault (1972) to describe what discourse analysis is and how it reveals historical frames of meaning, on Habermas' notion of "interests" (1971) to interpret the common meanings represented by the handbooks, and on Gilbert (1989) to explain the procedure for doing this kind of analysis. A more detailed discussion of the methodology than is possible here is available elsewhere (Wilson, 1993).

To analyze professional literature, content analysis is the obvious technique for revealing historical frames of meaning; methodologically, however, such a process is at best ambiguous. Revealing textural meaning requires what Foucault (1972) terms discourse analysis:

> Generally speaking, the analysis of discourse operates between the twin poles of totality and plethora. One shows how the different texts with which one is dealing refer to one another, organize themselves into a single figure, converge with institutions and practice, and carry meanings that may be common to a whole period. Each element considered is taken as the expression of the totality to which it belongs and whose limits it exceeds. And in this way one substitutes for the diversity of the things said a sort of great, uniform text, which has never before been articulated, and which reveals for the first time what men [sic] "really meant" not only in their words and texts, their discourses and their writings, but also in their institutions, practices, techniques, and objects that they produced. In relation to this implicit, sovereign, communal "meaning," statements appear in superabundant proliferation, since it is to that meaning alone that they all refer and to it alone that they owe their truth. . . . (p. 118)

The key notions here are to identify the meanings "common to a whole period" which form a "great, uniform text." In brief, getting at the meaning common to a historical period is the point of this analysis.

With respect to an interpretive framework for understanding the common frame of meaning in the handbooks, Habermas (1971) has argued that the construction of knowledge is tremendously influenced by "interests," which he defines as human needs arising from fundamental categories of human social organization, namely work, interaction, and emancipation. In his view, different knowledge is produced for particular human uses and is therefore always in the service of identifiable interests. Specifically, in his analysis "empirical-analytic" science is ontologically linked to issues of control: Humans utilize scientific inquiry in order to control natural and social phenomena. Control is the central issue of the professionalization movement. I draw upon Habermas because his concept of interests can be used in the task of critiquing implicit assumptions that constitute the "taken-for-granted" world view (Apple, 1979; Franklin, 1974; Schutz, 1967) underlying the adult education professionalization movement. Implicit assumptions are challenged by questioning what purposes and whose interests the knowledge serves. The concept of interests provides an analysis for going beyond the explicit expression of knowledge to understand the human motivations and uses for creating it (Bernstein, 1976; Franklin, 1974; Giroux, 1980; Habermas, 1971).

The present analysis derives from Franklin (1974) who used Habermas' notion of interests to uncover the great, uniform text connecting science with social control in American curriculum theory. His work exemplifies how interests can be used to interpret historical discourse. His purpose was "to uncover and identify the existence and nature of certain basic intellectual structures" (1974, p. 14). Franklin was not concerned with tracing specific historical influences from one individual to another, claiming correctly that this is nearly impossible to historically substantiate. Rather, for him Habermas' idea of interests enabled him to bypass these issues of historical imputation and go directly to the "implicit and unconscious similarities" (Franklin, 1974, p. 15; in Foucault's lexicon, the "discourse") that shape traditions of intellectual thought such as the one of social control he was examining. Similar analyses directed at revealing common meanings and the assumptions upon which they rest have been developed in curriculum studies (Apple, 1979), the sociology of school knowledge (Whitty, 1985), citizenship education (Giroux, 1980), literature (Eagleton, 1976; Kelley, 1974; Taxel, 1984), and cinematography (Wright, 1975). Gilbert (1989) provides specific questions which were used to analyze the literature of adult education in terms of revealing the historically relevant assumptions that guided the discourse of professionalization:

1. What topics, propositions or broad concepts provide the organizing structure of the discourse?

2. How do concepts, terms, metaphors, jargon and other stylistic devices elaborate the structure of the discourse?

3. What are the underlying problems which have generated the discourse? How has the discourse articulated these problems? From whose perspective?

4. What theories provide the descriptions and explanations thought relevant? What relationships, causes, consequences are proposed? On what premises is the account based and what assumptions are made in the course of the explanation?

5. What perspectives, questions, and theories are not acknowledged? (p. 65)

These questions directly address the meanings common to a whole period and help to reveal the discourse represented by the adult education handbooks.

The data—in Foucault's terms, the text—for this study were the seven editions of handbooks published between 1934 and 1989 by the American Association of Adult Education, the Adult Education Association, and the American Association for Adult and Continuing Education (see the 1989 edition for a complete listing of editors, authors, and topics). These books represent historical and episodic frames of reference with respect to issues, theory, research, and practice of American adult education. My argument is not that the handbooks represent the field so much as they represent the interests of those who have been seeking to professionalize the field. In this respect the handbooks offer an opportunity to exemplify and illustrate the discourse representative of the professionalization movement. That the handbooks were first instituted in the 1930s and have been published approximately every 10 years or so is significant in order to see how this frame of reference emerged and how consistent it has remained. Because the handbooks are a historical and deliberate attempt to codify the knowledge which allegedly guides the practice of adult education, they represent a unique chart of the intentions of the field over time as well as provide access to the world views from which those intentions derive.

SCIENCE, PROFESSIONALIZATION, AND THE ADULT EDUCATION HANDBOOKS

In very broad strokes, there are two phases to the evolving story of the seven handbooks. In the first phase, the 1934 and 1936 handbooks comprise an initial attempt to describe the various components of the field through a systematic listing of program and institutional examples. The 1948 handbook begins to demonstrate the shift away from the cataloging of the early editions to an emerging reliance on scientific knowledge to define the field; it also presents the first version of the "common concerns" and the anxiety regarding professionalization which will continue to dominate the field for the next 40 years. The 1960 edition marks the full emergence of adult education as a field of academic study and the complete adoption of empirical-analytic science as the ideology to sustain its professionalization efforts. The second phase, encompassing the 1970, 1980–81, and 1989 handbooks, represents largely a period of consolidation and refinement because the handbooks in most respects continue the interests and conventions adumbrated in 1948 and established by the 1960 edition. Each phase, though, has as its central theme the growing concern with professionalizing the field through the use of science.

Early Empiricism and the Emergence of Adult Education as a Field of Study

The 1934 and 1936 handbooks can be seen as early attempts to systematically array knowledge about the field of adult education; this is done almost exclusively through a listing of program and institutional examples in catalog fashion.

These two handbooks are nearly identical in form, content, and intent. They are written almost exclusively by institutionally-based representatives of different organizational and programmatic interests in adult education. Because of the institutional location of the writers, much of the knowledge presented is apparently derived from the practice of these institutional contributors; that is, the knowledge presented in the handbooks appears to represent the experience of practitioners in explicit institutional and programmatic areas of adult education in the 1930s such as settlement organizations, voluntary associations, libraries, prisons, schools, worker education programs, and Americanization programs. This anecdotal information is countered by the explicit use of quantitative descriptions of institutional and programmatic manifestations of adult education in the 1930s. There are numerous examples of primitive statistical description supporting the presence of adult education in American institutional life. Actually, the handbooks themselves, both in their individual entries as well as their overall effect, are largely directories or catalogs of those organizations and programs, accomplished chiefly by short, narrative descriptions followed by extensive listings of exemplars. They are, in fact, an extensive catalog of institutionally-located adult education programs in the United States in the 1930s.

These two handbooks provide a medium for presenting what Cartwright called the "facts" of adult education, which he described as a product of "the first studies of adult education in the United States initiated by the Carnegie Corporation in 1924" (1934, unpaginated preface). By the 1934 and 1936 editions, these "facts" are fundamentally defined as the enumeration of the programmatic presence of adult education in the American institutional life of the 1930s. Consequently, many of the entries in these two handbooks are based on "surveys of various aspects of activity . . . descriptive and critical reports on specific enterprises . . . and research studies in theory or practice" which are essential to "creating a body of sound theory and constructive practice" (Beals, 1936, p. 13). Very early we see the invocation of empirical-analytic science to sustain an emerging concern for professionalization—a framework ideologically inchoate in the 1930s that will emerge clearly in the 1948 edition. Thus, while many of the entries report only anecdotal and practice-derived information, many others explicitly report on or refer to survey studies conducted under the auspices of the Carnegie Corporation and the American Association of Adult Education in the late 1920s and early 1930s. The significance of these two editions lies in their early use of survey research, which chiefly focuses on counting and identifying programmatic and institutional manifestations of the field, in order to define the contours and parameters of adult education. These two editions represent an exhaustive survey of the institutional presence of adult education in American society and an appeal to the value of systematic inquiry. Given these benchmark editions, there is little wonder why Knowles (1962) would acclaim the success of American adult education in becoming institutionalized. They are, however, clearly the anomalies in the sample because they are almost exclusively derived from the institutional practice of adult education in the 1930s. The point is to show the first stirrings of this professionalization movement by showing how much a departure subsequent editions are from these two.

The 1948 edition is perhaps the pivotal piece in the emergence of scientific knowledge as the basis for professionalizing the practice of adult education. While still retaining the heritage of content and form of the 1930s editions, this volume represents a transition because new categories of content, as well as new forms for expressing it, emerge in this edition that prove to be precursors for all subsequent editions. First is the reporting of actual research studies that propose empirically defined principles of practice. For example, Brownell (1948) describes principles of leadership in community development, while Ogden and Ogden (1948) report that participation and collaboration were crucial elements in community development. Houle (1948), in reporting on his study of adult education in the armed forces during and after World War II, argues that the programs were "an experiment in the education of adults without parallel in any civilian undertaking" (p. 276). Significantly, Houle argues that "while it was impossible to record proper objective evidence on which generalizations might be based" (p. 278), the study nonetheless produced "far-reaching" implications for the practice of adult education.

Indeed, he was correct then in presenting such currently well-accepted notions as the relation of prior schooling to involvement in adult education, the need to start education at the level of the adult, and the need to orient adult instruction to tasks. Also new to this edition are embryonic discussions of practice as a general process, irrespective of specific institutional or programmatic context (as already noted, the previous editions had focused exclusively on reporting specific examples of practice). For example, Hallenbeck (1948) defines adult education as "a process, not an end" (p. 245) in defining the professional training for practitioners. Essert (1948) and Rogers (1948) both discuss the process of using groups in adult education.

The salience of the 1948 edition, however, lies in describing and categorizing the field in terms of three broad categories: common concerns, institutions, and programs; this systematic arrangement becomes the model for every subsequent handbook. Thus the 1948 edition, in a crucial conceptual departure from its predecessors, presents an attempt to "theorize" the field itself (it must be noted that Knowles [1960] claims this was accomplished in Ely's *Adult Education in Action* [1936] although I believe her categories are somewhat different than those in 1948). Previous editors had arranged content alphabetically. The 1948 edition is arranged in sections. One is on programs ("areas of interest, activity, and need"); a second is on institutions ("institutional resources"); and, tellingly, a third is called "common concerns," in which professional preparation of practitioners, methods of instruction, and collaboration are central issues. The notion of common concerns is especially important because it is the first organizational and topic indicator of the field's interest in professionalizing by defining a core body of knowledge through empirical-analytic science.

Significantly, it is in the common concerns section that Hallenbeck (1948) connects the professionalization of the field with training adult educators. This concern, first initiated in the 1930s by listing academic programs and university courses in adult education (it is revealing that there were 49 colleges and universities offering courses in adult education listed in the 1936 handbook), will become one of the prominent issues in every subsequent edition. Hallenbeck argues that there are three elements in defining a profession: a body of knowledge, specific training, and jobs. With respect to the body of knowledge, Hallenbeck proposes that history and philosophy of adult education, adult psychology and learning, methods and materials, and program administration be the central topics in training adult educators (these had been typical adult education courses in colleges and universities in the 1930s; clearly they have remained so since). Thus Hallenbeck is the first in the handbooks to make the argument that the field of adult education will become more professionalized as it conducts research to develop principles of practice by which to train adult educators. It is this central common concern—the need to develop empirically-based theory to guide practice—around which the field will be increasingly organized in subsequent editions. It is in this respect that embryonic discussions of adult education as a general process irrespective of institutional or programmatic context, gain import and why specific research studies proposing principles for the scientific practice of adult education are so prophetic. Thus this edition foreshadows how the field of adult education itself is becoming an object of study. The effect of these common concerns and the organizational scheme of the 1948 edition is to demonstrate a definitional ordering of the field, that is, to make an effort to define and integrate its diverse elements by articulating it as a scientific process rather than as a set of exemplars. So, it is not surprising to see adult educators in the 1950s and especially 1960s enthusiastically endorsing a technical scientific approach to education. Further, it would truly be surprising if the field had not adopted this framework of professionalizing practice since science has been central to the professionalization of American education since the turn of century (Feinberg, 1975).

The inchoate transitions of the 1948 edition fully emerge in the 1960 edition. In solidifying the changes of 1948, the 1960 edition squarely locates the use of scientific knowledge as central to the definition and professionalization of adult education. While continuing the convention of presenting the field as theory ("common concerns"), programs, and institutions, the dominant concern of this handbook is to develop the scientific study and definition of the field and through the use of systematic, empiric study to increasingly professionalize its practice. That is, there is a "continuing need for experimentation and research so that adult educators make crucial decisions on the basis of dependable evidence, rather than on intuition and limited experience" (Schmidt & Svenson, 1960, p. 94). This is the characteristic stance: Scientific research is thus explicitly proposed in this handbook as solving problems of practice. Scientifically resolving practice problems is routinely connected to professionalization. Houle (1960) laments the lack of professionalization in adult education because "many of the fundamental principles which underlie successful theory and practice have yet to be discovered" (p. 128). Thus the common concern continues to be the definition of the field by developing empirically-based principles of practice, which Kreitlow (1960, p. 115) refers to as "a common frame of reference." Consequently, survey research studies dominate this edition, which Kreitlow argues is essential in order that "hypotheses . . . be established . . . that can be tested experimentally" (1960, p. 108). Verner says that "adult educators need . . . more substantive knowledge so that they can perform their function properly . . . " (1960, p. 166), which he defines as research being "structured on prior research so that a consistent body of knowledge is accumulated" (p. 171). The intention of this research is to develop scientifically-tested principles that will improve the practice of adult education by contributing to the development of a core body of professional knowledge.

The development and use of research in this edition to describe adult education is integrally connected to the professionalization of the field. Hallenbeck in 1948 had begun enumerating the parameters of professional training by defining graduate school curricula. This is a major concern in the 1960 edition. Houle argues that "the group of present practitioners of adult education cannot yet meet . . . accepted canons of a profession" (1960, p. 124). A significant part of the problem is that there is at that time only a small group of professionally "trained" adult educators. Too many practitioners were still practicing on the basis of experience and intuition, not yet guided by empirically-based theory. The central problem which this handbook attempts to address is stated by Kreitlow:

> At this point in its development, adult education research cannot be compared with research in physics or even sociology. At the same time, unless the improvement of research continues as it has in the past decade, too long a time may ensue before we know some of the answers that administrators of adult programs, teachers in adult programs, and citizens who support the programs, need to know. (1960, p. 108)

Thus scientific research in this handbook is presented as solving problems of practice by enabling the practitioner to make better decisions about what to do. Indeed, this volume demonstrates that the earlier purpose of cataloging exemplars is now completely overshadowed by the reporting of research.

Because this edition represents the culmination of emergent patterns from earlier editions and sets the pattern for later ones, it signals the end of the first phase of the evolution of the adult education handbooks. With the categorical parameters established in this edition, adult education successfully negotiates the transition from being a field of practice to a field of study. While the professional anxieties regarding this transition have continued to plague the field since 1960, the evidence of this handbook in conjunction with subsequent editions indicates how successful this edition was in substantiating an empirical-analytic ideology of the field in terms of defining common programmatic, institutional, and theoretical concerns. Thus, the 1960 edition adds ample evidence for claims about the field's technical orientation (Brookfield, 1989a; Cunningham, 1989; Law, 1988; Law & Rubenson, 1988; Welton, 1987). But I want to argue that, rather than an emergence, this is the culmination of a movement that had begun 30 years before.

Science and the Body of Knowledge in Adult Education

These categories of definition and professionalization, constructed through the use of scientific research, become the primary conceptual categories of the remaining three handbooks. Thus, the subsequent editions of the handbook in 1970,

1980–81, and 1989 neither seriously challenge the professional reliance upon empirical-analytic knowledge nor significantly alter the organizational scheme of common concerns established in 1948 and 1960.

The dominant concern of the 1970 handbook remains identical to the 1960 edition: to bring conceptual order to the field through research in order to professionalize its practice. Schroeder argues that from 1930 to 1946 the field began to search for a definition and that the "period 1947–1964 was characterized by intensified movement toward greater professionalism and . . . a proliferation of written materials concerned with definitions and delineation of adult education as a field of research, professional study and practice" (1970, p. 27). Developing a body of "tested" knowledge and disseminating it to practitioners is the central mission of adult education as a field of study in 1970. Continuing the precedent of 1960, the 1970 handbook demonstrates its chief function is to report research. But the problem of the 1960 edition remains the same in the 1970 edition: How can the professionalization process proceed without the production of more and better research? The editors' framework is clear in this respect:

> Perhaps most striking is the paucity of data concerning both the field as a whole and its various components. Several authors have ruefully confessed they had few reliable statistics upon which to base their chapters. Others offer mute testimony by their reliance on the two or three publications that speak quantitatively of such matters as clientele, subjects studied and institutional enrollments. (Smith, Aker, & Kidd, 1970, pp. ix–x)

The handbook content in part negates this claim because there are substantial amounts of quantitative description which continue the tradition so effectively solidified in the 1960 edition.

Although the 1980–81 multi-volume handbook appears at first to significantly alter the established traditions of the handbooks, it actually is the most pronounced example of the dominance of scientific knowledge in adult education. It is almost exclusively focused on empirically developing theory and principles of practice in adult education. Continuing the concerns of previous editions, this edition is replete with injunctions for defining the field by developing a body of knowledge based in empirical-analytic research that will produce a unifying order which will professionalize practice. Peters sets the orientation of this handbook by connecting the use of research to bringing more unity to the field in order to continue its professionalization: "Few tasks are as challenging to the adult educator as the problem of finding order with the collage of organizations, programs, clientele, and concepts that depicts the nature of adult education" (1980, p. xi). Finding order is the essential mission of this edition. In response to this major concern regarding unity, the 1980–81 edition is in a profound sense attempting to conceptualize the entire field as an integrated entity. For example, Boyd and Apps' volume on "redefining the discipline of adult education" attempts to account for the entire field: "Our model for adult education now has three dimensions. . . . By visualizing a cube—each plane represents one of our educational dimensions, one may locate a given program in terms of three coordinates: its transactional mode, client focus, and predominant system" (1980, p. 10). Thus Boyd and Apps attempt to describe the field as an interlocking array of features that can categorize any instance of adult education. Peters' volume, ironically entitled *Building an Effective Adult Education Enterprise*, is an elaborate and eloquent argument to use systems theory to develop "an essential unity to the field" (Peters, 1980, p. xi); nearly the entire volume is about the study of the field, not its actual practice. Schroeder's chapter on a typology of learning systems may well be the jewel in the empiric crown; it attempts to systematically array all the identifiable components in a system that is defined by measurable quantities in order to "help practitioners become more discriminating in their use of knowledge and researchers more realistic and generative in their search for knowledge" (1980, p. 41). Perhaps Boshier's model of adult education is an appropriate final example of the empirical-analytic orientation of this edition: "The purposes of adult education are best represented on two axes which lie in an orthogonal relationship to each other. These axes allow the portrayal of the extent to which an adult education institution or activity is learner centered or societal centered" (1981, p. 237).

In effect, this edition completes the adoption of the empirical-analytic model of knowledge first intimated in the 1930s, for its scholars attempt to integrate the entire field using theoretical propositions supported by research as well as to indicate directions for continued systematic inquiry. Defining the field from a unified perspective in order to develop tested, empirical propositions is central to the field's identity at this point, which Long describes as increasing "the accumulation of tested and verified truth" (1980, p. 7).

The significant aspect of the 1989 handbook is that it explicitly reinvokes the organizational and definitional parameters adumbrated in 1948, fully realized in 1960, and conventionalized by 1970: common concerns, institutions, and program areas. The difference in this handbook is that the field is contemplated from both a sense of integration and a sense of diversity, thus ameliorating the almost feverish quest for unity in the 1980–81 edition. Common concerns for all adult educators are focused on those issues dealing with the professional practice of adult education and the educational process: "What adult educators do constitutes a common core of practice that unites an otherwise diverse field" (Merriam & Cunningham, 1989, p. xvii). Central to all practice is an interest in facilitating adult learning and designing effective programming. These concerns are presented as transcending what Merriam and Cunningham describe as "the staggering number of diverse institutions" (1989, p. 273) and program areas of adult education. In order to define both the diversity and the unity of the field in terms of a body of knowledge, the contributors continue to rely as in past editions almost exclusively on scientific knowledge. As in the past as well, professionalization depends upon "identifying good principles of practice and by disseminating those principles through various forms of training and related literature" (Galbraith & Zelenak, 1989, p. 131). The framework of common concerns first introduced in 1948 lives on in the first two sections of this handbook, "Adult Education as a Field of Practice" and "Adult Learners and the Educational Process." It is here in these two sections that the "common components of practice" (Merriam & Cunningham, 1989, p. xvii) are addressed.

The significant change in this edition, however, is a focus on presenting definitional classifications of adult education programs, institutions, and theory rather than on developing principles of practice. That is, perhaps because there is a maturing quiescence regarding the unity anxiety of earlier editions, the central intent is to provide classifications of practice based on literature reviews of research and thought, rather than to emphasize empirically-developed principles of practice. Classifications, or categorizations, are used to describe knowledge about the common concerns of adult education, its institutions, and its programs. Many chapters focus on this. For example, Courtney classifies definitions of adult education into five perspectives:

> First, it has been seen as the work of institutions and organizations. Second, it has been described as a special kind of relationship, as in the concept of andragogy. . . . Third, it has been considered a profession or scientific discipline. Fourth, it has been seen as stemming from historical identification with spontaneous social movements. Finally, it has been distinguished from other kinds of education by its goals and functions. (1989, p. 17)

Beder (1989) classifies philosophies; Brookfield (1989b) describes facilitating paradigms; Cookson (1989) classifies international adult education; Boucouvalas and Krupp (1989) describe different adult development perspectives; Steele (1989) classifies major evaluation models.

Beginning in the 1930s as programmatic and institutional catalogs, the handbooks have become by 1989 episodic statements of the definitional character of the field based on bibliographic collections of the field's most recent research. The 1989 edition is in fact a catalog of research findings, just as the 1960, 1970, and 1980–81 handbooks had been. While retaining the "handbook" theme, this edition demonstrates just how far the series has moved from its original intentions. Furthermore, what is evident, from the earliest editions on, is a constantly growing and largely uncritical endorsement of empirical-analytic science for professionalizing the practice of adult educators and the increasing role of university researchers in that process. While continuing to reify its practical heritage, the field has nonetheless sought to sanctify its professionalization movement through the auspices of univer-

sity study, just as nearly any other emergent professional group
has sought to do in the twentieth century (Cervero, 1988;
Houle, 1980; Larson, 1979; Schön, 1983). It is to that "peculiar
institution" that I now turn.

SCIENCE AND THE CONTROL OF
PROFESSIONALIZATION

A central element in the argument of this paper is that
the discourse in the adult education handbooks represents the
interests of those wishing to professionalize the practice of
adult education. The changing definition of the handbooks is
clear in this respect. Originally conceived as a reference compilation enumerating the institutional and programmatic presence of adult education in the United States, they soon became
a compilation of research dedicated to scientifically improving
the practice of adult education. Thus the handbooks represent
the movement away from the cataloging of practice exemplars
to a field of university-based scientific study of practice. Using
the image which first appeared in 1948, I have tried to depict
the stated common concern. This expressed common concern
has had to do with unifying a diverse field of practice by standardizing it through the development of empirically-based principles. Explicitly, this has meant organizing our understanding
of the field as theory, institutions, and programs. This definitional order emerges in 1948 and has remained conceptually
stable since then. The consequence of this concern is more
subtle. Its presence emerges only by looking at the "great, uniform text" that the handbooks represent, for it is not an image
purveyed simply by various identifiable persons but an intellectual structure which pervades the emergence of the field
itself as a professional occupation. It is in this sense that we
have to see the issue not just as a matter of improving practice
but one of controlling the profession itself.

The central premise of Habermas' epistemology is his ontological argument that knowledge exists to further some human purpose. In terms of a body of knowledge predicated on
the natural science model of empirical inquiry, that human
interest is control. In Habcrmas' terms, "empirical-analytic"

knowledge is instrumental in that it functions to control something. The handbooks represent just how systematic and pervasive this drive and its intellectual underpinnings have been. The question then becomes, what has the dominance of empirical-analytic knowledge in adult education been designed to control? The answer to that question has to do with the control of knowledge itself and thus the control of the professionalization process of adult education. I think the handbooks demonstrate very clearly how scientific knowledge has been used to define the field and thus control the development of professionalization. In the introduction I drew upon Schön's (1983) depiction of how theory is to be developed scientifically in research institutions and then applied to well-defined problems by practitioners: "professional activity consists in instrumental problem solving made rigorous by the application of scientific theory and technique" (p. 21). The handbooks explicitly demonstrate this as their chief function, their stated common concern. The tradition of using empirical-analytic knowledge to define the field of adult education in order to systematize its practice is intimated in the 1930s handbooks and clearly evident from 1948 on.

To understand the connection between science and control, we have to look further. With its shift from archiving to constructing knowledge, the modern research university has become a magnet for occupations seeking to professionalize (Houle, 1980; Larson, 1979; Schön, 1983): "In the first seventy-five years of the twentieth century, as formal higher education was rapidly expanding, preparatory training programs of professionals seemed to move inexorably toward the sponsorship of universities" (Houle, 1980, p. 30). Therefore, in addition to the epistemological connection, Schön's analysis shows that it is no historical accident that university-affiliated contributors (professors, deans, continuing educators, and administrators) provided a fourth of the entries in 1948, and that by the 1980s provided nearly every entry in the handbooks. So a shift in authorship from the dominance of practitioners in the 1930s is certainly indicative of a shift in control of what counts as valuable knowledge in the field. Schön's analysis, however, while carefully articulating the epistemological relation between empirical-analytic knowledge ("technical rationality" in his lexicon) and professionalization and charting its historical consequences, does not explicitly deal with the issue of control which Habermas' analysis introduces.

Larson (1979), though, in her analysis of universities, professionalization, and market share, helps us to see the issue of control more clearly. She argues that, in order for a profession to transact its service in a market economy, it has to develop standardized forms of knowledge ("cognitive exclusivity") upon which to base its service, and it has to standardize the practice of the service in order to become a recognizable commodity in a service economy. Defining a service expertise, however, not only depends upon developing and controlling a body of knowledge; it also depends on controlling the training of practitioners, which can be accomplished by locating both knowledge production and professional training in the same institutional framework, the modern research university. Thus the dominance of empirical-analytic knowledge in adult education is directly related to researchers' attempts to professionalize practice through the systematic study of the field in order to develop scientific principles of practice. In this way, the field could not professionalize its practice until it could produce both standardized service and recognizable providers (practitioners) of that service. In other words, a profession cannot control its market in a service economy until it is routinely recognized as a provider by the consumer. This is a way of accounting for the constant delineation of common concerns in the handbooks since 1948 and the connection of those concerns to developing principles of practice. That is, professionalization depended on developing an exclusive knowledge base and locating both the development of that knowledge and the training of providers in the same institutional location. The foremost task of the handbooks is to provide an identifiable body of knowledge that will standardize the training of adult educators, which, by standardizing practice, makes adult education an identifiable service commodity.

Controlling knowledge production is therefore essential to defining what constitutes the profession. Scientific knowledge has been essential to the development of a unique body of knowledge, to the training of practitioners, and thus to the development of adult education as a profession. This is what the discourse in the handbooks represents. Without this basis in a scientifically-derived body of knowledge, there would be no professional activity to transact in a service economy. This may well be the central problem of the professionalization movement in adult education as well as a way of understanding why adult education has been unable to garner the professional recognition it has so consistently sought.

By way of closure, I would like to raise two related points as issues needing further consideration. The first is the "so what" question: This account isn't very interesting because it doesn't tell us anything. Of course, the analysis presented here is at best tentative and clearly exception can be taken. But the discourse is just as clearly evident—the dominant intellectual framework for understanding adult education has been this scientific ideology. I believe it helps in understanding how the field has arrived at its present configuration. It leads me to want to argue that the best way to understand the modern period of adult education is to recognize that this scientifically-driven professionalization movement emerged much earlier than we have typically supposed. It is conventionally claimed (Brookfield, 1989a; Cunningham, 1989; Law, 1988; Taylor et al., 1985; Welton, 1987) that the social movement heritage met its demise in the 1950s with the emergence of the professionalization movement. Certainly the analysis contained here alters that timeline, for I want to argue that the 1950s and 1960s represent the culmination of this movement, not its emergence.

It may well be that there has been no shift in modern times (dated from the 1920s on) of the field from emancipatory interests to technical ones, not, that is, if the analysis is constrained to mainstream activities sponsored by the various adult education associations. I further suspect that we can find evidence for this interpretation in the early days of the field's association activities. But perhaps more important is the result of this movement, which has consistently devalued the "practical" roots of the field by passing them off as unprofessional because of their experiential and intuitive nature. If the field is to achieve greater success as a helping profession and achieve the public identity it desires, we cannot afford to adhere so strictly to a narrow scientific view of practice. Alternative frameworks for understanding and acting effectively in our educational world are increasingly apparent. If the field continues to privilege the natural science model of inquiry as the major legitimate means of improving practice, then we will continue to remain limited in our appeal to practitioners and fail to expand our potential.

REFERENCES

Apple, M. (1979). *Ideology and curriculum*. London: Routledge & Kegan Paul.

Beals, R. (1936). American association for adult education. In D. Rowden (Ed.), *Handbook of adult education* (pp. 12–16). New York: American Association for Adult Education.

Beder, H. (1989). Purposes and philosophies of adult education. In S. Merriam & P. Cunningham (Eds.), *Handbook of adult and continuing education* (pp. 37–50). San Francisco: Jossey-Bass.

Bernstein, R. (1976). *The restructuring of social and political theory*. New York: Harcourt, Brace, Jovanovitch.

Boshier, R. (1981). Adult education: Issues of the future. In B. Kreitlow (Ed.), *Examining controversies in adult education* (pp. 235–256). San Francisco: Jossey-Bass.

Boucouvalas, M., & Krupp, J. (1989). Adult development and learning. In S. Merriam & P. Cunningham (Eds.), *Handbook of adult and continuing education* (pp. 183–200). San Francisco: Jossey-Bass.

Boyd, R., & Apps, J. (1980). A conceptual model for adult education. In R. Boyd & J. Apps (Eds.), *Redefining the discipline of adult education* (pp. 1–13). San Francisco: Jossey-Bass.

Brookfield, S. (1989a). The epistemology of adult education in the United States and Great Britain: A cross-cultural analysis. In B. Bright (Ed.), *Theory and practice in the study of adult education: The epistemological imperative* (pp. 141–173). London: Croom-Helm.

Brownwell, B. (1948). The Montana study. In M. Ely (Ed.), *Handbook of adult education* (pp. 113–117). New York: Institute of Adult Education, Columbia University.

Cartwright, M. (1934). Preface. In D. Rowden (Ed.), *Handbook of adult education* (unpaginated). New York: American Association of Adult Education.

Cervero, R. (1988). *Effective continuing education for professionals.* San Francisco: Jossey-Bass.

Cookson, P. (1989). International and comparative adult education. In S. Merriam & P. Cunningham (Eds.), *Handbook of adult and continuing education* (pp. 70–83). San Francisco: Jossey-Bass.

Courtney, S. (1989). Defining adult and continuing education. In S. Merriam & P. Cunningham (Eds.), *Handbook of adult and continuing education* (pp. 15–25). San Francisco: Jossey-Bass.

Cunningham, P. (1989). Making a more significant impact on society. In B. A. Quigley (Ed.), *Fulfilling the promise of adult and continuing education* (pp. 33–46). New Directions for Continuing Education, no. 44, San Francisco: Jossey-Bass.

Eagleton, T. (1976). *Marxism and literary criticism.* Berkeley: University of California Press.

Ely, M. (1936). *Adult education in action.* New York: American Association of Adult Education.

Essert, P. (1948). The discussion group in adult education. In M. Ely (Ed.), *Handbook of adult education* (pp. 269–275). New York: Institute of Adult Education, Columbia University).

Feinberg, W. (1975). *Reason and rhetoric: The intellectual foundation of 20th century liberal education policy.* New York: John Wiley.

Flexner, A. (1916). Is social work a profession? *School and Society, 1,* 901–911.

Foucault, M. (1972). *The archeology of knowledge and the discourse on language.* (A. M. Sheridan Smith, Trans.). New York: Pantheon.

Franklin, B. (1974). The curriculum field and the problem of social control, 1918–1938: A study in critical theory (Doctoral dissertation, University of Wisconsin-Madison, 1974). *Dissertation Abstracts International, 35,* 5776A.

Galbraith, M., & Zelenak, B. (1989). The education of adult and continuing education practitioners. In S. Merriam &

P. Cunningham (Eds.), *Handbook of adult and continuing education* (pp. 124–133). San Francisco: Jossey-Bass.

Gilbert, R. (1989). Text analysis and ideology critique of curricular content. In S. de Castell, A. Luke, & C. Luke (Eds.), *Language, authority and criticism: Readings on the school textbook*, (pp. 61–73). London: Falmer.

Giroux, H. (1980). Critical theory and rationality in citizenship education. *Curriculum Inquiry, 10* (4), 329–366.

Habermas, J. (1971). *Knowledge and human interests.* (J. Shapiro, Trans.). Boston: Beacon. (Original work published 1968).

Hallenbeck, W. (1948). Training adult educators. In M. Ely (Ed.), *Handbook of adult education* (pp. 243–249). New York: Institute of Adult Education, Columbia University.

Houle, C. (1948). An unparalleled experiment in adult education. In M. Ely (Ed.), *Handbook of adult education* (pp. 276–280). New York: Institute of Adult Education, Columbia University.

Houle, C. (1960). The education of adult educational leaders. In M. Knowles (Ed.), *Handbook of adult education in the United States* (pp. 117–128). Chicago: Adult Education Association of the USA.

Houle, C. (1980). *Continuing learning in the professions.* San Francisco: Jossey-Bass.

Kelley, R. (1974). Literature and the historian. *American Quarterly, 26,* 141–159.

Knowles, M. (1960). *Handbook of adult education in the United States.* Chicago: Adult Education Association of the USA.

Knowles, M. (1962). *The adult education movement in the United States.* New York: Holt, Rinehart & Winston.

Kreitlow, B. (1960). Research in adult education. In M. Knowles (Ed.), *Handbook of adult education in the United States* (pp. 106–115). Chicago: Adult Education Association of the USA.

Larson, M. (1979). *The rise of professionalism: A sociological analysis.* Berkeley: University of California Press.

Law, M. (1988). Adult education, McCarthyism, and the Cold War. In C. Warren (Ed.), *Proceedings of the 29th adult edu-*

cation research conference (pp. 181–186). Calgary, Canada: University of Calgary.

Law, M. & Rubenson, K. (1988). Andragogy: The return of the Jedi. In M. Zukas (Ed.), *Proceedings of the transatlantic dialogue: A research exchange* (pp. 232–237). Leeds, UK: School of Continuing Education, University of Leeds.

Long, H. (1980). A perspective on adult education research. In H. Long & Hiemstra (Eds.), *Changing approaches to studying adult education* (pp. 1–21). San Francisco: Jossey-Bass.

Merriam, S., & Cunningham, P. (Eds.). (1989). *Handbook of adult and continuing education.* San Francisco: Jossey-Bass.

Ogden, J., & Ogden, J. (1948). Special projects in adult education. In M. Ely (Ed.), *Handbook of adult education* (pp. 118–125). New York: Institute of Adult Education, Columbia University.

Peters, J. (Ed.). (1980). *Building an effective adult education enterprise.* San Francisco: Jossey-Bass.

Rogers, M. (1948). Autonomous groups. In M. Ely (Ed.), *Handbook of adult education* (pp. 143–152). New York: Institute of Adult Education, Columbia University.

Schmidt, W., & Svenson, E. (1960). Methods in adult education. In M. Knowles (Ed.), *Handbook of adult education in the United States* (pp. 82–95). Chicago: Adult Education Association of the USA.

Schroeder, W. (1970). Adult education defined and described. In R. Smith, G. Aker, & J. Kidd (Eds.), *Handbook of adult education* (pp. 25–44). New York: Macmillan.

Schroeder, W. (1980). Typology of adult learning systems. In J. Peters (Ed.), *Building an effective adult education enterprise* (pp. 44–77). San Francisco: Jossey-Bass.

Schön, D. (1983). *The reflective practitioner: How professionals think in action.* New York: Basic.

Schutz, A. (1967). *The phenomenology of the social world.* (G. Walsh & F. Lehnart, trans.). Geneva, NY: Northwestern University Press. (original work published 1932).

Smith, R., Aker, G., & Kidd, J. (Eds.). (1970). *Handbook of adult education.* New York: Macmillan.

Steele, S. (1989). The evaluation of adult and continuing education. In S. Merriam & P. Cunningham (Eds.), *Handbook of adult and continuing education* (pp. 260–272). San Francisco: Jossey-Bass.

Taylor, R., Rockhill, K., & Fieldhouse, R. (1985). *University adult education in England and the United States: A reappraisal of the liberal tradition.* Beckenham, UK: Croom Helm.

Taxel, J. (1984). The American Revolution in childen's fiction: An analysis of historical meaning and narrative structure. *Curriculum Inquiry, 14*(1), 7–55.

Verner, C. (1960). The literature of adult education. In M. Knowles (Ed.), *Handbook of adult education in the United States* (pp. 162–178). Chicago: Adult Education Association of the USA.

Welton, M. (1987). Vivisecting the nightingale: Reflections on adult education as an object of study. *Studies in the Education of Adults, 19*(1), 46–68.

Whitty, G. (1985). *Sociology and school knowledge: Curriculum theory, research, and politics.* London: Metheun.

Wilson, A. (1993). Discourse analysis and hermeneutics: Methodological considerations in analyzing intellectual traditions in adult education history. Fourth Visiting Scholar Conference in the History of Adult Education. Syracuse, NY: Department of Adult Education, Syracuse University.

Wright, W. (1975). *Six guns and society: A structural study of the western.* Berkely: University of California Press.

Michael R. Welton (1942–   ) is professor of adult and continuing education in the School of Education, Dalhousie University, Halifax, Nova Scotia. Professor Welton received his B.A. and M.A. degrees in social anthropology, and his Ph.D. in Educational Foundations at the University of British Columbia.

For over thirty years, Welton has been involved in the education of adults. He has taught adult literacy classes in Nigeria, writing in the community college, directed a writing project involving First Nations' students, and taught university courses in adult education.

Dr. Welton has two intellectual passions: history and critical social theory. He believes that our present understanding of and practices in adult education take on full meaning when we examine them in light of our traditions and those of other cultures. A society's institutions thwart human development unless they are purposefully learner-centered, developmental, and emancipatory. Welton relies upon the work of German philosopher, Jurgen Habermas, for a framework that has enough ontological depth and sociological breadth to encompass the complexities and conundrums of adult learning. In the following essay which examines critical theory's contribution to understanding adult learning, Welton demonstrates how Habermas's ideas allow us to think imaginatively about knowledge, learning, and the human condition.

MICHAEL R. WELTON

16 The Contribution of Critical Theory to Our Understanding of Adult Learning

At first glance, Jürgen Habermas seems an unlikely candidate for attention from the American adult education community. Born in Dusseldorf, Germany, in 1929, Habermas came of age in National Socialist Germany. During his formative years, Habermas experienced the irrationality and barbarism of Nazism. How was it conceivable that Germany, the home of great apostles of enlightenment such as Luther, Kant, Hegel, and Marx, could descend into gas chambers and torchlight parades? Was it really possible to create a rational society after Auschwitz? How was it possible for a scientifically literate and technologically sophisticated society to place its knowledge

From An Update on Adult Learning Theory, *edited by S. B. Merriam.* New Directions for Adult and Continuing Education, no. 57. *Copyright © by Jossey-Bass, Inc. Publishers. Reprinted with permission.*

and technique in the service of evil? Was it possible for human beings to free themselves from irrational ways of ordering their common life? These questions, originating in Habermas's childhood and teenage years, have been central to his writings over the last three decades.

In this chapter, I examine Habermas's ideas about human knowing, language, and social evolution. I argue that Habermas provides us with a fresh way of looking at adult learning in social and historical contexts. This is his major strength. But I also argue that Habermasian insights hold promise for our education practice.

KNOWLEDGE, LEARNING, AND
THE HUMAN CONDITION

Critical theory is often identified with a talented group of German thinkers who were associated with the Institute of Social Research in Frankfurt (Theodor Adorno, Max Horkheimer, Herbert Marcuse, and Walter Benjamin). These men believed that life had to be transformed. When they began writing in the early 1920s, they had to make sense of the carnage of battlefields such as the Somme and to grasp the meaning of the Russian Revolution. As the 1920s unfolded into the global depression of the 1930s, they tried to understand the rise of fascism, the collapse of liberal democracy, the growth of new forms of production, and the birth of mass culture. In the 1920s, influenced by Marx's writings, they still believed that the industrial working class was the group that would bring about a more just and free society. By the outbreak of World War II, these Frankfurt thinkers had abandoned several fundamental Marxian axioms. They no longer believed that the industrial working class (the "proletariat") would usher in a better world.

Habermas is a critical theorist of the second generation. He agreed with his Frankfurt teachers that Marxism had to be updated for a new time. He did not accept the brooding pessimism of his mentors. Habermas set out on a very ambitious journey. He wanted to travel back to Marx to find out where he went wrong and then travel forward to his own time to scout the intellectual scene for ideas to make sense of the changed world of post-World War II Europe and America. He appreciated Marx's bold and scholarly attempt to explain why nineteenth-century industrial capitalism produced simultaneously abundant wealth and mammoth misery. But he thought that Marx was wrong to believe that he was writing a "science" of society. Habermas believed that Marx had overestimated the place of science in human life. But what was the proper role of natural scientific knowing in our world? And how could a theory purporting to explain and change the world be justified?

Habermas believed that the natural scientific way of knowing is not the only valid kind of knowledge. In his celebrated and controversial *Knowledge and Human Interests*, Habermas (1972) offered a way of thinking about human knowledge and learning that eventually captured the imagination of many adult education thinkers. From its inception as a university-based field, the study of adult education has been plagued by the (almost) intractable problem of how to define the boundaries of the field. Theorists and practitioners have been struck by the diversity of adult education practices and have almost despaired of finding any underlying unity in the diversity. Habermas developed a way of thinking about the relationship between knowledge, learning, and the human condition that provided a powerful means of understanding the unity in the diversity of human learning processes and outcomes.

Habermas contended that knowledge can take three different forms: technical, practical, and emancipatory. All societies exist in a material environment and must interact with nature to produce their existence. Habermas named this learning domain "labor." Humankind's interchange with nature generates a *technical* interest in prediction and control. All societies, from tribal to modern, learn along the axis of interaction with nature. Only in modern societies is learning about nature expressed in the natural scientific form known as positivism. But all societies also involve "symbolic interaction," the communication of persons with one another. Human interchange creates a *practical* interest in the understanding of meaning. Contemporary social sciences and humanities (anthropology, sociology, literary criticism, history) are called hermeneutical sciences (hermeneutics is the science of interpretation) because they study how human beings make meaning and reach consensus. Finally, every society manifests various forms of power relations among members. *Emancipatory* knowledge derives from humankind's desire to achieve emancipation from domination, whether domination of nature over human life or the domination of some individuals or groups over others. For Habermas, then, knowledge is the outcome of human activity motivated by interests that guide and shape their learning processes.

Human beings learn through the generation of application of technical knowledge (there is cumulative growth in technical and scientific knowledge) and through the generation and application of practical and moral knowledge (there are changes over time in our beliefs, values, and rules governing our interactions). The emancipatory interest is derivative of the others and the most significant. The forms of knowledge guided by the technical and practical interests are always open to questioning and reexamination. But reason also demands explicitly nondistorted communication. A critical social science cannot rest satisfied with discovering regularities in our social action. It must also ask whether our beliefs, values, and interactions express dominative relations that can, in principle, be changed. Each learning domain has its own logic and cannot be reduced to any other (Giddens, 1985; Bernstein, 1985; Held, 1980).

Habermas's theory of knowledge-constitutive interests has captured the imagination of many adult educators and social thinkers. The idea that not all learning can be pressed into a single mold spoke to educators living and working in a world in which technical control over things and people seemed all-pervasive. A philosophy of adult learning influenced by Habermas starts with the affirmation that human beings are *material* and *historical* beings who have the potential to learn about nature, others, and the self. This learning is cumulative through time and is embodied in our ideologies, institutions, and social practices. It is also true, claims Habermas, that human learning can be blocked and distorted. In sum, human beings have the capacity to become active, reflective creatures. But the conditions of our lives (the institutions and values that shape us) often prevent us from acquiring the competencies needed to develop and unfold our many-sided potentialities. The clearest articulation of this philosophy of adult learning is in Fay's (1987) *Critical Social Science: The Limits to Liberation*. This framework is also implicit in Michael Collins's (1991) *Adult Education as Vocation* and my book, *Toward Development Work* (Welton, 1991).

The work of Jack Mezirow illustrates a second way in which adult educators have incorporated Habermasian ideas about the different forms of human knowledge. He analyzes Habermas's work to help him think about the fundamental purpose of the adult educator. Mezirow deserves considerable credit for introducing Habermasian ideas to a field known for its pragmatism. In his writings over almost two decades, Mezirow has been arguing that the cardinal purpose of the educator of adults is to foster critical reflection, namely, to help learners "become critically aware of the cultural and psychological assumptions that have influenced the way we see ourselves and our relationships and the way we pattern our lives" (Mezirow, 1978, p. 101). Mezirow believes that Habermas has established beyond reasonable doubt the existence of three distinct learning domains, each governed by a particular knowledge interest. Each "learning domain suggests . . . a different mode of personal learning and different learning needs" (Mezirow, 1981, p. 143). In *Transformative Dimensions of Adult Learning*, Mezirow (1991) draws on a wide range of sources to make his case. He thinks that the emancipatory interest of human beings is of cardinal significance because our critical reflection on learning blockages has the potential to change the way in which we as human beings communicate with others and nature.

Habermas's reflection on learning domains opens up previously closed lines of questioning. Should adult educators go along with corporate-defined agendas for the training of workers? Should we accept the restricted ways in which competence is defined by some educators and policymakers? Habermasian-influenced adult educators think of worker education as the process of becoming knowledgeable about the

way in which the structure of work enables or impedes human
development and learning, including acquiring the ability to
participate freely in communication processes within the enterprise and learning to be skillful in executing technically
appropriate job tasks (Marsick, 1987; Hart, 1992).

IMPORTANCE OF LANGUAGE

Habermas's (1984, 1987) theory of communicative action
is based on the idea that all human communication involves
validity claims, and that an ideal speech situation is presupposed every time we use language. According to Habermas,
when one person says something to another, that person makes
the following claims (implicitly and sometimes explicitly): (1)
What is said is comprehensible, that is, it obeys certain rules
of language so that there is a meaning that can be understood
by the other. (2) The propositional content (the factual assertions) of whatever is said is true. (3) The speaker is justified
in saying whatever is said. In other words, when we use speech
in any given context, we invoke certain social rights or
"norms." And (4) the speaker is sincere in whatever is said,
that is, he or she does not intend to deceive the listener.

To illustrate Habermas's abstract concept of an ideal
speech situation, let us suppose that in response to a traveler's
question a ticket clerk at a railway station says, "That will
be $25 for a cheap day return." The passenger might not in-
itially know what the phrase "cheap day return" means. When
the clerk explains what the phrase means, he or she is justifying the first claim. It is implicit in what the clerk says that
factual content of the statement is true: It actually does cost
$25 for the ticket (the second validity claim). It is also likely
that the passenger will take for granted that it is appropriate
for the clerk to pronounce authoritatively about the price of
the ticket (the third validity claim). And it is also assumed
that the clerk sincerely believes what he or she says (the fourth
validity claim; see Giddens, 1985, pp. 128–29).

Habermas argues that these four validity criteria serve
as a measuring stick for every interaction. They are implicit
in all communication, but we become especially aware of
them when we are forced, during a conflict, to justify our ar-

guments. In every interaction (face-to-face, organizational, and political-economic policy-making levels), a speaker may speak more or less comprehensibly, sincerely, appropriately, and truthfully. Each of the four criteria allows us to see when interpersonal agreement has been distorted, and how different types of misinformation influence participation in face-to-face and collective decision making.

The first criterion, comprehensibility, requires that people reveal what they mean to one another. Adult learners cannot learn about themselves and others when speech is ambiguous, confused, or nonsensical. At the organizational level, for instance, jargon may be used to exclude others from understanding important matters. The second criterion, sincerity, demands that listeners check the speaker's intentions. The communicative learning process is ruptured when listeners cannot trust the speaker and believe that, despite rhetorical reassurances, the real motive of the speaker has been disguised. Critically reflective learning exposes unexpressed interests (for example, an instrumental or strategic interest in controlling the agenda to maximize control over select resources).

The third criterion, appropriateness or legitimacy, asks, "Is this right?" Here, the concern is with determining proper roles and contexts. How responsive is the speaker to the views of others? Are professionals dominating the discourse? Critically reflective learning positions one to say, "I don't need to accept that," and to ask if decisions are being made in a participatory manner. The final criterion, truth, is guided by the checking of evidence. The question "Is this true?" directs attention to whether information is withheld, responsibility obscured, or need misrepresented. To what extent are decisions being made on insufficient or inadequately interpreted data? Is the learning process democratized or collaborative?

Imagine a community meeting in a rural township. Adult educators have been working for months with local communities to help them understand the impact of a proposed waste disposal site on the ecosystem and to explore alternatives. At the meeting, politicians, businesspeople, environmentalists, and local people are scheduled to speak. From the outset, community members do not trust the politicians and businesspeople to speak sincerely or truthfully. As these individuals

speak, community members soon realize that the fourth validity criterion, truthfulness, has not been met. The politicians
have not mentioned an authoritative environmental impact
study that pointed to the serious threat to the fragile ecosystem if the waste disposal site is approved. The business views
are questioned because they are perceived to reflect narrow
interests. And the community members are also very angry
that the learning process regarding waste disposal was not
open and collaborative. Indeed, the adult educators had to fight
each step of the way to be allowed to even see background
documents.

Each of these criteria—comprehensibility, sincerity, legitimacy, and truthfulness—helps the adult educator to identify the particular competencies required of learners to demystify
distorted speech, expose unexpressed interests, and democra-
tize their common life. The concept of an ideal speech situation enables us to compare reality with a fixed standard and
to assess the extent to which our modern institutions approxi-
mate the ideal.

Habermas is not advocating an ideal form of life in which
violence, manipulation, and conflict disappear. Indeed, he believes that "relations of force" are often "inconspicuously set"
in the "very structures of communication" and prevent humans from mutual understanding (Habermas, 1979, pp. 119–
120). Habermas encourages us to overcome the obstacles that
inhibit undistorted and noncoercive communication. For adult
educators, this means the cultivation of pedagogical practices
that enable all learners to enter into a communicative relationship obligated to make their utterances intelligible, to provide good grounds for their assertions, and to justify their
values in a sincere way. Fundamentally, Habermasian-influenced adult educators attempt to create rule-structured
communication conditions that enable free and noncoercive
learning to occur.

SOCIETY AND PERSONAL WORLDS

Habermas, like his Frankfurt teachers, is profoundly
aware of the dark side of our modern technological societies.

The evidence is everywhere: the degradation of ecosystems, the reduction of politics to the administration of things, the triumph of instrumental rationality, and the spiritual aridity of mass consumerism. The iron cage and not the promised land of universal freedom appears to have greeted us down modernity's bewitching road. But Habermas does not share his mentor's perception that modern history is one long nightmare. He thinks that modern societies manifest both potential and pathology.

Living in the modern world demands that we give valid reasons for our thinking and action. By so doing, we are shaken free from taken-for-granted ways of seeing and acting. We cannot simply depend on someone else's view of truth, goodness, or beauty. Modernity pushes us all toward being active and reflective persons. But the process of becoming an autonomous, reflective person is not an easy pathway. In our modern age, we are attempting to steer our way through a world of great risk and anxiety. The modern self is threatened by feelings of powerlessness, meaninglessness, and uncertainty. But, Habermas insists, we cannot return to the cocoon of traditional, dogmatic societies. We must learn to see the new possibilities of personal and social learning about meaning that are opening up before us.

Habermas uses the concepts of system and lifeworld to understand how much communicative rationality exists in the modern world. For Habermas, the system has to do with the economy, coded as money, and the state administrative system, coded as power (which he calls the state and corporate steering apparatuses). Systems are defined as organizations of purely strategic actions; that is, people in command positions in systems use a form of reason that represses human norms or values. The objects of corporate and state administrative decisions are acted on from the outside in a way that is inaccessible to reflection. Habermas claims that the capitalist economic system, the legal-rational political system, and even the modern mass communications system employ media such as money and power in a largely coercive, anticommunicative way.

For Habermas, the lifeworld is where "everyday practice" and "everyday communication" occur. The lifeworld is communicatively shared. In our families, places of worship, and schools, we acquire a background of shared meanings. This background of shared meanings makes ordinary symbolic interaction possible. It also provides the background for the legitimation of society and patterns of self-formation. It is in the lifeworld that we come to understand our ethical obligations to family, friends, and society. Adequate socialization processes require competent reference persons to help individuals to become communicatively competent actors.

Habermas does not think that the lifeworld and system world act on each other to mutual benefit. He uses the metaphor "colonization of the lifeworld" to show how the system has become uncoupled from communicatively shared experience and is now steered by the media of money and power. The uncoupling metaphor, however, should not be interpreted to mean that the economic and state administrative systems are detached totally from the lifeworld. The lifeworld always remains related to or embedded in the system. But the lifeworld is now subjected to incessant pressure from the economy and the state. Family and daily work life are pressed into the service of the imperatives of an instrumental rationality. Human beings as childrearers, partners, workers, clients, citizens, and consumers struggle against the process of being turned into objects of corporate and state management. Systemic imperatives, then, threaten to disempower men and women who have the capacity to be empowered, reflective actors.

Collins argues that a "thoughtful pedagogy" must be committed to sustaining lifeworld interests. Like Habermas, Collins is alarmed at the extent of the erosion of skills within lifeworld contexts. Professional experts have colonized areas that "formerly belonged to the everyday lifeworld of reasonably competent, attentive adults" (Collins, 1991, p. 94). Here one thinks of health care, home economics, and community-based services. For example, consider the way in which professional medical experts have, over time, rendered so many of us dependent on their knowledge and services. As we have become more dependent, we have been blocked from learning to be knowledgeable about our mental and physical health. Many of us can scarcely identify where the spleen is located! In the area of home economics, our dependence on prepackaged foods

has robbed us of knowledge about food, its nutrients, preparation, and meaning. We no longer have much sense of the
relationship between our health and well-being and the foods
that we eat. Many other examples could be given.

A thoughtful and enlightened pedagogy would, therefore,
be impelled by a vision of a lifeworld and system world acting
on each other to mutual benefit. Adult educators would work
within industrial and bureaucratic organizations, steered by
an ideology of technique, to create democratic learning communities. Adult educators would also support community-
based initiatives, such as antinuclear and other new social
movement actions, to "protect life-world interests" (Collins,
1991, p. 97). Adult educators who agree with Habermas's indictment of modern technological society must help adult
learners acquire the requisite competencies to engage in free
and noncoerced dialogue and to work with others to recreate
institutions, large and small, that do not "nullify . . . genuine
democratic discourse" (Collins, 1991, p. 112).

CONCLUSION

In this chapter, I have tried to sketch Habermas's main
ideas and point to their significance for North American adult
educators. Habermas is a very complex thinker, and the academic discussions of his work are very intricate, sometimes
ambiguous, and often difficult to grasp. Nonetheless, his thought
opens up new and interesting ways of thinking about adult
learning in historical and social contexts.

First, the idea that there are three distinct types of knowledge—technical, practical, and emancipatory—offers the North
American adult education community one promising way of
building an adequate philosophical framework for our field of
study and, in particular, for our understanding of adult learning and the nature of knowledge. Second, Habermas's theory
of communicative action provides adult educators who are
committed to an emancipatory education practice with an
ideal standard for their pedagogical work. He challenges adult
educators to consider why we have been blind to the ways in
which institutions enable or constrain our capacity to learn

to be the kind of persons we most want to be. Third, Habermas helps us think about how adult educators can assist in creating developmental, learner-centered, and emancipatory institutions within which individuals can find purpose and identity and become "active, innovative, responsible, and thus happy persons" (Bellah and others, 1991, p. 50). Habermas believes that while all institutions are educative, not all are true learning communities. An institution, whether family, corporation, or state agency, may be organized to block free and noncoerced learning processes. Habermas encourages us to ask whether our institutions, large and small, truly enable human beings to unfold their potentials (cognitive, moral, technical, aesthetic) in their daily routine interactions. Fourth, Habermas provides adult educators with a language to think about the pathologies and potentialities of modern technological societies. He encourages us to understand that technical rationality is only one valid way of knowing, and that our technological knowledge about how to "master" nature ought to be in the service of our moral vision of a developmentally humanist society (one that distributes learning chances equitably throughout the society). Fifth, Habermas's ideas about the interplay of system and lifeworld help us to understand the adult educator's vocation. Collins's idea of a "thoughtful pedagogy" committed to sustaining lifeworld interests represents an important way of formulating the central purpose of the North American adult educator.

References

Bellah, R. N., and others. *The Good Society*. New York: Knopf, 1991.

Bernstein, R. "Introduction." In R. Bernstein (ed.), *Habermas and Modernity*. London: Polity Press, 1985.

Collins, M. *Adult Education as Location*. York: Routledge & Kegan Paul, 1991.

Fay, B. *Critical Social Science: The Limits to Liberation*. Ithaca, N.Y.: Cornell University Press, 1987.

Giddens, A. "Jürgen Habermas." In Q. Skinner (ed.), *The Re-*

turn of *Grand Theory in the Human Sciences*. New York: Cambridge University Press, 1985.

Habermas, J. *Knowledge and Human Interests*. Portsmouth, N. H.: Heinemann Educational Books, 1972.

Habermas, J. *Communication and the Evolution of Society*. Boston: Beacon Press, 1979.

Habermas, J. *Theory of Communicative Action*. Vol. 1. Boston: Beacon Press, 1984.

Habermas, J. *Theory of Communicative Action*. Vol. 2. Boston: Beacon Press, 1987.

Hart, M. *Working and Educating for Life: Feminist and International Perspectives on Adult Education*. New York: Routledge & Kegan Paul, 1992.

Held, D. *Introduction to Critical Theory: Horkheimer to Habermas*. London: Hutchinson, 1980.

Marsick, V. (ed.). *Learning in the Workplace*. London: Croom-Helm, 1987.

Mezirow, J. D. "Perspective Transformation." *Adult Education*, 1978, 28 (2).

Mezirow, J. D. "A Critical Theory of Adult Learning and Education." *Adult Education Quarterly,* 1981, 32 (1), 3–27.

Mezirow, J. *Transformative Dimensions of Adult Learning*. San Francisco: Jossey-Bass. 1991.

Welton, M. R. *Toward Development Work*. Geelong, South Victoria, Australia: Deakin University Press, 1991.

Frank Youngman (1948–) is an Englishman who has worked at the University of Botswana since 1975. Formerly the director of the Institute of Adult Education and dean of the Faculty of Education, he is now a faculty member in the Department of Adult Education.

Youngman aligns himself with the social action tradition within adult education and undertakes teaching, research and writing on the political economy of adult education from a socialist perspective. He is particularly concerned with the role of adult education in addressing the challenges of underdevelopment, especially in South Africa. Youngman regards adult education as part of the wider provision of learning opportunities in society, and therefore he also participates actively in the study and development of other forms of education. He was a member of the Presidential Commission which reviewed Botswana's educational system in 1992–93. He has published widely on many aspects of adult education, including the book, *Adult Education and Socialist Pedagogy* (1986).

The following selection, "The Political Economy of Literacy in the Third World," was first published in the International Council for Adult Education journal, *Convergence* (Vol. XXIII, No. 4, 1990). In the article, Youngman applies the perspective of socialist pedagogy to the issue of literacy in the Third World. He observes that literacy is not merely a technical issue, but one grounded in a structural context, and "related to questions about the nature of the societies within which we work." Youngman discusses the intricate relationships among social interests, knowledge production and literacy, arguing that literacy can either "reinforce unjust, unequal and undemocratic societies or contribute to the possibility of building more just, fair and democratic systems."

FRANK YOUNGMAN

17 The Political Economy of Literacy in the Third World

INTRODUCTION

The designation of 1990 as International Literacy Year by the United Nations has provided the impetus for renewed concern with the issue of adult literacy. Many adult educators throughout the world are involved in special activities to make the year and are planning longer term programs to address the problem of illiteracy on a sustained basis. Furthermore the

Education for All initiative (sponsored by the World Bank, UNICEF, Unesco and UNDP) has focused international attention on the question of basic education, of which adult literacy is an integral part.

Although there remains a problem of adult illiteracy in the industrial countries (see, for example, *Convergence Vol. XX, No. 2, 1987*), by far the highest illiteracy rates are experienced in the underdeveloped countries of Africa, Asia and Latin America. The statistics speak for themselves. . . . In 1990 there is an estimated illiteracy rate of two percent in the industrialized countries and of 34 percent in the Third World. A total of 865 million people in the Third World are illiterate, a figure that is projected to increase to 898 million by the year 2000. (Because of population increases, the absolute number of illiterates will rise, even though the percentage of adults who are illiterate should decline).

The countries of the Third World therefore continue to be faced with a problem of massive proportions. Despite some national success stories in the past (such as Cuba), many countries today appear to be making little progress and some (such as Mozambique) are even having their achievements reversed. Yet journals such as *Convergence* report the efforts of adult educators and grassroots groups working against the odds in local struggles for literacy which provide a basis for optimism. The international mobilization stimulated by International Literacy Year and the World Charter on Education for All has put literacy high on the agenda of educational policy-makers as well as adult education practitioners.

THE PERSPECTIVE OF POLITICAL ECONOMY

Participants in the workshop were keen to explore the nature of adult literacy activities and how they relate to the wider society. As one of them put it, "How can we be certain that our efforts in literacy are changing society for the better?" I suggested that the perspective of political economy is helpful for considering questions like this because it focuses attention on the need to analyze the economic and political context of adult education activities such as literacy programs, so that the consequences of different kinds of programs are questioned. The approach has been well articulated by Patrick Healey in an article in *Convergence (Vol. XVI, No. 4, 1983)* in which he posed two basic questions:

- Who gains and who loses by adult education?
- Why does this occur?

The first question draws attention to the fact that adult education benefits some groups in society rather than others. For example, agricultural extension programs in the Third World tend to benefit the rich peasants and to exclude those with limited or no resources, thus reinforcing the social divisions in the countryside. The second question pushes us towards developing appropriate tools of social analysis and improving our understanding of the social forces which influence adult education.

It is a perspective which generates a critical approach to adult education because it questions our taken-for-granted assumptions, such as all literacy programs being a "good thing." It challenges us to consider how literacy is affected by the nature of society and how societies are affected by different kinds of literacy work. A society whose economic policies are based on the International Monetary Fund's concept of structural adjustment and associated cut-backs in public expenditure, will be unable to provide adult literacy opportunities on a large scale. A literacy primer which embodies gender stereotypes will reinforce the social inequality of women and men. The political economy approach argues that adult education activities are shaped by their economic and political context and in turn have an effect on that context.

Thus the essence of the political economy perspective is that it takes us beyond purely educational concerns to wider concerns about the role of adult education in society. This spirit was captured by the Director-General of UNESCO, Frederico Mayor, in his Keynote Address to the Fourth World Assembly on Adult Education, when he said "Literacy is too often seen in only educational terms; in fact it is a societal problem."

LITERACY IS NOT A TECHNICAL ISSUE

The perspective of political economy proposes that the problem of adult literacy must not be conceived simply in technical terms, but rather it must be related to questions about the nature of the societies within which we work.

In this viewpoint, a literacy class is not only a place where a range of cognitive skills are learned, it also carries a variety of social and political messages. For example, the content of the primers used may reflect the interests, values and vocabulary of a dominant land-owning class rather than the needs of the landless peasants who form the literacy group. Similarly, the processes of interaction in the literacy class may perpetuate inequalities in the relationship between women and men. Thus choices of target population, method, curriculum, language of instruction, the timing and location of classes and so forth, which may appear on the surface to be purely technical, are in fact profoundly influenced by the political and economic context in which they take place.

The value of the political economy approach is that it politicizes our thinking about literacy, so that we relate our concern with literacy to questions of power in society. This is important because International Literacy Year has brought to the fore many advocates of adult literacy whose support has a variety of rationales and whose programs would have diverse consequences. The fundamental questions—literacy for what? literacy for whom?—are of renewed significance.

THE STRUCTURAL CONTEXT OF LITERACY

The analytical task set by political economy is therefore one of uncovering the patterns of power that exist in society, and to show how these influence the nature of literacy activities. In Healey's words, who gains and who loses from a given literacy program?

In any society, there are a variety of social divisions, but the most fundamental relate to the productive basis of society, where differences in access to and control over productive resources is the foundation of the divisions of class. The different classes in society are defined by the part groups play in production (peasants and workers, for example) and by their relationship to each other (workers vis-á-vis capitalists, for example). Classes are unequal in their power to decide what is produced and who benefits from production, and in their influence on other spheres of society. An analysis of the class structure in the Third World also has to take into account the place of the national economy within the overall world economic system, which is dominated by the advanced capitalist countries. This means there is an external influence on the dynamic of internal class relations, exemplified by the impact of bodies such as the World Bank and the International Monetary Fund, multinational corporations, and donor agencies. A cursory analysis of literacy programs in the Third World reveals the extensive involvement of foreign aid and technical personnel in their design and implementation.

Although production is a major determinant of social relationship, there are other very important divisions in society which intersect with and reinforce these class divisions. These include gender, race and ethnicity, and those divisions which are particular to a given society, such as caste in India. The sum total of these social divisions constitutes a structure of power disparities which significantly influences the form and content of literacy programs. The structure is not abstract because it is embodied in people and in their social relationships affecting, for example, the social dynamics of a literacy class.

Tools of social analysis are therefore very useful to adult educators so that they can understand the structural context of literacy and its implications for their work. And popular educators, such as those of the Women's Resource Centre for the Philippines, have shown how useful these tools are also for adult learners to understand their own situation and how it might be changed. The realization of the possibility for change in society is based on the fact that the structural analysis of the political economy approach has a historical dimension, showing how structures have developed and changed over time. Contemporary patterns of power in society have evolved through social action and therefore can be changed by social action. Thus there can be changes to who gains and who loses from literacy programs.

LITERACY, KNOWLEDGE AND SOCIAL INTERESTS

The divisions in society inevitably lead to conflicts and struggles as the different groups pursue their own interests. It is clear, for example, that the factory-owner's interest in increased profits and the factory-worker's interest in higher wages represents a basic conflict in society. It is necessary also to recognize that educational institutions and programs are greatly affected by these different economic and social interests. There is a link between social power and the kind of knowledge that gets diffused through educational activities.

This linkage is evident at the levels of content and of processes so that both the curriculum of literacy materials and what goes on during literacy classes carry messages about society and the distribution of power in society. Thus materials which promote individual entrepreneurship and teacher-learner relationships which are authoritarian both legitimate a certain kind of society. Hence literacy activities encode expectations about what is normal and reasonable in the social relations between classes, sexes, races and ethnic groups.

The important analytical tools in this respect are the concepts of ideology and hegemony. Ideology refers to a system of ideas, beliefs and values which promotes the interests of a particular class or social group, for example, racism. Hegemony refers to the situation in which the ideology of a dominant class or social group is diffused throughout society, so that all classes or groups tend to accept as common sense a set of ideas and values which in fact do not promote the interests of the majority. Education is a major agency for the transmission of this dominant culture and many national literacy programs have this effect. But of course there are literacy programs which have been designed specifically to challenge the dominant ideology, such as those programs reported in *Convergence Vol. XXIII, No. 1, 1990*, aimed at empowering women in Nepal and blacks in South Africa.

This is the basis of the question which Freire has put to

us so insistently over the years—in favour of whom or what do we promote a particular kind of literacy? In terms of the above discussion, is the effect of a particular literacy program to sustain hegemony or to develop counter-hegemony?

LITERACY AND THE STATE

The question of whose interests are being served by literacy programs cannot be fully considered without taking into account the role of the state, as the majority of literacy activities are provided and controlled by the state. The literacy programs carried out by the organizations of civil society, such as churches, community-based groups and non-governmental organizations, are relatively insignificant in the quantitative terms of enrollment numbers, and even these are at least partially shaped by state power. The dominant role of the state requires that adult educators refine their analysis of its nature.

Political economy proposes a theory of the state which regards it not as a neutral instrument of the common good working in the general interest of all citizens, but as an arena of class conflict. The state is a complex of public institutions which the economically dominant classes in society seek to control or influence in order to advance their own interests. Although other classes are sometimes successful in influencing the state (for example, to extend trade union rights or welfare benefits), their relative weakness puts them at a disadvantage. Thus state intervention in education tends towards strengthening the legitimacy of the dominant classes and towards sustaining the existing economic system. In this way, public education is an important element in the organization of ideological hegemony.

The state characteristic of much of the Third World has a tendency to instability and authoritarianism, with low levels of national productivity restricting state revenues and public services. Nevertheless, expenditure on education has been made as a response to mass demands for improved standards of living and as a means of gaining legitimacy. State-run adult literacy programs, such as those in Iran and Brazil in the 1970s, can be seen as efforts to build support for the economic and political order. Literacy as a means of social control is evident in more unstable situations, such as the literacy activities in Waslala in northern Nicaragua in 1977–79 carried out as part of counter-insurgency operations against the Sandinistas and their sympathizers.

Of course, some states in the Third World have represented the interests of the popular classes and have pursued development strategies intended to restructure the socioeconomic order, reduce external dependency, and extend democracy. In this context, state-sponsored literacy programs are aimed at expanding the capability of workers and peasants to be involved in the economic and political decisions affecting their lives. Such programs are exemplified by the literacy campaigns in Mozambique in the late 1970s and the National Literacy Crusade in Nicaragua in 1980. But these examples are rare, and on the whole, state support for literacy serves to reinforce patterns of domination and subordination in society.

KINDS OF LITERACY

The central conclusion to be drawn from the political economy approach to literacy is that we cannot talk about a single kind of literacy. There are different kinds of literacy related to the struggles of different groups in society. As Freire has argued, there is no such thing as neutral education. To polarize, there are basically two kinds of literacy. There is the kind of literacy which helps to socialize learners into an uncritical acceptance of the status quo. This is the kind of literacy which promotes hegemony, which Freire calls literacy for "domestication" and which in their book *Literacy, Schooling and Revolution* (Philadelphia: Falmer, 1987) Lankshear and Lawler call "improper" literacy. And there is the kind of literacy which helps learners to understand and act to change those social relations and practices which reinforce unequal patterns of power. This is the kind of literacy which promotes counter-hegemony—Freire's literacy for "liberation," Lankshear and Lawler's "proper" literacy.

Thus when analyzing literacy activities, we must identify to what extent the activities serve to reinforce unjust, unequal and undemocratic societies or contribute to the possibility of building more just, fair and democratic systems.

THE SOCIAL RESPONSIBILITY OF
THE ADULT EDUCATOR

But we are not just analysts of society and the context of literacy work. Theory must be a guide to practice and as adult educators we are all involved in practice of some kind. Whatever the nature of this involvement, be it as popular educators, trainers, administrators, policy-makers or researchers, our own work serves social interests. Hence we cannot avoid the major issue of what kind of literacy practice we should advocate. This is not a question which can be given a utopian answer as it must be rooted in the realities of our situations. And the realities of the contemporary Third World are often bleak. At the macro level, there are repressive regimes, limited democracy, economic stagnation and decline, external debt and imperialist intervention, civil wars and growing poverty. At the micro level, there are families, jobs, economic survival and personal security to consider. The conditions facing the progressive adult educator in the Philippines, Palestine, South Africa or El Salvador are only extreme examples of the difficulties many literacy workers face throughout Asia, Africa and Latin America. But whatever our situation, we have to take responsibility for the social consequences of our work.

The political economy of literacy confronts us with a number of questions we need to ask ourselves:

- Do I have a critical understanding of existing society and a vision of an alternative future?
- Do I have a practical commitment to changing my society so that it is more equal, fair and democratic?
- Do I want to develop literacy activities which challenge the cultural and ideological hegemony in my society?
- If I do, what are the possibilities within state-sponsored programs? Are such programs always inimical to the people's interests or can they be a place for alternative action?

- What are the possibilities within non-governmental programs? Are such programs always working in the people's interests? Can literacy be linked to those social movements directed to building a new society?

These are some of the questions which arise from considering the political economy of literacy. Gramsci wrote of "the pessimism of the intellect and the optimism of the will" and while an analysis of the Third World today might lead to pessimism, the economic and political crisis itself erodes popular support for the status quo and provides possibilities for concerted literacy action for social change and a better future.

NOTES AND REFERENCES

Readers who may wish to explore the ideas presented here in greater depth are referred to the following books:

Freire, P. and Macedo, D. 1987. *Literacy: Reading the word and the world.* London: Routledge and Kegan Paul.

Torres, C. A. 1990. *The Politics of Non-Formal Education in Latin America.* New York: Praeger.

Youngman, F. 1986. *Adult Education and Socialist Pedagogy.* London: Croom Helm.

bell hooks (Gloria Jean Watkins, 1952–) holds a M.A. degree from the University of Wisconsin and a Ph.D. from the University of California at Santa Cruz in English Literature. She has held positions as a lecturer at the University of Southern California, the University of California at Riverside, Occidental College, San Francisco State University, and the University of California at Santa Cruz. In 1985 she became an assistant professor of African American Studies and English literature at Yale University where she taught until assuming her current position as associate professor in American Literature and Women's Studies at Oberlin College in Ohio.

The title of hooks' first book, *Ain't I a Woman: Black Women and Feminism* published in 1981, reflects the focus of her work as a writer, professor, feminist theorist, and social activist. This book was recognized in 1992 by *Publishers Weekly* as "one of the 20 most influential women's books of the last 20 years." hooks is an outspoken critic of the functions of race and gender in contemporary culture, and her work has received acclaim for its theoretical rigor, intellectual integrity, breadth of knowledge, and passion. Her other publications include *Feminist Theory: From Margin to Center* (1984), *Talking Back: thinking feminist, thinking black* (1989), *Yearning: Race, Gender, and Cultural Politics* (1990), *Breaking Bread: Insurgent Black Intellectual Life* (1992), *Black Looks: Race and Representation* (1992), and *Sisters of the Yam: Black Women and Self-Recovery* (1993). Although a prolific writer and an articulate spokesperson for those who are oppressed and exploited, hooks has said that it is in her role as teacher that she is doing her most important work. For her, teaching is one of the most substantial forms of political resistance.

In the following selection from *Talking Back: thinking feminist, thinking black*, hooks describes her vision of the radical and transformatory nature of feminist pedagogy. According to hooks, feminist education should be a place where there is a sense of struggle against issues of sexism and racism and acknowledgment of the union of theory and practice. It needs to be a place where students and teachers work together to overcome the estrangement and alienation that have become the norm in education and in society, and most importantly "feminist pedagogy should engage students in a learning process that makes the world more rather than less real."

bell hooks

18 toward a revolutionary feminist pedagogy

My favorite teacher in high school was Miss Annie Mae
Moore, a short, stout black woman. She had taught my mama
and her sisters. She could tell story after story about their
fast ways, their wildness. She could tell me ways I was like
mama, ways I was most truly my own self. She could catch
hold of you and turn you around, set you straight (these were
the comments folk made about her teaching)—so that we
would know what we were facing when we entered her classroom. Passionate in her teaching, confident that her work in
life was a pedagogy of liberation (words she would not have
used but lived instinctively), one that would address and
confront our realities as black children growing up in the segregated South, black children growing up within a white-supremacist culture. Miss Moore knew that if we were to be
fully self-realized, then her work, and the work of all our progressive teachers, was not to teach us solely the knowledge
in books, but to teach us an oppositional world view—different
from that of our exploiters and oppressors, a world view that
would enable us to see ourselves not through the lens of racism
or racist stereotypes but one that would enable us to focus
clearly and succinctly, to look at ourselves, at the world around
us, critically—analytically—to see ourselves first and foremost
as striving for wholeness, for unity of heart, mind, body, and
spirit.

It was as a student in segregated black schools called
Booker T. Washington and Crispus Attucks that I witnessed
the transformative power of teaching, of pedagogy. In particular, those teachers who approached their work as though it
was indeed a pedagogy, a science of teaching, requiring diverse
strategies, approaches, explorations, experimentation, and

risks, demonstrated the value—the political power—of teaching. Their work was truly education for critical consciousness. In these segregated schools, the teachers were almost all black women. Many of them had chosen teaching at a historical moment when they were required by custom to remain single and childless, to have no visible erotic or sexual life. Among them were exceptional teachers who gave to their work a passion, a devotion that made it seem a true calling, a true vocation. They were the teachers who conceptualized oppositional world views, who taught us young black women to exult and glory in the power and beauty of our intellect. They offered to us a legacy of liberatory pedagogy that demanded active resistance and rebellion against sexism and racism. They embodied in their work, in their lives (for none of them appeared as tortured spinsters estranged and alienated from the world around them) a feminist spirit. They were active participants in black community, shaping our futures, mapping our intellectual terrains, sharing revolutionary fervor and vision. I write these words, this essay to express the honor and respect I have for them because they have been my pedagogical guardians. Their work has had a profound impact on my consciousness, on my development as a teacher.

During years of graduate school, I waited for that phase of study when we would focus on the meaning and significance of pedagogy, when we would learn about teaching, about how to teach. That moment never arrived. For years I have relied on those earlier models of excellent teaching to guide me. Most specifically, I understood from the teachers in those segregated schools that the work of any teacher committed to the full self-realization of students was necessarily and fundamentally radical, that ideas were not neutral, that to teach in a way that liberates, that expands consciousness, that awakens, is to challenge domination at its very core. It is this pedagogy that Paulo Freire calls "education as the practice of freedom." In his introduction to Freire's *Pedagogy of the Oppressed*, Richard Shaull writes:

> Education either functions as an instrument which is used to facilitate the integration of the younger generation into the logic of the present system and bring about conformity to it, or it

becomes "the practice of freedom," the means by which men and women deal critically and creatively with reality and discover how to participate in the transformation of their world.

A liberator feminist movement aims to transform society by eradicating patriarchy, by ending sexism and sexist oppression, by challenging the politics of domination on all fronts. Feminist pedagogy can only be liberatory if it is truly revolutionary because the mechanisms of appropriation within white-supremacist, capitalist patriarchy are able to co-opt with tremendous ease that which merely appears radical or subversive. Within the United States, contemporary feminist movement is sustained in part by the efforts academic women make to constitute the university setting as a central site for the development and dissemination of feminist thought. Women's Studies has been the location of this effort. Given the way universities work to reinforce and perpetuate the status quo, the way knowledge is offered as commodity, Women's Studies can easily become a place where revolutionary feminist thought and feminist activism are submerged or made secondary to the goals of academic careerism. Without diminishing in any way our struggle as academics striving to succeed in institutions, such effort is fully compatible with liberatory feminist struggle only when we consciously, carefully, and strategically link the two. When this connection is made initially but not sustained, or when it is never evident, Women's Studies becomes either an exotic terrain for those politically chic few seeking affirmation or a small settlement within the larger institutional structure where women (and primarily white women) have a power base, which rather than being oppositional simply mirrors the status quo. When feminist struggle is the central foundation for feminist education, Women's Studies and the feminist classroom (which can exist outside the domain of Women's Studies) can be places where education is the practice of freedom, the place for liberatory pedagogy.

At this historical moment, there is a crisis of engagement within universities, for when knowledge becomes commoditized, then much authentic learning ceases. Students who want to learn hunger for a space where they can be challenged intellectually. Students also suffer, as many of us who teach do, from a crisis of meaning, unsure about what has value in life, unsure even about whether it is important to stay alive. They long for a context where their subjective needs can be integrated with study, where the primary focus is a broader spectrum of ideas and modes of inquiry, in short a dialectical context where there is serious and rigorous critical exchange. This is an important and exciting time for feminist pedagogy because in theory and practice our work meets these needs.

Feminist education—the feminist classroom—is and should be a place where there is a sense of struggle, where there is visible acknowledgement of the union of theory and practice, where we work together as teachers and students to overcome the estrangement and alienation that have become so much the norm in the contemporary university. Most importantly, feminist pedagogy should engage students in a learning process that makes the world "more rather than less real." In my classrooms, we work to dispel the notion that our experience is not a "real world" experience. This is especially easy since gender is such a pressing issue in contemporary life. Every aspect of popular culture alerts us to the reality that folks are thinking about gender in both reactionary and progressive ways. What is important is that they are thinking critically. And it is this space that allows for the possibility of feminist intervention, whether it be in our classroom or in the life of students outside the classroom. Lately, there has been a truly diverse body of students coming to my classes and other feminist classes at universities all around the United States. Many of us have been wondering "what's going on" or "why are all these men, and white men in the class." This changing student body reflects the concern about gender issues, that it is one of the real important issues in people's private lives that is addressed academically. Freire writes, "Education as the practice of freedom—as opposed to education as the practice of domination—denies that we are abstract, isolated, independent, and unattached to the world; it also denies that the world exists as a reality apart from us."

To make a revolutionary feminist pedagogy, we must relinquish our ties to traditional ways of teaching that reinforce domination. This is very difficult. Women's Studies courses are often viewed as not seriously academic because so much

"personal stuff" is discussed. Fear that their courses will be
seen as "gut" classes has led many feminist professors to rely
more on traditional pedagogical styles. This is unfortunate.
Certainly, the radical alternative to the status quo should never
have been simply an inversion. That is to say, critical of the
absence of any focus on personal experience in traditional
classrooms, such focus becomes the central characteristic of
the feminist classroom. This model must be viewed critically
because a class can still be reinforcing domination, not transforming consciousness about gender, even as the "personal"
is the ongoing topic of conversation.

To have a revolutionary feminist pedagogy we must first
focus on the teacher-student relationship and the issue of
power. How do we as feminist teachers use power in a way
that is not coercive, dominating? Many women have had difficulty asserting power in the feminist classroom for fear that
to do so would be to exercise domination. Yet we must acknowledge that our role as teacher is a position of power over
others. We can use that power in ways that diminish or in
ways that enrich and it is this choice that should distinguish
feminist pedagogy from ways of teaching that reinforce domination. One simple way to alter the way one's "power" as
teacher is experienced in the classroom is to elect not to assume the posture of all-knowing professors. This is also difficult. When we acknowledge that we do not know everything,
that we do not have all the answers, we risk students leaving
our classrooms and telling others that we are not prepared. It
is important to make it clear to students that we are prepared
and that the willingness to be open and honest about what
we do not know is a gesture of respect for them.

To be oppositional in the feminist classroom one must
have a standard of valuation that differs from the norm. Many
of us tried new ways of teaching without changing the standards by which we evaluated our work. We often left the classroom feeling uncertain about the learning process or even
concerned that we were failing as teachers. Let me share a
particular problem I have faced. My classroom style is very
confrontational. It is a model of pedagogy that is based on
the assumption that many students will take courses from me
who are afraid to assert themselves as critical thinkers, who

are afraid to speak (especially students from oppressed and exploited groups). The revolutionary hope that I bring to the classroom is that it will become a space where they can come to voice. Unlike the stereotypical feminist model that suggests women best come to voice in an atmosphere of safety (one in which we are all going to be kind and nurturing), I encourage students to work at coming to voice in an atmosphere where they may be afraid or see themselves at risk. The goal is to enable all students, not just an assertive few, to feel empowered in a rigorous, critical discussion. Many students find this pedagogy difficult, frightening, and very demanding. They do not usually come away from my class talking about how much they enjoyed the experience.

One aspect of traditional models of teaching I had not surrendered was that longing for immediate recognition of my value as a teacher, and immediate affirmation. Often I did not feel liked or affirmed and this was difficult for me to accept. I reflected on my student experiences and the reality that I often learned the most in classes that I did not enjoy and complained about, which helped me to work on the traditional assumption that immediate positive feedback is the signifier of worth. Concurrently, I found that students who often felt they hated a class with me would return later to say how much they learned, that they understood that it was the different style that made it hard as well as the different demands. I began to see that courses that work to shift paradigms, to change consciousness, cannot necessarily be experienced immediately as fun or positive or safe and this was not a worthwhile criteria to use in evaluation.

In the feminist classroom, it is important to define the terms of engagement, to identify what we mean when we say that a course will be taught from a feminist perspective. Often the initial explanations about pedagogy will have a serious impact on the way students experience a course. It is important to talk about pedagogical strategy. For a time, I assumed that students would just get the hang of it, would see that I was trying to teach in a different way and accept it without explanation. Often, that meant I explained after being criticized. It is important for feminist professors to explain not only what will differ about the classroom experience but to openly acknowledge that students must consider whether they wish to be in such a learning space. On a basic level, students are often turned off by the fact that I take attendance, but because I see the classroom experience as constituting a unique learning experience, to miss class is to really lose a significant aspect of the process. Whether or not a student attends class affects grading and this bothers students who are not accustomed to taking attendance seriously. Another important issue for me has been that each student participate in classroom discussion, that each student have a voice. This is a practice I think is important not because every student has something valuable to say (this is not always so), but often students who do have meaningful comments to contribute are silent. In my classes, everyone's voice is heard as students read paragraphs which may explore a particular issue. They do not have the opportunity to refuse to read paragraphs. When I hear their voices, I become more aware of information they may not know that I can provide. Whether a class is large or small, I try to talk with all students individually or in small groups so that I have a sense of their needs. How can we transform consciousness if we do not have some sense of where the students are intellectually, psychically?

Concern with how and what students are learning validates and legitimates a focus, however small, on personal confession in classroom discussions. I encourage students to relate the information they are learning to the personal identities they are working to socially construct, to change, to affirm. If the goal of personal confession is not narcissism, it must take place within a critical framework where it is related to material that is being discussed. When, for example, I am teaching Toni Morrison's novel, *The Bluest Eye*, I may have students write personal paragraphs about the relationship between race and physical beauty, which they read in class. Their paragraphs may reveal pain, woundedness as they explore and express ways they are victimized by racism and sexism, or they may express ideas that are racist and sexist. Yet the paragraphs enable them to approach the text in a new way. They may read the novel differently. They may be able to be more critical and analytical. If this does not happen, then the paragraphs fail as a pedagogical tool. To make feminist classrooms the site of transformative learning experiences, we must constantly try new methods, new approaches.

Finally, we cannot have a revolutionary feminist pedagogy if we do not have revolutionary feminists in the classroom. Women's Studies courses must do more than offer a different teaching style; we must really challenge issues of sexism and sexist oppression both by what we teach and how we teach. This is truly a collective effort. We must learn from one another, sharing ideas and pedagogical strategies. Although I have invited feminist colleagues to come and participate in my classes, they do not. Classroom territoriality is another traditional taboo. Yet if we are to learn from one another, if we are to develop a concrete strategy for radicalizing our classrooms, we must be more engaged as a group. We must be willing to deconstruct this power dimension, to challenge, change, and create new approaches. If we are to move toward a revolutionary feminist pedagogy, we must challenge ourselves and one another to restore to feminist struggle its radical and subversive dimension. We must be willing to restore the spirit of risk—to be fast, wild, to be able to take hold, turn around, transform.

Elizabeth J. Tisdell (1955–) received a bachelor's degree in mathematics from the University of Maine in 1977, and an M.A. in religion and religious education from Fordham University in 1979. From 1979 to 1989, she worked as a campus minister on two different college campuses both teaching in the academic curriculum, and providing programs dealing with spirituality and social justice issues for both traditional-age and returning adult students. In 1992, she graduated from The University of Georgia with an Ed.D. in adult education and an emphasis in women's studies. Currently she is assistant professor in the Department of Graduate Programs in Education at Antioch University, Seattle.

Emancipatory education and learning in higher education has been the focus of Tisdell's research. Her dissertation study focused both on how power dynamics are manifested in adult higher education classes, and how structured power relations based on gender, race, and class can be challenged. Tisdell's subsequent research examines faculty perceptions of how the inclusion of gender or multicultural course content affects the classroom dynamics in higher education classes.

In the following article, Tisdell discusses the ways in which structured power relations based on gender, race, and class are manifested. She also discusses two primary models of feminist pedagogy and examines the ways in which the feminist pedagogy literature offers new strategies for challenging structured power relations in the adult learning environment so that emancipatory learning can occur. Finally, she suggests that the feminist theory and pedagogy literature are beginning to have an impact on the field of adult education, offering new ways of theorizing about adult learning as well as new ways of managing the emancipatory adult classroom environment.

ELIZABETH J. TISDELL

19 Feminism and Adult Learning: Power, Pedagogy, and Praxis

We were in an adult learning class. There were eighteen students in the class, thirteen women and five men. I was a student in the class, and our task on that night was to break into four small groups to discuss and then present or act out a particular theory of adult learning. Members of my group had done their homework well; we had a good handle on Bandura's social learning theory, the theory that we were to present, so we busily began planning our presentation. We decided that Paul, the only male student in our group, would be the narrator while the rest of us would act out what he, as narrator, explained. As each group made their presentations, we were entertained and amazed by both the creativity of our peers and what we had learned in the process about adult learning theory. But when all was said and done, the not-so-readily apparent dynamics were, to me, far more fascinating. Even though there were two to three times as many women as men in the class and in each group, every group had done what my group had: chosen a male student for the lead role in the presentation.

It was not that each group consciously decided that the person in the lead role should be male. After all, such choices are usually made unconsciously, and often it does not matter how "politically correct" or intellectually sophisticated one's rational thinking is about gender, race, or class issues. In fact, in the scenario described above, I was the one who suggested quite offhandedly that Paul be the narrator. I was not thinking that we needed a male leader, nor was I even thinking about the fact that Paul was male. Rather, I was intent on the task at hand—how to put our skit together to portray Bandura's social learning theory. One might think that this is an isolated instance. After all, somebody had to be in the lead role, and it just happened to be Paul this time. True enough, but when all four groups also chose a male for the lead role, especially when the number of males was so limited in this class, it seemed that there was something more going on than met the eye.

Situations like these are not merely coincidental. It is no secret that males (and others who benefit from systems of privilege in our culture, such as those who are white, middle-class, or able-bodied) are often chosen for leadership positions over females (or racial minorities, members of the working class, or people with disabilities) in the professional world of work. But they are also more often in leadership roles, either overtly or covertly, in less formal situations, such as in voluntary organizations, in social gatherings, and, as we have seen in the above vignette, in the adult education classroom. It is not necessarily that these males consciously "take over" the groups in which they participate, or that women (or members of those less privileged populations cited above) consciously acquiesce or set the males up to be in leadership positions instead of themselves.

This process of putting (mostly white) men in either informal or formal leadership positions is instead more unconscious in nature. It is probably a result of the fact that we are, after all, accustomed to having men in leadership positions in all places in our society. The adult education classroom is no exception. Men, especially white men, have been socialized to be in leadership roles. Not only do they often willingly volunteer for such roles, but they also have been socialized to speak with a more authoritative style than women, which makes them more likely to be chosen for such roles. Women, on the other hand, have been socialized to be in support roles, to defer to men, and to take care of people, sometimes at their own expense. They may contribute to the process of putting men in leadership roles by suggesting a particular man for one of those roles, especially if they perceive that he wants to be in that role, in order to take care of him. Or women can simply refuse to volunteer for a variety of reasons. No matter what the reasons are, the reality is clear: In general, males and those who benefit from greater privilege in our society because of their race, class, age, or experience have more power than do women, racial minorities, and members of the working class in the adult education classroom. The question is, What can be or is being done about it?

The role of adult education in changing the nature of unequal power relations between privileged and oppressed groups is a concern expressed in the adult education literature (for example, Collard and Law, 1989; Cunningham, 1988; Freire, 1971). Cunningham (1988) has argued that adult educators have an ethical responsibility to create environments where people can come to an understanding of how the realities of their lives were created. This means helping people explore what the nature of structured power relations has to do with the realities of their personal lives. For example, what does being born black, or being born into a working-class family, or being female from a particular religious tradition mean in regard to how much opportunity, power, or control one has in one's family, workplace, and personal life? And what are the spoken and unspoken rules regarding how an individual from one such background is supposed to act in groups (including classroom groups) with people who have different status? The creation of an environment where students can examine the connection between their personal situations and the structured power relations between privileged and oppressed groups in our society leads to a more conscious and informed understanding of their lives and may contribute to their emancipation.

The question of how best to educate for social transformation has no easy answer. It has long been an issue for adult educators interested in emancipatory education. The recent feminist pedagogy literature offers new insights that may prove useful for adult education practitioners who try to educate for social transformation. In order to outline how feminist theory and feminist pedagogy can offer new insights both to the field of adult learning and to those educators interested in educating for social transformation, the following discussion has three parts. First, an explanation of feminist pedagogy and an examination of its underlying assumptions are provided. Second, how feminist theory and pedagogy offer new insights for an understanding of learning in adulthood is considered. Finally, the impact of feminist pedagogy literature on the field and the implications of incorporating feminist theory and pedagogy in the practice of adult education are discussed.

WHAT IS FEMINIST PEDAGOGY?

A wide body of literature reflects the orientation known as feminist pedagogy. While the various strands of feminist pedagogy have been influenced by different educational models, all strands share a concern with the following issues: (1) how to teach women more effectively so that they gain a sense of their ability to effect change in their own lives, (2) an emphasis on connection and relationship (rather than separation) with both the knowledge learned and the facilitator and other learners, and (3) women's emerging sense of personal power. All of the feminist pedagogy literature is emancipatory in the broad sense in that it is concerned with women's personal empowerment (Hayes, 1989; Maher, 1987).

However, it is important to point out that not all of the feminist pedagogy literature deals with the nature of structured power relationships or with women's collective experience as an oppressed group. The strand of the feminist pedagogy literature that stops short of dealing with structured power relations deals only with women's personal empowerment from a developmental-psychological perspective. Maher (1987) has suggested that the wide body of literature coming to be labeled feminist pedagogy can be divided into two major subgroups that have been influenced by two major educational models. She called these two models the "liberatory" model and the "gender" model and examined the strengths and weaknesses of each. The philosophical assumptions of each of the models are examined below.

Liberatory Model. The liberatory or emancipatory model of feminist pedagogy deals with the nature of structured power relations and interlocking systems of oppression based on gender, race, class, age, and so on. In particular, versions of the liberatory model attempt to account for and deal with why it is that women (and minorities) are often silenced or absent or that their contributions are overlooked or discounted in the public arenas of our society, including government, industry, education, and in the classroom at all education levels. These models of feminist pedagogy have critical theory and the work of the neo-Marxist education theorists, along with feminist reinterpretations of those theories, at their root. Feminist education theorists who write from the perspective of the liberatory model have been heavily influenced by Freire's (1971) work, but they have also been critical of Freire and Marxist education theories because their primary focus has been on class-based oppression. Freire and his followers have not dealt adequately with oppression based on gender, race, or interlocking systems of oppression such as gender and race, or gender and class, or gender, race, and class.

Most feminist emancipatory education theorists operating from the liberatory perspective are influenced by a socialist-feminist or feminist-materialist theoretical understanding of society and its power relations. The underlying philosophical assumption of feminist materialism is that the material realities of people's lives—the physical realities of maleness or femaleness, race, material needs for food and shelter, and so on—shape or affect all other aspects of people's sociocultural lives, including their values (Chafetz, 1988).

Consider education as a sociocultural value. There is likely to be a difference in the value that a white middle-class male versus a black working-class woman with two children place on education because of the difference in the material realities that inform each of their lives. Consider the experience of both of them when in an educational situation. In order to even be able to take part in that educational activity, the black working-class woman is much more likely than the male to need someone to take care of her children. Once child care is arranged and she is present for the educational experience, she and the white middle-class male are likely to have very different experiences in the situation. The white middle-class male will probably feel much more validated by the experience. After all, most of the so-called experts in any field of study are likely to be white middle-class males, and most of the examples used in the books and curriculum materials are probably about people who are also white and middle class. Society at large has been taught to value what people that look, think, and talk like him have to say. But for the black woman, neither "the experts" nor most of the examples used in the books are about people that look, think, or talk like her. Moreover, she has probably been taught that her speech pattern is "incorrect," and she has to learn to write and speak in a style that some other group has determined is "correct"; therefore, the society is not predisposed to pay that much attention to what she has to say. In addition, because of her working-class status, she also has less money to spend on education or educational supports such as child care, transportation, tutors, and books. If she succeeds in spite of all of these obstacles, it is likely that she will be paid less than her white male counterpart in the workplace for the same job. Thus, it is easy to understand why she might value formal education less than the white middle-class male. It has different returns for her because of the material realities of her life—her different gender, her different race, and her different class background.

For some of the reasons noted in the above example, many feminist emancipatory education theorists suggest that the oppression of women in both the paid work force and the domestic labor realm is *reproduced* by events in the classroom. Because the curriculum, the knowledge base, and the examples used in the books and materials are created by and are primarily about the white middle-class male experience, white middle-class males are more likely to be successful both in the education system and in a society that accords greater value to that experience. Therefore, white male privilege is reproduced by the system. Because the experience of women of all races is either absent or is presented in the curriculum in a way that reinforces their subservience, they are taught in both overt and covert ways to be subservient in the education system as well as in society. Thus, the oppression of women in general is reproduced. This is true for race and class relations as well (Weiler, 1988).

Reproduction theory accounts for how power relations in society are partially reproduced by the education system. It does not, however, account for the fact that a number of women and members of minority and working-class groups have been as successful as their white male counterparts and have assumed leadership positions both in the education system and in society. For this reason, other feminist education theorists operating from the liberatory model focus more on the forms of resistance that women and minorities adopt in order to create meaning in the education system and in a society that has been designed to help reproduce the existing power relations. Resistance theorists are concerned with how teachers and students *produce* meaning through their own resistance and their own cultural experience.

Feminist resistance theorists discuss the many ways in which women and girls have resisted adoption of the values of the white middle-class culture. In a study examining black and white working-class women's ways of knowing in community-based adult education programs, Luttrell (1989) found that the women of both races resisted placing too much importance on the white middle-class value on knowledge advanced by school authorities. Both the black and white women distinguished between common sense and intelligence. Common sense, a characteristic that both the black and white women attributed to themselves, was defined as the ability to negotiate working-class culture and to solve day-to-day problems. Intelligence was not as clearly defined, but, overall, a distinction was made between school-based intelligence and "real intelligence."

Real intelligence was seen as the ability to teach oneself a skill such as how to fix a car or play a musical instrument. In defining who had real intelligence, the white women gave only male examples. They included the manual labor typical of males, such as the ability to fix mechanical items, in their examples of real intelligence, but the skilled labor required of them as women—the ability to sew, quilt, or cook—was never cited as instances of real intelligence. The black women, on the other hand, saw the work that they did as requiring real intelligence; many also specifically cited the ability to deal with racism and survive as instances of real intelligence. While the black women defined themselves as having real intelligence, they "attribute black men's power to black men's superior knowledge" (Luttrell, 1989, p. 43), saying that black men have the ability to convince black women to do just what the women said they would never do. Thus, even though the black women saw themselves as having real intelligence, black men's intelligence was seen as superior to their own. Both the black and white women resisted adoption of the white middle-class value of the importance of school-based knowledge. But both groups adopted the gender-oppressive value of male intellectual superiority, although in different ways.

In summary, there appear to be three central themes in feminist resistance theory (Weiler, 1988). First, all people have the capacity to be the creators and producers of meaning in their lives and to resist the forces of oppression. Second, the forms that such resistance takes are influenced by multiple factors of oppression, including race, class, gender, age, sexual orientation, and ethnicity. Third, the various forms of resistance that people use, based on the multiple factors of race, class, gender, and so on, may sometimes propagate other forms of oppression or domination of themselves or other people.

Gender Model. The liberatory model of feminist emancipatory education focuses on the structured power relations and interlocking systems of oppression that affect women's lives both in society and in the classroom. The gender model, on the other hand, deals directly with women's socialization as nurturers. The gender model is emancipatory in the personal psychological sense, but it is not emancipatory in terms of dealing with the power relations of the larger social structure.

Belenky, Clinchy, Goldberger, and Tarule's (1986) book, *Women's Ways of Knowing: The Development of Self, Voice, and Mind,* is probably the most often-cited work in contemporary feminist pedagogy operating from the gender model. The authors interviewed a total of 135 women of different races, classes, and ages about the ways in which they best came to know and learn. They found that women learn best in environments that emphasize connected teaching and learning. In these environments, women begin to recognize their own ability to think independently, to think critically, and to come to their own conclusions. It is also in these connected teaching-learning situations that many women come to recognize and hear their own voices.

Connected teachers, as defined by Belenky, Clinchy, Goldberger, and Tarule (1986), see the teacher as midwife. The teacher's task is to draw students out, to "assist the students in giving birth to their own ideas, in making their own tacit knowledge explicit and elaborating on it" (1986, p. 217), and to support the evolution of the students' own thinking. In connected teaching, the student begins to integrate the private and the public, the personal and the political. For example, a woman in an algebra class might finally understand how to calculate percentages when she realizes that she has always been able to figure out how much to leave for a 15 or 20 percent tip in a real-life situation. Or a woman in a psychology class might make the connection between the societal forces that reinforce male privilege when she realizes that most psychological theories have been based on research conducted with white male samples.

It is clear that Belenky, Clinchy, Goldberger, and Tarule (1986) are concerned about the personal empowerment and individual development of the student as well as how that sense of personal power can be developed through overt and hidden aspects of the curriculum. While, ideally, the relationship between the personal and the collective comes to light in the education process, Belenky, Clinchy, Goldberger, and Tarule appear to be primarily concerned with the students' emerging sense of personal power and ability to effect change in their lives. These authors would probably argue that change in one's personal life ultimately effects social change, but they appear to be only secondarily concerned with structural change and political action. Other educators, such as those who operate with the liberatory model discussed earlier, are more concerned with the role of education in structural change, and they more directly deal with power issues not only in society but also in the classroom. As Maher (1987) has suggested, a synthesis of both the liberatory and the gender models may offer new possibilities for teaching and learning.

FEMINIST PEDAGOGY AND ADULT LEARNING

Based on the above discussion, what insights does the feminist emancipatory education or feminist pedagogy literature offer for learning in adulthood? A synthesis of both the liberatory and the gender models initially offers three primary and interrelated insights for adult learning.

First, it is clear that the feminist emancipatory education literature suggests that women may have different learning needs from men. Nearly all education systems may have been initially designed for the education of men, with a knowledge base predominantly based on a rationality that was socially constructed by white males. Belenky, Clinchy, Goldberger, and Tarule (1986) suggest that women seem to do best in learning environments where affective forms of knowledge or knowledge that comes from life experience are valued. In short, they do best in learning environments where there is an effort to relate theoretical concepts to real-life experience.

Clearly, the idea of capitalizing on students' life experiences and relating theoretical concepts to those experiences is not new in the adult education literature. Nevertheless, the feminist pedagogy literature centers on the importance of women in particular reclaiming and validating the learning that comes from their life experience *as women*. Because women have a different relationship to the structures of power from that of men, there has been a tendency to dismiss or discount their learning that comes from experience in the private realm.

Belenky, Clinchy, Goldberger, and Tarule's (1986) connected teaching methods and learning environments seem to help women begin to see themselves as creators of knowledge. The creation of connected learning environments helped at least some women in their study begin to integrate subjective knowledge, where truth is perceived as personal, private, and internally derived, with procedural knowledge, where objective procedures are used for deriving or obtaining knowledge. Women who were able to integrate subjective and procedural forms of knowledge came to see themselves as more independent thinkers, and Belenky, Clinchy, Goldberger, and Tarule report that these women were more concerned with moral and spiritual values and began to translate their moral views and commitments into action. When attempting to solve moral dilemmas and to translate ideas into action, they tended to ask questions related to context. Thus, connected learning environments may help women see themselves as independent thinkers and constructors of knowledge, which is more likely to lead to social action.

Second, implicit in the discussion of the feminist emancipatory education literature is attention to the sociocultural context where power relations based on the interlocking systems of oppression abound. These power relations are always present and clearly affect learning. Power disparities between women or racial minorities and the white male majority are present in both hidden and overt ways in adult education curricula. As Hugo (1989), Collard and Stalker (1991), and Colin and Preciphs (1991) have pointed out, literature that deals with power issues related to women and minorities is often absent in adult education curricula, and the literature that does deal with women and minorities often portrays them only in non-authoritative roles, which contributes to the reproduction of unequal power relations in society. The feminist emancipatory education literature calls attention to these issues and underscores the importance of directly dealing with these issues in the sociocultural context—through the choice of what to include in the overt curriculum and in attending to what gets taught through the hidden curriculum by the way in which the class or education program is conducted.

Third, the feminist emancipatory education literature contributes to the adult learning literature in the direct discussion of how to deal with power issues in the learning environment that affect the learning process. There is considerable discussion in the feminist pedagogy literature about the power disparity between the teacher and the student, and how professors, as authorities of their own knowledge, should deal with power issues that come up in their classes. Much of the literature deals with concrete examples based on experience. Since this power disparity is a central theme in much of the feminist emancipatory education literature and of interest to adult educators who want to attempt to deal with power issues and alter the nature of structured power relations in the classroom, some brief examples are in order here.

Gardner, Dean, and McKaig (1989) discuss the reality of trying to deal with power issues in a women's studies class. Gardner, the professor of the class, discusses her effort to make a "truly feminist" classroom. She relinquished most of her authority and took on a passive role in the first part of the class because she did not want to exercise power and domination in her classroom. She found, however, that as a result of relinquishing her own authority as teacher, the feminist majority, those who considered themselves "the enlightened," dominated the class, and those students who either had less of a background in feminism or were less sure of their political position felt silenced. "The students used differences in knowledge to create a distinct hierarchy in the classroom with knowledge being a source of power over others" (Gardner, Dean, and McKaig, 1989, p. 65). A similar dynamic emerged when discussing topics of class, where women from working-class backgrounds felt silenced.

These dynamics caused Gardner to rethink her own position on the issue of teacher authority. She reclaimed some of her authority as teacher and encouraged the class members to critique the power dynamics that emerged in the class. This helped the students grapple with the nature of power relations in a concrete situation. Gardner then concluded that, as an instructor, she can use the power of her role as teacher to facilitate the emancipation of women students.

Black feminist theorist bell hooks also addresses this issue of teacher authority in the feminist classroom. She acknowledges that there is a power disparity between teachers and students in classrooms and that it needs to be dealt with openly. She suggests, however, that teachers can use their power in ways that enrich students by directly challenging unequal power relations based on gender, race, and class. Hooks's model of feminist pedagogy differs from the model described by Belenky, Clinchy, Goldberger, and Tarule (1986) in that her style is more confrontational.

> It is a model of pedagogy that is based on the assumption that many students will take courses from me who are afraid to assert themselves as critical thinkers, who are afraid to speak (especially students from oppressed and exploited groups). The revolutionary hope that I bring to the classroom is that it will become a space where they can come to voice. Unlike the stereotypical model that suggests women best come to voice in an atmosphere of safety (one in which we are all going to be kind and nurturing), I encourage students to work at coming to voice in an atmosphere where they may be afraid or see themselves at risk [hooks, 1989, p. 53].

hooks (1989) argues that teachers need to be proactive in confronting unequal power relations. Thus, she uses the power of her role to directly challenge the unequal power relations of society. Her perspective, as well as that of Gardner, Dean, and McKaig (1989), on how to deal with power issues in higher education classrooms while bearing in mind the sociocultural context of the students and the learning situation, may offer insights to other adult educators on how to do the same in their own learning environments.

IMPLICATIONS FOR PRACTICE

The feminist pedagogy and feminist theory literature is just beginning to have an impact on the field of adult education. While there is a body of literature that examines the nature of power relations in the adult education field, there is at present a limited literature base that specifically examines power relations based on gender and race. Colin and Preciphs (1991) have discussed the fact that the curricula in most adult education settings still represent the white worldview. Collard and Stalker (1991) and Hugo (1989) have also pointed out that there has generally been a lack of attention to feminist theory, which uses gender as a unit of analysis in theory development in adult education and adult learning. Hugo (1989) has suggested that feminist theory should be used to critique existing theories in adult education and to offer new insights to the field of adult education. The recent critiques by both Hart (1990) and Clark and Wilson (1991) of Mezirow's theory of perspective transformation (Mezirow and Associates, 1990) have been informed by a feminist analysis. Hart (1992) analyzes work and education from a feminist perspective and makes an outstanding contribution to the workplace learning literature. Thus, there is evidence that the feminist theory and feminist pedagogy literature are in fact beginning to have an impact on the field of adult education and on adult learning theory.

But the feminist pedagogy literature is also beginning to have an impact in the practical realm of adult education. As we come to better understand the ways in which women and minorities know and learn, practitioners who want to raise consciousness or challenge power relations in the adult learning environment are beginning to adopt teaching strategies intended to directly challenge structured power relations. What are some of these teaching strategies and what are the practical implications of the feminist pedagogy literature for adult educators who want to engage in emancipatory education practices?

First, adult educators who want to adopt feminist and emancipatory education practices should carefully consider how their curriculum materials for their classes or learning activities serve to challenge the nature of structured power relations based on gender, race, and class. As Wood (1988) has suggested, decisions about what to include in the curriculum are political considerations. When choosing curriculum materials to address issues related to women and racial minorities, one might consider if such materials examine these issues from the perspective of unequal power relations or from the standpoint of gender or racial differences only. Since books related to content areas often do not include chapters dealing with women and minority issues, it may be necessary to include additional books or articles that specifically address gender, race, and class issues related to the course content or learning opportunity.

Second, adult education instructors who want to challenge structured power relations based on gender, race, and class need to adopt teaching strategies that contribute to the achievement of this goal. Instructors must develop and experiment with teaching strategies that prove over time to be emancipatory. As Belenky, Clinchy, Goldberger, and Tarule (1986) found, teaching strategies that unite theory and practice, that value affective forms of knowledge, and that require reflection on how the course content relates to students' life experiences seem to contribute to the ability of women to find voice. Such an approach may also work for minority students. However, the adoption of such an approach does not mean that critical reflection and discussion of highly theoretical material are unnecessary or impossible in a feminist or emancipatory education classroom, or that students in such classrooms are not challenged (hooks, 1989). Rather, discussion of highly theoretical concepts must be integrated with a consideration of how they relate to the lives of real people, including the students in the class. Such an approach is not only intellectually stimulating, it also makes the educational experience more meaningful and may be more likely to lead to social action.

Third, while the choice of emancipatory teaching strategies is an individual decision, it is worthwhile for all university departments to develop new courses specifically designed to deal directly with power relations based on gender, race,

and class. Development of new learning opportunities dealing
with these issues is important, but integration of these issues
into the existing curriculum and learning activities is also important for all content areas. Adult educators outside academia
might also consider the development of programs that deal
with power issues related to their own content areas, such as
how these issues might be addressed in the workplace.

Finally, adult educators who are interested in challenging
unequal power relations based on gender, race, and class may
attempt to address the ways in which their own unconscious
behavior in the learning environment either challenges or reproduces society's inequitable distribution of power. We have
all unconsciously internalized to some degree the values of
the dominant culture. In attempting to increase our consciousness about power relations in the classroom, we may want to
consider such issues as the gender, race, and class of the majority of characters in our illustrative stories and examples,
who are affirmed (by both facilitators and students) as leaders
of the class and how, with whom we have more eye contact,
and on whom we rely to carry the discussion (Tisdell, 1992).
We may want to watch ourselves on videotape or consider in-
viting a trusted colleague or friend to observe the way in which
we conduct a learning session, paying attention to these issues.
One cannot change what one is not conscious of, and the reproduction of power relations happens largely through unconscious mechanisms.

In conclusion, the feminist pedagogy literature is in fact
beginning to have an impact on the field of adult education.
In the coming years, as theorists continue to use feminist
theory to critique present theories of adult learning, those
theories are likely to be revised. Further research on the adult
learning patterns of women and members of minority groups
may also lead to the development of new adult learning theories. And as practitioners continue to adopt some of the principles of feminist pedagogy in their own teaching, there may
be an increased sensitivity to gender and minority issues
among students and practitioners, leading to even greater insights into the nature of feminist pedagogy and the education
of women and minorities. Thus, we look to the future with
a growing awareness of gender and minority concerns. May

this growing awareness help lead to the emancipation of ourselves and our students.

REFERENCES

Belenky, M. F., Clinchy, B. M., Goldberger, N. R., and Tarule, J. M. *Women's Ways of Knowing: The Development of Self, Voice, and Mind.* New York: Basic Books, 1986.

Chafetz, J. *Feminist Sociology: An Overview of Contemporary Theories.* Itasca, Ill.: Peacock, 1988.

Clark, M. C., and Wilson, A. "Context and Rationality in Mezirow's Theory of Transformational Learning." *Adult Education Quarterly*, 1991, *41* (2), 75–91.

Colin, S., and Preciphs, T. K. "Perceptual Patterns and the Learning Environment: Confronting White Racism." In R. Hiemstra (ed.), *Creating Environments for Effective Adult Learning.* New Directions for Adult and Continuing Education, no. 50. San Francisco: Jossey-Bass, 1991.

Collard, S., and Law, M. "The Limits of Perspective Transformation: A Critique of Mezirow's Theory." *Adult Education Quarterly*, 1989, *39* (2), 99–107.

Collard, S., and Stalker, J. "Women's Trouble: Women, Gender, and the Learning Environment." In R. Hiemstra (ed.), *Creating Environments for Effective Adult Learning.* New Directions for Adult and Continuing Education, no. 50. San Francisco: Jossey-Bass, 1991.

Cunningham, P. "The Adult Educator and Social Responsibility." In R. G. Brockett (ed.), *Ethical Issues in Adult Education.* New York: Teachers College Press, 1988.

Freire, P. *Pedagogy of the Opressed.* New York: Herder & Herder, 1971.

Gardner, S., Dean, C., and McKaig, D. "Responding to Differences in the Classroom: The Politics of Knowledge, Class, and Sexuality." *Sociology of Education*, 1989, *62*, 64–74.

Hart, M. "Critical Theory and Beyond: An Emancipatory Education and Social Action." *Adult Education Quarterly*, 1990, *40* (3), 125–138.

Hart, M. *Working and Educating for Life: Feminist and In-*

ternational Perspectives on Adult Education. New York: Routledge & Kegan Paul, 1992.

Hayes, E. R. "Insights from Women's Experience for Teaching and Learning." In E. R. Hayes (ed.)., *Effective Teaching Styles*. New Directions for Adult and Continuing Education, no. 43. San Francisco: Jossey-Bass, 1989.

hooks, b. *Talking Back: thinking feminist, thinking black*. Boston: South End Press, 1989.

Hugo, J. "Adult Education and Feminist Theory." In P. M. Cunningham and J. Ohliger (eds.), *Radical Thinking in Adult Education*. Occasional Papers No. 1. Battle Creek, Mich.: Kellogg Foundation, 1989.

Luttrell, W. "Working-Class Women's Ways of Knowing: Effects of Gender, Race, and Class." *Sociology of Education*, 1989, *62*, 33–46.

Maher, F. A. "Toward a Richer Theory of Feminist Pedagogy: A Comparison of 'Liberation' and 'Gender' Models for Teaching and Learning." *Journal of Education*, 1987, *169* (3), 91–100.

Mezirow, J., and Associates. *Fostering Critical Reflection in Adulthood: A Guide to Transformative and Emancipatory Learning*. San Francisco: Jossey-Bass, 1990.

Tisdell, E. J. "Power Relations in Higher Education Classes of Nontraditional-Age Adults: A Comparative Case Study." Unpublished doctoral dissertation, Department of Adult Education, University of Georgia, 1992.

Weiler, K. *Women Teaching for Change*. South Hadley, Mass.: Bergin & Garvey, 1988.

Wood, G. "Democracy and the Curriculum." In L. Beyer and M. Apple (eds.), *The Curriculum: Problems, Politics, and Possibilities*. Albany: State University of New York Press, 1988.

Sue Blundell (1947–   ) has a B.A. in classics and a Ph.D. in Greek philosophy from Westfield College, University of London. She has worked in adult education for many years, and currently teaches Greek Cultural History to mature students studying for part-time degrees at Birkbeck College, University of London, and at The Open University, the U.K.'s foremost distance learning institution. She has published a book, *The Origins of Civilization in Greek and Roman Thought* (Croom Helm, 1986), and her book on *Women in Ancient Greece* was published in 1995 by The British Museum Press and Harvard University press.

In the courses which she teaches on the history of women in ancient Greece, she is aware of the dangers of ghettoization and of reinforcing the image of women as victims. She is firmly convinced that the rediscovery of women's history still has a contribution to make to their liberation, but believes that much more thought needs to be given to the incorporation of this strand of history into the mainstream of education.

In the article "Gender and the Curriculum of Adult Education," Dr. Blundell reviews feminist discourse from four perspectives—liberal, radical, Marxist and socialist—and assesses the potential each holds for bringing about change in the adult education curriculum. The following selection is her analysis and critique of one of these perspectives, radical feminist discourse, and its implications for curriculum.

SUE BLUNDELL

20 Gender and the Curriculum of Adult Education

Note. Three of the discourses mentioned below—liberal, Marxist and socialist—have not been included in this excerpt.

In the field of adult education, curriculum theory is for the most part conspicuous by its absence, although the work of Colin Griffin (1983) has gone some way towards filling this significant gap. But Griffin would be the first to admit that his analysis takes little or no account of the issue of gender. Since women constitute a majority of both the students and the teachers in adult education, this omission would appear

From International Journal of Lifelong Education, Vol. 11, No. 3 (July-September 1992), 199–216. Taylor & Francis Publishers. Reprinted with permission.

225

to be a serious one. To date, much has been achieved by women scholars in terms of hauling gender into the debate about the school curriculum;[1] and some very useful studies of the patriarchal bias within the curriculum of higher education have been undertaken.[2] But as yet there has been no detailed research which has focused on gender issues in relation to the curriculum of adult education, although books by Thompson (1983) and Hughes and Kennedy (1985), which set out to define and describe the essential characteristics of adult women's education, have offered some very helpful insights. In this article I shall be building on the work done by all of these women in outlining some basic analytical approaches to the gender implications of the adult curriculum.

My discussion will be structured around the four major discourses—liberal, radical, Marxist and socialist—which exist within the social and political theory of feminism. These discourses, which Sue Middleton (1984) among others has distinguished, seem to me to offer the most useful way into this subject if we are to examine the fundamental question which it raises: the question of whether the curriculum of adult education has any contribution to make to the liberation of women.

There is no doubt in my mind that this is the ultimate goal which an adult education programme for women should be aspiring to achieve; equally, I am convinced that as it is presently constituted adult education has very little to offer in this direction. There are, I think, two basic reasons for this failure: first, because the 'little home-maker' approach to women's education has by no means been eradicated from our adult centres; and second, because that part of the curriculum which on the face of it appears to be gender-blind is in fact profoundly male-centred. At present, what the traditional adult education curriculum is offering to women is either a reinforcement of their time-honoured domestic role, or selective admission to a system of knowledge which is defined, transmitted and controlled by men. It is through the medium of the four discourses that I shall be assessing the significance of the adult curriculum for women, and exploring the strategies for transforming it. . . .

THE RADICAL PERSPECTIVES AND
THE PATRIARCHAL CONSTRUCTION OF KNOWLEDGE

The radical perspectives on women embrace three major discourses—the Marxist feminist, radical feminist and social-ist feminist discourses. Though these differ in their broad analyses of the nature of women's oppression and in some aspects of their prescriptions for change, they do have certain fundamental points in common. One is their belief that women *are* oppressed (as distinct from the liberal view that they are 'disadvantaged'), and that this oppression is one way or another intrinsic to our social structure, so that some kind of social transformation will be required before women can be liberated. Another point in common, more specifically linked to the discourse on education, is the view that one facet of the oppression of women is their subordination within a knowledge system which is patriarchally constructed. Before examining these discourses separately and giving some account of their differences, I shall set out the main features of the view of knowledge which they share.

No one has done more than the radical feminist Dale Spender to illuminate the multifarious means by which male power in our society gets translated into male control of the definition and distribution of knowledge—means which include the control of language and the 'power of naming' (Spender 1980), the patriarchal bias of academic subjects (Spender 1981b), and the stranglehold on powerful positions within the academic professions (Spender 1981a). Under the last heading, she notes the way in which all the agencies that have a hand in the generation of academic knowledge—publishers of books and periodicals, professional associations, conferences, academic boards, examination boards, and of course the academic departments within the universities—are dominated by men. As a result, Spender says, 'men are able to exclude women from the construction of knowledge: they can exclude them as subjects when they set up research which is problematic to men, they can exclude them as researchers and theorists by not allocating funding to projects which are perceived as

problematic to women, and by "disallowing" women's un-
funded research' (Spender 1981a: 159).

The construction of academic knowledge is not just an
issue within higher education: academic definitions influence
what counts as knowledge in secondary schooling; and adult
education, to the extent that it either reproduces the knowledge categories of schooling or delivers a watered-down version
of what is taught in universities, is thoroughly permeated by
this male-centred knowledge. It is, moreover, a knowledge
which successfully masks its patriarchal bias: in many if not
all of the academic disciplines, male experience is represented
as constituting universal experience,[3] a distortion which the
strategy of 'adding women on' cannot fundamentally alter. The
typical analytical scenario which this procedure produces goes
something like this: 'people say, do or think (a), (b), or (c) (but
oh, by the way, women on the other hand say, do or think
(x), (y), and (z)'. Not only does this offer no challenge to the
universalizing of male values (i.e. men = people) but, by making a special case out of women, it helps to reinforce the im-
pression that women are 'deviants' who do not conform to
the norm of human experience.

What is true of the academic world at large is also true,
needless to say, of the discipline of education. Sandra Acker
(1981) draws attention to the way in which sociologists of education have used data derived from predominantly male
sources in constructing general theories, and is highly critical
of the 'new' sociology of education for failing to tackle this
masculine bias. Theorists like Michael F. D. Young,[4] who have
been instrumental in developing new approaches to the sociology of education, have been at pains to point out the way
in which the construction of knowledge serves to legitimize
the existing relations of production within capitalist society;
but they have produced little or no discussion of the role which
knowledge plays in legitimizing existing *gender* relations.
Much the same could be said of Griffin's theoretical work on
adult education (1983). Like the new sociologists, Griffin is
primarily concerned with knowledge construction as a function of the social relations of production: in spite of the important role which adult education plays in the education of
women, gender relations are not accorded a single mention.

This said, I have to admit that the analysis of the relationship between the patriarchal construction of knowledge and the reproduction of gender relations, and of the relationship between gender relations and the relations of production, is a thorny and controversial area of theory. It is at this point that the three remaining feminist discourses begin to part company, so I deal with this topic under the separate sections devoted to them.

THE RADICAL FEMINIST DISCOURSE

Radical feminists see patriarchy as the root cause of women's oppression: for them, the domination by men is not a function of capitalism; rather, it precedes capitalism and is one of the principal elements in its evolution. According to this analysis, patriarchy is a universal and enduring facet of human social organization because it is grounded in woman's capacity for child-bearing and in the sexual division of labour to which this has given rise. The resulting separation between the female domestic sphere and the male public sphere has placed political and cultural power in the hands of men, and they have used this power to assign a high value to their own social role, and a low value to the role of women.[5] In this discourse, then, gender division is seen as the basis for a system of oppression—patriarchal oppression—which is quite independent of class division.

For this reason, the radical feminist analysis of the education system is a reasonably straightforward one, since it tends to concentrate on the manifestations and reproduction of patriarchal power, and can, by the criteria of its own analysis, safely ignore the interconnections between patriarchal power and the relations of production. The deconstruction of the knowledge content of education in this discourse relies heavily on identifying the areas of direct male control, and on assembling the evidence for overt and hidden male bias in the curriculum. On the positive side, radical feminists are concerned with constructing a new, women-centred knowledge to replace the old male-centred variety; and with getting women into a position where they can distribute and reproduce this knowledge. Thus, according to Spender,

> while males control education there is no direct means for women to pass on their understandings. What women know frequently dies with them, until feminists periodically rediscover them and their writing and attempt to reconstruct women's heritage and tradition. Each generation of women forges understandings about subordination, within their own lifetime and from the circumstances of their own lives, but because these meanings do not become the general currency of the culture they are not passed on to the next generation with the result that neither women nor men know about the women who have gone before. (Spender 1982: 18)

Although writers like Spender are certainly not without hope that the male-centred knowledge system at present dominant in education can ultimately be changed, they see change as something that will be generated through the construction of the 'viable woman-centred alternative' (Spender 1982: 144); and it is on the latter that their attention is naturally focused. Moreover, so far as Spender is concerned, the changes which are envisaged for men's education do not apparently involve any radical transformation of its knowledge content, but rather a recognition of its lack of objectivity—an abandonment, in fact, of the *concept* of objectivity. Men will have to accept the limits of their own subjectivity, and in so doing they will be immediately stripped of much of their assumed authority: 'If there are to be men's "truths" which originate in men's subjectivity, and women's "truths" which originate in women's subjectivity, then it is obvious that there must be more than one "truth".... No one group will have a privileged way of knowing...' (Spender 1982: 148–9).

In constructing a curriculum for women's education, radical feminists build on the separateness of the male and female identities and make it into a virtue. One important feature of their prescriptions has been to advocate the setting up of separate, women-controlled institutions for the education of women, or, as the next best thing, of women-only, women-taught courses within our existing educational institutions.[6]

In both cases the areas of knowledge explored can be subsumed under the general heading of women's studies.

There are many different ideas about how precisely the knowledge content of women's studies should be constituted, but most writers agree that one vital element is their interdisciplinary nature, and the challenge which this offers to the patriarchal definitions of knowledge. Many are also anxious to dispel the notion that women's studies involves the study only of women and not of men. According to Evans (1982), many liberal male academics assume that the objective behind women's studies is the examination of a neglected bit of the world, and for this reason they do not see it as offering any challenge to either the traditional disciplines or the traditional methods of enquiry. It is only through the recognition of the crucial role which the deconstruction of male knowledge has to play in women's studies that this marginalization can be avoided. As Fitzgerald has written, 'women's studies . . . challenges the ways in which social structures (the curriculum very much included) create and foster ideas about ourselves and the world. . . . Questioning the underlying assumptions about the truth and supposedly objective knowledge of academic fields is to recognise that the very chopping up and categorising of knowledge in the academy is itself a political act' (Fitzgerald 1978: 3).

Few radical feminists, however, would go so far as Mary Evans does when, in acknowledging that there are some aspects of the patriarchal disciplines which women can turn to their own uses, she warns of the danger of refusing the accumulated knowledge of the past 2,000 years (Evans, 1982: 70). Generally speaking, other radical feminists have not followed Evans in her emphasis on the knowledge content of the women's studies curriculum, or in her insistence that the significance accorded to women's subjective experience should not lead to a downgrading of theoretical and analytical research (Evans 1982: 67). In most of the discussions of the philosophy of women's studies, there has been a tendency to concentrate on its methodology, as presenting the most obvious contrast to the operations of the patriarchal curriculum. Spender, in describing the way in which women's studies developed out

of the women's movements of the late 1960s and early 1970s,
gives a telling account of this practice:

> Unlike men, we had no received tradition in which to operate.
> . . . There were no established authorities whose reputations
> were vested in a particular theory and who sought to initiate
> us into seeing things their way. In short, there was no hierarchy.
>   In the absence of experts, courses, books, models, theories,
> we were all on an equal footing. No-one was more learned, no-
> one had access to a privileged way of knowing; there could be
> no division into teachers and students, for we were all engaged
> in the same process of trying to generate knowledge about
> women, and the venture was co-operative, not competitive . . .
> there could be no privileged or authoritative group who could
> rule that the knowledge of some women was valid, while that
> of others was not. . . . If we were to have descriptions and ex-
> planations about the existence of women, then *all* women
> should be included in the frame of reference, *all* women had
> to have a voice and be accommodated. (Spender 1982: 144–145)

What Spender is outlining here is a perfect example of the
concept of the learner-centred curriculum which writers like
Knowles and Freire were fostering in the 1970s.[7] As in the
prescriptions of Knowles, we get the same stress on self-directed learning, applicability to the learner's role in life, the
problem-centred approach, and above all the importance of personal experience: to quote Spender once more, 'by demonstrat-
ing that all those who are involved in women's studies can
make knowledge and are not passive dependents waiting to
receive it, we have challenged some of the foundation stones
of education and of male supremacy' (Spender 1982: 146). We
are also very close to Freire here, with his strictures on the
banking concept of education, and his insistence on breaking
down the contradiction between teacher and learner. His notion of the 'teacher-student' (Freire 1972: 53) comes to mind
when we read Janet Robyns's account of her experience of a
women's studies group: 'The "teacher" did not remain the
same person. In sharing our knowledge, our thoughts and experiences, the "teacher" rotated among us. Each functioned
as teacher at times because each had something to offer. There
was no knower/non knower, judge/judged hierarchy' (Robyns
1977: 3).

To my mind, one of the most striking *differences* between these feminist accounts and the writing of Knowles and Freire is that they are describing something that actually happened, while Knowles and Freire seem to remain very much on the level of theory. My own experience of the feminist consciousness-raising groups of the 1970s tells me that the absence of the teacher/learner distinction was a reality among those groups, and that this was linked with the 'bottom-up', non-institutional character of the movement. No experience which I have had in adult education, either as teacher or student, has ever matched this. And it is difficult to imagine how in an institutional setting it ever could. Certainly in the works of Freire and of Knowles's disciples there is no shortage of accounts of how theory has been translated into practice; and in my own work as a teacher I have attempted to follow some of their principles. But I have never been convinced by anything that I have read or done that someone who enters a room as a 'teacher' (or, even worse, an 'investigator', to pick up on one of Freire's terms) can leave it as 'just one of the girls'.

Spender is well aware that, with the development of a body of knowledge and the entry of women's studies into the educational institutions, there is a danger that the practice will no longer match up to this non-competitive model of education developed by the early women's movement: 'where the possibility of "transmission" exists—with all its concomitant attributes of hierarchies and competition—it may be very important for feminism to focus on past achievements and to keep the co-operative model in mind . . . ' (Spender 1981a: 171). Nevertheless, as Spender says, the feminist model of education can still make itself felt in institutionalized courses. The stress which is placed on the value of personal experience, the abandonment of sterile and dishonest notions of objectivity, and the non-hierarchical social conditioning which many women have received all make it likely that, even if the teacher cannot entirely disappear, her role can at least be minimalized. Women-only classes in adult education, in my experience, come far closer to the learner-centred model of the curriculum than do mixed classes. At the same time, the relative informality of adult education classes, the large numbers of women attending them, and the potential for innovation which they offer are all factors which make the adult education institute fruitful territory for the introduction of women's studies.

To appreciate what women on an individual level have to gain from learning in a women-only environment, we need only refer to the experience of one of Dale Spender's interviewees:

> After institutionalised education you feel worse. After feminist education you feel better. I left university convinced I was dim, I was always sure everyone around me was brighter than I was, and I was always frightened of being found out. I was frightened of the world. I felt incompetent. I had the mentality of a victim. All that changed after my women's studies course. I felt much more in charge of my own life, though I was more aware of the things that were against me. But I felt capable, I thought it was possible to do something about them. (Spender 1981: 171)

These words evoke perfectly the way in which a patriarchal education can terrorize and demoralize women, and the way in which, on the contrary, a women-only education can empower and gladden them. They represent, I think, a huge indictment of our current education system.

The concept of women-only courses does, however, throw up a number of problems. First, there is the obvious, organizational problem that at present the law permits the advertisement of women-only provision in only two instances: where it provides for women 'who have not been in regular full-time employment for some time because of domestic or family responsibility'; and where it provides training for employment in work in which women are locally or nationally under-represented. Clearly, we have to campaign for a change in the law if general women's studies courses are ever to be provided on an effective basis. A second problem is the one that Evans (1982) highlights: in stressing the tremendous value of the learner-centred methods of feminist education, we should not lose sight of its knowledge content. If we immerse ourselves in the subjective experiences of subordination, and do not apply any hard analysis to the political and social structures which determine that subordination, then we run the risk of producing only individual responses to a collective oppression. Women's education, in other words, can easily become depoliticized, and for this reason it is important to develop a theoretical perspective for women's studies which endeavours to integrate method with content.

Maggie Coats (1989: 33–34) has drawn attention to other problems which are intrinsically linked to the separatism of women's studies. One is the danger that women-only provision might seem to imply identical provision for all women—that all women experience the same conditions of existence and have identical needs. This would be to ignore the effects of class, race, sexual orientation, disability and age. The second difficulty arises from the fact that for many women, women-only provision is traditional, since they are going to move on to education or training in mixed situations. It is important, therefore, that issues of transition and progression should be addressed within all-women groups—we cannot afford to ignore the existence of the other sex.

What these two difficulties highlight is the fundamental danger inherent in women-only provision, the danger that it might lead to the ghettoization of women's education. Our education system does not exist in isolation, but is an element within social and cultural structures which persistently undervalue women. If a significant number of women were to opt for the total separatism which seems to be advocated by Spender, then we could end up with a kind of educational apartheid, involving a traditional, high-status curriculum for men, and an innovative but low-status curriculum for women. To guard against this, we will need to foster the kind of theoretical perspective which can address questions of patriarchal domination. But we will also need to ensure that there is a continual flow of women out of separate provision and into the mainstream of education, where they must hold on to what they have learnt from each other and struggle to achieve the transformation of patriarchal definitions and practice. . . .

Notes

1. See Middleton (1984) for a perceptive and critical survey of some of this research.

2. See Spender (1981b), and Acker, in Acker and Piper (1984: 25–48).

3. A number of papers have been published which examine the patriarchal bias of particular disciplines: see, for example, a paper by Kelly (1985), in which she puts forward the view that science is masculine not merely because it is perceived as such, but also because it is packaged as such; and an influential article by Ardener (1972), in which he claims that the analytic tools which a male-oriented intellectual tradition has supplied to social anthropologists equip them only to respond to the world views of male informants, and neither to hear nor to understand the views held by women. Probably the most successful and detailed critique of a patriarchal discipline has been the one that Ann Oakley (1974) has applied to sociology. More recently, Jean Grimshaw (1986) has examined some of the basic tenets of philosophy from a feminist perspective.

4. Young's *Knowledge and Control* (1971) is generally seen as the definitive work which helped to launch the new sociology of education. To be fair to Young, he has in a recent paper (Young 1988: 10) set out as one of the weaknesses of the new sociology of education the fact that it has neglected questions of race and gender.

5. See Firestone (1979), Ortner (1974) and Rosaldo (1974).

6. See Rich (1975) and Spender (1981b: 127).

7. See Freire (1972) and Knowles (1978).

References

Acker, S. 1981, No-woman's-land: British sociology of education, 1960–1979. *Sociological Review*, Vol. 29, No. 1, pp. 77–104.

Acker, S. 1984, Women in higher education: what is the problem?, in Acker and Piper (1984), pp. 25–48.

Acker, S. and Piper, D. (Eds) 1984, *Is Higher Education Fair to Women?*, Guildford, SRHE & NFER-Nelson.

Ardener, E. 1972, Belief and the problem of women, reprinted in S. Ardener (1975).

Coats, M. 1989, The case for women-only provision and a women-centered curriculum, in Cole (1989), pp. 33–36.

Evans, M. 1982, In praise of theory: the case for women's studies. *Feminist Review*, No. 10, pp. 60–74.

Firestone, S. 1979, *The Dialectics of Sex*, London, Women's Press.

Fitzgerald, A. 1978, Teaching interdisciplinary women's studies. *Faculty Newsletter*, Great Lakes College Association, 27 March.

Freire, P. 1972, *Pegagogy of the Oppressed*, Harmondsworth, Peguin.

Griffin, C. 1983, *Curriculum Theory in Adult and Lifelong Education*, London, Croom Helm.

Grimshaw, J. 1986, *Feminist Philosophers: Women's Perspectives on Philosophical Traditions*, Brighton, Wheatsheaf.

Hughes, M. and Kennedy, M. 1985, *New Futures: Changing Women's Education*, London, Routledge.

Kelly, A. 1985, The construction of masculine science. *British Journal of Sociology of Education*, Vol. 6, No. 2, pp. 133–154.

Knowles, N. 1978, *The Adult Learner: A Neglected Species*, Houston and London, Gulf.

Middleton, S. 1984 The sociology of women's education as a field of academic study. *Discourse*, Vol. 5, No. 1, pp. 43–62.

Oakley, A. 1974, *The Sociology of Housework*, London, Martin Robinson.

Ortner, S. B. 1974, Is female to male as nature is to culture?, in Rosaldo and Lamphere (1974), pp. 67–87.

Rich, A. 1975, Towards a woman-centred university, in Howe (1975), pp. 15–46.

Robyns, J. 1977, Reproductive versus regenerative education; the extension of English education through reference to feminism, unpublished Associateship Report, University of London, Institute of Education.

Rosaldo, M. Z. 1974, Women, culture and society: a theoretical overview, in Rosaldo and Lamphere (1974), pp. 17–42.

Spender, D. 1980, *Man Made Language*, London, Routledge.

Spender, D. 1981a, Education: the patriarchal paradigm and the response to feminism, in Spender (1981b), pp. 155–173.

Spender, D. (Ed.) 1981b, *Men's Studies Modified: The Impact of Feminism on the Academic Disciplines*, Oxford Pergamon,

Spender, D. 1982, *Invisible Women. The Schooling Scandal*, London, Writers and Readers Publishing Cooperative.

Thompson, J. (Ed.) 1980, *Adult Education for a Change*, London, Hutchinson.

Young, M. F. D. 1971, *Knowledge and Control: New Directions for the Sociology of Education*, London, Collier-Macmillan.

Young, M. F. D. 1988, *Curriculum and Democracy: Lesson from a Critique of the 'New Sociology of Education'*, Occasional Paper No. 5, University of London, Institute of Education, Centre for Vocational Studies.

Mechthild U. Hart (1948–　) earned her M.A.T. in music and German at the University of Munich, her M.A. in German literature and Ph.D. in adult education at Indiana University. After coming to the United States she became active in a variety of community organizations. She helped organize a women's bookstore and a battered women's shelter, and she participated in different peace organizations. Since 1987, she has been teaching and advising at the School for New Learning's alternative B.A. and M.A. programs for working adults at DePaul University, Chicago.

Most of her work in community groups was of a cooperative, educational nature, intensifying her interest in adult education as an important political force to bring about social change. Her community-based work in adult education, her practical experiences with political organizations, and the development of an international and feminist theory perspective provide the philosophical underpinnings for her book, *Working and Educating for Life: Feminist and International Perspectives on Adult Education* (1992). Since the publication of her book she has integrated her interest in work and mothering by teaching, writing and talking about "motherwork." She looks at mothering as a form of necessary, life-sustaining work which is being threatened by growing poverty.

In the following selection, Hart gives a summary of some basic questions concerning the epistemological, ethical, and interactive dimensions of mothering, and how these questions can provide a basis for developing alternative educational concepts and practices. Her main point is that such an alternative vision of adult education "takes as its starting point a model of work which is oriented towards the production, sustenance and improvement of life."

MECHTHILD U. HART

21 Subsistence Knowing

THE PRODUCTIVE PROCESS OF EDUCATION

In the most general terms, education can be considered a process which produces (or helps to produce) the capacity for speech and action, or the ability to participate in the human community as an autonomous, critical, and active member. More specifically, autonomy, critical ability, and capacity for competent action imply the individual's capacity for experience itself, where active participation in reality and critical judgement about the consequences of one's action are fully intertwined. In other words, education helps to produce the capacity for having 'fruitful experiences' in the sense Dewey described. This means not only that the individual learner must be able to recognize and actualize the educative potential contained in experience, but also be able to organize her experiences in such a way that they are or become educative. The capacity for experience therefore indicates a practical and critically reflective involvement in social reality from the centre of one's own subjectivity. The latter likewise has to be reflected upon and understood in a process of a critical and creative engagement with one's own inner nature.

Some of the components of this education may look familiar: to learn from and through experience, and to organize educational experiences in ways that are conducive to this learning. These are not only cherished principles of adult education, but also the basis of the 'experiential learning theory' which was developed by Kolb (1974), based on Lewis' 'action theory', Dewey's model of learning, and Piaget's theory of cognitive development. However, from the perspective of production for life, we need to go beyond this theory. Although experiential learning theory stresses the primacy of experience, it lacks essential elements when looked at from a comprehensive critical perspective. Instead of dialectical unity it poses polar relationships between thinking and acting, or experiencing and reflecting; it provides no impetus or vehicle for a critical examination of power relations as, in fact, it lacks a comprehensive notion of critique; it therefore has no future-oriented, Utopian dimension. Finally, experiential learning theory remains entirely within the confines of individualistic thinking. Because a communal orientation is entirely absent, by implication the relationship of self and others is stated in terms of the primacy of the former. Interaction or communication, reciprocity or mutuality are therefore not integral elements of experiential learning theory, as they must be for an education for life.

The points I am raising in this chapter do not only bear similarity to experiential learning theory, but also to many suggestions and ideas presented in the emerging field of a feminist pedagogy.[6] Despite similarities and points of agreement, and a grounding of ideas in female experience, none of the proposed theories and methods of a feminist pedagogy have been systematically developed out of a theory of women's productive work and of a corresponding epistemoloy. Furthermore, no connection has been made between a feminist pedagogy and epistemology from the larger, more encompassing perspective of subsistence production.

When looking at education as a productive process, modelled after the rationality of production for life, one can see many important parallels with the work and epistemology of mothering. In fact, the basic premises underlying mothering also structure education for life. At the centre of a productive educational process lies the same dialectical unity of the particular and the general, of mimesis and reflection, of attending to the concrete and assuming the critical distance of judgement which characterizes the work of the mother. From this basic relationship all others flow, and it recurs in different forms and guises in all other important educational relationships. This is the same as saying that education for life does not allow for creating *artificial dichotomies* in any of its basic relationships, be it between the role of teacher and the role of student, between authority and obedience, process and content, thought and emotion, self and other, subjectivity and objectivity, empathy and critique, caring and judgement, knowledge and knowledge acquisition, and transforming and submitting to reality. While these pairs represent different poles of a relationship, they never assume the character of static opposites, ordered into hierarchies. Each of the individual elements may occur as a distinct moment in the educational process. However, they never crystallize into separate entities but constantly interweave and interlace within a context of live interaction.

VALIDATION OF SUBJECTIVITY

In the educational process 'mimetic nearness' refers, above all, to the validation of the individual learner's subjectivity. Within an explicitly educational context, the acknowledgement of another's unique individuality is a deliberate, purposeful activity based on the assumption that true learning

is dependent on such an acknowledgement. It can therefore
not simply be a formal gesture in the sense of a statement
like 'I grant you the right to be your own person' but has to
be expressed in action, above all in the willingness and deliberate attempt to know the individual learner as a unique
human being. Knowing the learner here has two components:
understanding the learner's reality as much as possible from
her perspective, and knowing her in the sense of being attuned
to, 'dwelling in' the unique qualities of her person. The latter
form of knowing can be described as empathy, the former as
a way of consciously participating in the learner's reality in
order to understand it, and the meaning she herself gives to
it. We can see how acknowledging the learner's experience and
individuality implies a movement between attentiveness and
empathy, and drawing conclusions and making judgements.
Because it is not possible to simply 'crawl into another person's
mind and meaning' by separating 'our interpretations from
connections with our own hermeneutical situation' (Habermas
1983: 11), to understand someone else's experience always implies, however subtly, to judge.

To understand means to recognize the other's reasons for
her opinions, interpretations and actions, and to recognize
someone's reasons is impossible without reasoning oneself, i.e.
without assuming an evaluative stance: we inevitably agree
or disagree with the other person's reasons, or we deliberately
withhold judgement, for which we likewise must be able to
give reasons. Thus, to take the other's perspective, or to at
least partially identify with her means both to 'feel with' the
other, and to participate in the other's reasonableness (or un-
reasonableness), to become aware of the rational-emotional
ground of the other's behaviour and self-identity. Because em-
pathetic understanding and judgement are so intricately intertwined, we can speak of a form of 'rational love' which neither
signifies symbiotic merging nor indiscriminate acceptance.

Here the overwhelming importance of self-knowledge
that was emphasized in connection with mothering or caring,
emerges again. Although we cannot slip out of our own hermeneutical situation, our own assumptions about and interpretations of reality, we can nevertheless critically examine
them if we do not want to run the risk of projecting our own

judgements and interpretations onto the other person. In other words, as educators and co-learners we need to be (or become) critically aware of the various bases for our judgements and evaluations, requiring ongoing self-reflection. The non-cognitive elements of empathy, where a person's unique qualities are 'known' in a sensing, intuitive way are therefore always interlaced with moments of evaluative summaries of the other person's experience as well as with ongoing self-observation and self-criticism. In the context of adult learners, this is a requirement which extends to all participants of the educational situation.

From the perspective of a productive educational process, validating subjective experience and engaging in a relationship of empathy are not simply abstract moral imperatives, but structural requirements for the educational process to be successful, i.e. indeed to contribute to the individual learner's capacity to speak and act autonomously and in concert with others, and to the ability to organize her experience in ways that make it fruitful or educative. The learner's own 'hermeneutical situation,' the meanings and interpretations that structure her reality, as well as her unique personal and biographical characteristics and circumstances all enter and become part and parcel of the educational situation. Because it is this 'material' which is being worked on in the educational process, it needs to be understood and be consciously integrated into the educational process, in order for it to unfold and develop its potential.

ACKNOWLEDGING DIFFERENCE

A stress on individuality and uniqueness implies respect for, and a creative use of diversity and difference. At the same time, diversity and difference, like individuality, have a decidedly social dimension which may be founded on and arise out of social divisions and hierarchies. Unique individual differences will always combine with socially defined ones, where difference ceases to be politically neutral, but becomes translated into inequality. Thus, differences and diversities that emanate from the different realities and experiences of age, class, race, sex, or sexual orientation are all fully tied to power-bound, hierarchical social valuations and institutions. They are therefore all imprinted with the mark of inequality, and these differences, and the experiences of dominance and injustice contained in them, will inevitably unfold their internal dynamics in education, distorting it from within. Only a profound understanding of social reality with all its divisions and hierarchies will make these dynamics visible and will allow educators and learners to separate authentic difference from artificially created ones, and to be realistic about the limits to equality and mutuality that can possibly be established in their educational setting (see Hart 1990a).

THE COMMUNAL DIMENSION OF EDUCATION

In a productive educational situation the learners (and educators) therefore pay tribute to and appreciate individuality, diversity, and uniqueness, but they are united by the common desire to reach mutual understanding through and with those differences. Such an education must therefore foster a theoretical consciousness which is capable of understanding and criticizing individual experience, as well as the wish and ability for mutual understanding. In other words, it must foster relations of solidarity among the participants of the educational situation (Hart 1990a). As I discussed elsewhere (Hart 1990b), an education which is oriented towards cooperative relations among the participants needs to create moral environments which touch the deep structure of non-hierarchical, egalitarian relations. Such an environment would have to nurture 'progressive' needs or need structures, and corresponding identities which are free from the need to control (or be controlled). In other words, a moral ecology would have to be established which fosters virtues and ethical sensibilities needed for caring, egalitarian, communal relationships.

Educational theory is in dire need of a theory of community, and of educating for community, thus going beyond an analysis of educational practices which focus on transformative processes within the learner herself (see Hart 1990b, see also the conclusions reached in this book). It must also go beyond the strictly social realm. In the light of the main concerns of this book, education for life needs to pay attention to those competences and abilities which lead to a different attitude towards and relationship with nature, and with non-human living things. Thus, the ability for empathy and for caring is challenged as well in an attempt to understand, and at least partially to identify with and to attain 'mimetic near-ness' with creatures with whom we cannot communicate in the medium of language. Thus far, no educational theory has systematically explored the skills and competencies that would allow for such understanding and corresponding knowledge, and that would require intensive use of human intelligence and reason, a reason which has eliminated all traces of the pervasive need for hierarchy and control.

CREATING AND RECREATING KNOWLEDGE

Furthermore, productive education, like mothering, is at-tuned to development and change. One of its prime goals is to actualize the potential of the learners, to draw out latent possibilities, rather than to confront the learner with the com-pleteness of certain pre-determined or pre-defined knowledge or skills. The kind of knowledge that enters the educational process, and that is shaped and created by it, emerges as an ambiguous, provisional reality. Not only is knowledge con-stantly created and recreated in accordance with change and development, but it also has multiple sources: subjective and objective, social and individual, about self and about others. Since in principle all learners contribute equally to the process of truth-finding and knowledge-creating, in such an educa-tional situation it cannot be determined from the outset who will learn from whom. Furthermore, the different sources of knowledge combine in an endless variety of ways, assuming the multiple shapes of a knowledge which has absorbed indi-viduality and subjectivity, as well as the unique characteristics of a particular educational situation, without, however, losing its objective, generally valid core. This objective core is guar-anteed by the shared or common medium of the social world in which educator and learners participate, and by their shared and common interest in critically examining and re-visioning this world. Thus, only a critical as well as Utopian dimension prevents the stress on individual difference, contextuality and multiple realities degenerating into an inconsequential and ultimately incapacitating, disempowering relativism.

Knowledge, skills and abilities which are shaped as well as presupposed by an education for life are as varied and complex as the educational process outlined above. They range from the intuition-based, non-cognitive 'feel' for and awareness of one's own as well as the other participants' individual uniqueness and difference to a relentless critical scrutiny of individual and social phenomena. Intuitive knowing, based on the positive act of respect and affirmation is therefore fully intertwined with the critical, evaluative stance of participating in the other's reality. It is such a stance which gives meaning to the requirement of taking the other seriously. Empathy and criticism or evaluation are therefore not separate, but only different moments in a combined, dialectical process. Both are embedded in the overall concern for power-free forms of interaction and communication which likewise encompasses the motivational as well as cognitive—critical realm of acting and learning, requiring both a desire for such social relations as well as the ability to recognize and criticize existing structures of dominance. The latter, in turn, involves substantive information and knowledge about social reality and therefore sets certain requirements for the *content* of education.

If the learners want to criticize society and arrive at a reflected-upon understanding of their own experience within society, they have to draw on a reliable body of knowledge, whose validity and reliability must, however, be drawn into the same overall process of criticism, and must be set in relation to their own experience. Neither externally given, objective knowledge, nor the knowledge contained in individual experience, are sufficient for arriving at the truth about the whole of society. The effort of truth-seeking is a profoundly transformative one, where knowledge about one's self and about the world is constantly recreated in view of a future society. This necessitates the shaping of a historical awareness, or an ability for historical thinking, where the present is examined in terms of its roots in a reflected-upon past, and of the possibilities and potentialities yet to be unfolded in the future. Freire's method of conscientization, and the method of consciousness-raising as developed by the women's movement are both examples for such a transformative process.

The abilities, skills, and knowledge which would be presupposed as well as acquired through a productive education, i.e. one that is based above all on an affirmation of life rather than an affirmation of 'the bottom line,' are therefore fundamentally different from those we find in the list and catalogues of skills necessary for work of the future. Above all, these abilities move outside the orbit of technological control, and do not conform to the contours of hierarchical divisions as do the skills currently proposed and taught. They are based on, and in turn structure relationships or relational matrices which are reciprocal, egalitarian, and non-appropriating. To discuss, describe, and practise these abilities and skills, and to deliberately integrate them into educational theory and practice is a task that still awaits careful attention. It will have to be a collective, cooperative effort, addressing the issue from many different perspectives and experiential backgrounds, and drawing on many different existing critical analyses of education, work, and society.

Born and educated in Germany, Herbert Spiegelberg (1904–1990) is considered the foremost historiographer of the phenomenological movement—a modern philosophical movement that calls for the investigation and description of phenomena. Spiegelberg was a lecturer at the University of Munich before moving first to England, and then to the United States in the early 1940s. After teaching philosophy to undergraduates for twenty-two years at a small Wisconsin college, Spiegelberg accepted a position on the graduate faculty at Washington University in St. Louis where he taught until his death in 1990.

The author of a large number of books and articles on philosophy, Spiegelberg is perhaps best known for his two-volume history of the phenomenological movement. In addition to writing, his desire to "do" phenomenology led to a series of workshops at Washington University in which he promoted individual and group activities in phenomenology.

One of Spiegelberg's interests was in exploring the role of phenomenology in psychology and psychiatry. In the following article, "Putting Ourselves Into the Place of Others: Toward a Phenomenology of Imaginary Self Transposal," Spiegelberg takes a phenomenological approach to what he calls self transposal, or putting oneself in the place of others. As he points out, the understanding of self-transposal is fundamental to the fields of social psychology, group dynamics, communication, and education. Understanding reality from another's perspective is a basic principle of the growing number of adult educators who employ qualitative approaches to research and practice.

HERBERT SPIEGELBERG

22 Putting Ourselves into the Place of Others: Toward a Phenomenology of Imaginary Self-Transposal*

1. To dwell in general terms upon the imperative need and duty of maximum understanding of others in a world as shrunken in space and as divided in spirit as ours would be

From Human Studies, Vol. 3, No. 2, April 1980. Copyright (c) 1980 by Ablex Publishing Corporation.

*Revised version of "TOWARD A PHENOMENOLOGY OF IMAGINATIVE UNDERSTANDING OF OTHERS" Proceedings of XIIth International Congress of Philosophy VII (1953) 235–39.

trivial in theory and as ineffectual in practice. I shall
therefore concentrate on the concrete task of exploring
means for raising curtains, iron and otherwise, that
separate the mental and moral isolationists of our time,
especially in those almost desperate cases where the normal appeals to mutual understanding are no longer able to
penetrate the walls of accumulated misunderstanding.
Among the operations increasingly involved in this context is the act of putting ourselves into the place of others.
Social psychology, group dynamics, the study of communication and education are becoming aware of its
significance. But we still lack a phenomenological
clarification of the basic phenomena. The purpose of this
sketch is to outline some of the contributions which a
descriptive phenomenology can make to the solution of
this task. It is meant as a first account of the essential
nature of the phenomenon, regardless of whether it actually
occurs or is at least possible among human beings, such as
we know them.

2. The act of putting ourselves into the place of others
    belongs to the larger group of imaginative acts. Hence it
    shares the *general structure* of these acts with them. In
    this context I shall presuppose that the structure of these
    acts has been sufficiently explored by phenomenologists
    such as Jean-Paul Sartre, Eugen Fink, and others.

3. However, in the case of imaginative understanding of
    others, the following *modifications* of this general struc-
    ture must be considered.

    (a) In putting ourselves into the place of others, we deal
        with a very special kind of object of our imagination.
        For it is the real imagining subject who transposes
        himself imaginatively from his usual vantage point
        into the world outside. In self-transposal, as I shall
        call the putting of ourselves into the place of others,
        we leave the "origin" of the coordinate axis for our
        world, as it were.

    (b) The materials used in imaginary self-transposal are all
        supposedly real, not imaginary. All that is imaginary

about the product of this imagination is the relationship of these elements, inasmuch as the real self transmigrates imaginatively into the other's real place; in other words, self-transposal is merely an imaginary rearrangement of reality.

(c) This imaginarily transformed relationship is not merely imagined without any thought of whether or not the imagined object is real or not, as when we imagine ourselves to be healthy or sincere, which we may in fact happen to be. Here we are fully aware that the imaginary transposal is not only contrary to fact but also contrary to all normal possibilities: Not only are we riveted to our own place in reality, but it is downright preposterous to think that any such transposal can ever happen to us in the normal, and even in the abnormal, course of events. The type of imagination involved in self-transposal is thus of the nature of a deliberate fiction flying to the face of the facts.

4. Among the *distinguishing characteristics* of self-transposal, the following call for special investigation: (a) the "place" into which we transpose ourselves; (b) the "self" which is being transposed; (c) the position occupied by this self after the performance of the transposal.

(a) Little reflection is needed to realize that the place into which we are to transpose ourselves is more than the geographical spot, describable in terms of longitude and latitude, at which the other happens to be located. More is involved if we imagine ourselves to be in another's "shoes," "skin," or however else colloquial language expresses the fiction "if I were in your place." It is rather the whole perspective as seen from this place, the "viewpoint" and the view which opens up, into which we have to enter or slide, as it were. Nor is it only the point in space we have to take over, but just as well the point in time and its perspectives toward past and future as seen from the other's place. In other words, what we have to consider is the

whole "frame" of existence, which the other oc-
cupies.

In order to understand what this phrase implies, we ought
to remember the structure of man as a conscious existence, i.e.
as a being incarnated in a body and characterized by a mental
structure whose chief features have been indicated by
Husserl's familiar pattern *"ego cogito cogitata mea"* (I am
referring to referents). We shall, therefore, first consider what
is involved in taking over the *cogitata* or intended referents of
another person's life. Under this heading we have to consider
not only isolated *cogitata*, even if this might be enough for certain limited cases of self-transposal; rather we have to consider
these *cogitata* with their "horizons," and, ultimately, in the
context of the "life-world" *(Lebenswelt)* to which they belong.
This life-world is obviously not the 'objective world," as we
can determine it by the methods of physical science. What
matters is the world as an individual sees it, with an individual's selection, accents, limited information, as well as
with one's misinformation. This world includes, for instance,
the peculiar perspective or scheme of the body in which one
happens to be incarnated, rather than the scientific picture of
the organism. It comprises his environment as one conceives
of it: the natural world as one sees it, the social world as one
experiences it, the cultural world in which one lives, the
religious world to which one relates oneself, etc.

As to one's *"cogitations,"* or acts of reference toward the
world, we have to picture the network of thoughts and feelings
by which the other is in contact with the life-world and which
also has sedimented strata: an individual's more or less careful
or flighty perceptions, preferences and idosyncrasies, aspirations and resignations.

Finally, we have to consider the *cogitator*, the self of the
other at the source of individual acts of reference to one's
world. It is of paramount importance that we learn to put
ourselves into the frame of personality and mind at the root of
this world and of one's comportment toward it. What this
means is that we try to assume imaginatively not only an individual's physique, as far as this is included in the indvidual's
own self-experience: Even more important is that we take on

in imagination the individual's "personality," one's intellectual and moral equipment, temperament, and all that goes customarily by the name of character. An actor impersonating different roles knows best what this implies. Personality in the sense also includes the social role which a person is expected to fill in the framework of society. Otherwise, we cannot hope to "see the world through another person's eyes," as self-transposal should enable us to do.

A current idiom even has it that we imagine ourselves becoming the other's own self. I submit that the common phrase "if I were you" interpreted literally involves a contradiction in terms: an "I" that becomes a "you" is no longer an "I." In any case, such a complete absorption of the other would no longer be a self-transposal. What this phrase seems to suggest is the highest degree of taking over the part of the other, slipping, as it were, into another's shell, as it might occur when we experienced the feeling of existence peculiar to another, and lived under another's assumed name.

(b) Next, we shall consider who the self is that thus transposes itself into the place of the other. Most attempts at self-transposal suffer from the fact that the transposing self carries with itself its own equipment, physique, ideas, experiences, frame of mind, etc. It is obvious that such self-transposals have the character rather of invasions and occupations than of attempts to enter into the world and personality of the other; hence they do not stand a chance of giving us real understanding. Before any meaningful transposal can take place the transposing self has to strip itself of those peculiarities which are not essential to selfhood as such. Such radical and conscientious abstraction from one's own empirical personality is not an easy assignment. It requires negative imagination. This does not mean that we first convert ourselves into disembodied colorless pure selves. But it does involve our learning to detach ourselves from our regular existential involvements. One might well call this a type of phenomenological reduction in which all our empirical determinations are suspended, relativized, or neutralized. Thus, self-knowledge and self-discipline are prerequisites of any meaningful self-transposal. There is enough evidence, even of a psychological nature, to back up this conception of man.

(c) Putting oneself into the place of the other is obviously a transitory operation. If successful, it results in the self's occupying the other's place. Thus the question arises whether and to what extent we are to "stay put" in the station into which we put ourselves.

It is obviously out of the question to live the life of the other from the inside at the same rate and pace as would the other, thus abandoning one's own station completely, of only in imagination, to the extent of cutting off one's retreat to one's own place. At best, we can expect to stay there for an exploratory period, long enough to become oriented in another's existence and to experience the reactions of our remodeled and transposed ego to it. In fact, any understanding of the other by the self requires that we maintain our position outside the other, while moving back and forth between another individual's and our places. To *become* the other is no longer to *understand* the other. The exact determination of the optimum of sojourn in the other's place presupposes a much fuller phenomenology of the types and degrees of self-transposal than I can offer here, and specifically of the various stages of intuitive fulfilment that can be given to our imagining the lives of others.

5. Self-transposal is to be distinguished from such *related acts* as sympathy, empathy, identification, role-taking, and similar acts, but their exploration can help in bringing out the unique nature of the act of self-transposal.

6. Likewise, the question of the *varieties* of the act has to be postponed. Only one phenomenon shall be mentioned by way of contrast: There is such an act as putting the other into the place of oneself. It occurs particularly where we choose another person as a model, asking ourselves what

that person would do if in our place. Obviously, this reverse transposal makes sense only where we believe we know the other at least as well as ourselves.

7. What is the *epistemological validity* of the method of self-transposal? Offhand it would seem to be preposterous to claim knowledge of others by a type of imagination as extravagant in scope as the act of self-transposal has turned out to be. Yet we would do well to remember that scientific imagination has been recognized more and more as perhaps the most important step in the methodology of the sciences, much as it has to be buttressed by subsequent verification. Besides, Husserl pointed out that free variation in the imagination is the most effective method of phenomenology. Anyway, this method represents our only chance of penetrating minds different from our own. Realizing the precariousness and pretentiousness of such a method can provide one of the most necessary lessons in social humility and respect for others that a critical social philosophy can teach us.

8. Finally, the *ethical question* must be raised: Why should we be under any obligation to perform an operation as fantastic as pretending to be in another's place, which is contrary to fact and reasonable possibility? It would be relatively easy to summon up prudential reasons why putting ourselves into the place of others is our best chance for getting along with them. But this is neither necessary nor enough for a genuine ethical imperative. While a final answer has to be postponed, I submit that man's contingency and specifically the "accident" of his actual station (birth and environment)[1] makes it a matter of "fairness," of an existential moral exigency, to realize that what has happened to others might, as far as ethical claims are concerned, just as well have happened to us; in the words of John Bradford: "There but for the grace of God go I."

[1] *On this concept and its ethical significance see my " 'Accident of Birth' A Neglected Motif in Mill's Philosophy,"* Journal of History of Ideas, 22, (1961), 479–492.

Michael Collins (1939–) has had a wide range of experience in adult
education in both the United States and Canada. After receiving his doc-
torate in adult and continuing education in 1980 from Northern Illinois
University, Collins taught at Kansas State University before moving to
Canada where he is now on the faculty of continuing education at the
University of Saskatchewan, Saskatoon.

In addition to teaching and writing, Collins has been a director of adult
education for a school system in British Columbia, a consultant with Learning Resources Network, an ESL teacher to new immigrants in Birmingham,
U.K., and coordinator of a Canadian residential conference on prison education. He has been the book review editor for *Lifelong Learning: The Adult
Years* and is currently co-editor of the journal *Mass Media and Adult
Education*.

His research and publications reflect interests in adult basic education,
volunteerism, and the philosophy of adult education. Collins has been particularly interested in using a phenomenological approach to better
understanding the practice of adult education. In "Phenomenological
Perspectives: Some Implications for Adult Education," Collins presents some
of the major concepts in phenomenology, including the stock of knowledge,
multiple realities, intentionality, and critical reflection; he also discusses
their relevance for research and practice in adult education. Critical reflection, for example, especially as it is anticipative, can permit us to experiment
with visions of a future learning society, one that is "preferred to the
prescriptive formulations of standardized curricula."

MICHAEL COLLINS

23 Phenomenological Perspectives: Some Implications For Adult Education

"What is phenomenology?" is a question that has been
posed by virtually every scholar associated with the phenomenological movement, and it seems to have been answered differently by each one of them. According to Richard Zaner, "the
difficulties of introducing phenomenology are notorious, and
quite sufficient to dissuade even the hardiest of souls."[1] And
Alfred Schutz, who introduced Edmund Husserl's phenomeno-

*"Phenomenological Perspectives: Some Implications for Adult Education," by Michael
Collins. May 1983. Reprinted by permission of the author.*

logical approach to modern sociology, warns us that "an attempt to reduce the work of a great philosopher to a few basic
propositions understandable to an audience not familiar with
his thought is, as a rule, a hopeless undertaking."[2]

In view of these daunting caveats, one might justifiably
ask whether it is at all feasible, within the confines of a short
chapter, to begin even a tentative exploration of the relevance
of phenomenological perspectives for adult education.
However, both Schutz and Zaner, despite their earnest quali-
fications with regard to the immensity of the task, have joined
other outstanding students of Husserl's founding works in lay-
ing out the impressive potential of phenomenological insights
and methodology. Zaner tells us that "the sense of the
phenomenological method is very much like that of the ex-
plorer when he turns to the task of where he has been and how
he got there."[3] Provided the course is carefully laid out, *the
way is open for others to extend the exploration or intensify
the level of investigation at any juncture which relates to their
particular concerns.* This essay is more a preliminary survey of
the lay of the land than a full-scale exploration, but some of its
signposts will be of interest to adult educators. First we have to
launch off, mindful of Husserl's understanding of how difficult
it is to find the right beginning:

> In point of fact, the beginning is here the most difficult thing of
> all.....The new field does not lie spread before our gaze crowded
> with given products, so that we simply grasp them.[4]

Our intent in this essay is to impart a sense of what
phenomenology is about while addressing some leading
phenomenological concepts which have direct relevance for
research and practice in adult education. Of necessity, this involves us in over-simplification and, perhaps, inexactitude.
However, our endeavor is well justified if we are thereby encouraged to consult studies of scholars working in the
phenomenological "tradition," or to take up the more difficult
task of familiarizing ourselves with the details of Edmund
Husserl's transcendental phenomenology.

As we survey the concepts in this essay let us bear in
mind that the central concern of phenomenology is about
meaning. *Understanding—the apprehension of meaning in any*

context—requires a readiness to suspend taken-for-granted beliefs (attitudes) in favor of a critical stance towards everyday experiences. This turning away from an uncritical attitude towards the world in which we live is methodical rather than iconoclastic or deterministic. Far from denying the existence of the "real" world, this stance entails a rigorous assessment of what is typically accepted as reality in our day to day lives. Already we begin to recognize that a phenomenological perspective has important implications for the way we design, facilitate, and evaluate learning projects for adults.

Though the following descriptions of leading phenomenological concepts are somewhat truncated, readers will observe that they are interconnected. This is in keeping with a phenomenological orientation which consistently points to the essential inter-connectedness of objects and events which occur in the everyday world of human action.

STOCK OF KNOWLEDGE

An individual's stock of knowledge is formed as new elements of knowledge (cognitions) and their implications are integrated into the layers of previously acquired knowledge. Previously acquired knowledge itself influences the manner in which new knowledge is integrated. Our ability to make critical judgments is a dimension of the stock of knowledge. It accounts for our motivational traits and the way we experience our world.

The formation of our stock of knowledge, then, is auto-biographical. It is this autobiographical dimension which distinguishes each of us from all others. Both the content and the timing of our past experiences establish our uniqueness as individuals and they have a decisive influence on the way we deal with our day to day projects.

While the adequacy of our individual stock of knowledge varies according to the situation at hand, there is always some aspect of our past experience which we can bring to bear on a new problem. We are rarely in a complete state of not knowing.

Advocates of self-directed learning in adult education can gain theoretical support from further phenomenological investigations of the structures of the stock of knowledge. In the meantime, our present survey of the concept is sufficient for us to question the growing reliance on pre-packaged standardized curricula which are not designed to connect with a learner's personal stock of knowledge. A similar kind of problem emerges when we turn our attention to the accepted way of conducting needs' assessment surveys. Typically, the questions asked on a needs' assessment instrument are merely a reflection of the designer's stock of knowledge which fixes the limits of the inquiry. Their intent is to elicit a series of responses contrived by the designer of the instrument and, while the enunciation of such programmed responses represent an important dimension of setting goals and establishing the directions along which purposeful action can take place, they do not get at those motivations of adults which are embedded in their past experience.

Adult educators who work in the area of adult counseling, especially those who are wedded to the notion that their clients can be readily grouped according to pre-determined "cognitive styles," or any other psychologistic categories, might find it instructive to investigate with greater thoroughness the problem of the constitution of the individual's stock of knowledge.

LIFE-WORLD AND THE NATURAL ATTITUDE

The life-world is the arena for all direct experiences of human beings. According to Alfred Schutz:

> the life-world, simply, is the whole sphere of everyday experiences, orientations, and actions through which individuals pursue their interests and affairs by manipulating objects, dealing with people, conceiving plans and carrying them out.[5]

For the most part, in our routine day-to-day activities, we adopt the mental stance of the *natural attitude*. It is essentially an accepting stance which we often characterize as being "realistic." In the natural attitude we suspend all scepticism concerning the existence of the events and objects of our everyday world. Taking them for granted, we refrain from all possible doubt that the world and its objects (events) could be otherwise than they appear to us. It is a world of well-circumscribed objects and events which have determinate properties.

In the light of this account, let us envisage adult learning situations in which a deliberate effort is made to set aside temporarily all presuppositions learners have of the events of their day-to-day lives. By focussing, within the learning context, on those occurences of individual and community life which have previously been experienced in a taken-for-granted manner, we make them problematic. The reality of the life-world of the community and its individual members is not denied, but temporarily "put into brackets." In this manner, new themes and interpretations are constituted which form the content for an ongoing adult education program. Curriculum materials are either created within the adult learning context or are relevantly selected to meet the immediate purpose at hand.

The process we are describing is akin to that adopted with impressive results by Paulo Freire in "Third World" countries, except that it avoids the anomalous position of incorporating a deterministic Marxist interpretation of historical development within a program to empower adult learners. A deterministic Marxist interpretation of the life-world is just as questionable from our perspective as the determinism of behavioristic assumptions on which standardized curricula are based. Instead, we recommend the adoption of learning strategies suggested by the act of 'bracketing' and the phenomenological device of 'epoche.' This entails a deliberate, through temporary, suspension of the unquestioning acceptance of those everyday, habitual, interpretations and characteristics associated with the problem at hand. The adult educator is thus able to create a learning environment in which a greater understanding is acquired of those structures in the community which detract from or enhance the quality of everyday living. In taking a deliberate stance towards these structures, in determining whether to transform them or leave them alone, adult learners are identifying their situationally concrete *interest at hand*, thus providing the basis for contextually relevant programming.

MULTIPLE REALITIES

The life-world is our fundamental and paramount reality, but within it no two people experience the same situation in exactly the same way. Moreover, experiences which are readily accessible to some of us, or within our potential reach, are outside the reach of others. There are many different orders of reality. We confer the *accent of reality* upon them and make of them *finite provinces of meaning*. Adult educators are well advised to be constantly alert to the implications of imposing their own cognitions of the life-world onto the meaning structures of their clients' different orders of reality. This is of even greater importance where people from different cultural backgrounds are involved.

Where adult educators put into question their own life-world perspectives, the likelihood that they will impose inappropriate, preconceived views of what others should or should not learn is lessened. This entails adopting for themselves, and encouraging in adult learners, a commitment to systematic doubting—a willingness to suspend the taken-for-granted posture of the natural attitude. The programmatic intent is to bring about a greater understanding of the structures of our life-world, of its distinguishable realities, and of how the accent of reality is stamped upon it. Purposeful action to modify the life-world can emanate only from such an understanding.

TYPICALITY

Our experience of the everyday life-world takes place in terms of *typification*. Events and objects are not merely experienced in their uniqueness. They are not given to us in isolation. As we have already seen, they refer us to similar sorts of things within our stock of knowledge.

For all of our life-world situations, there can be traced within our stock of knowledge typical recipes for typical problems, and typical attitudes to guide typical behavior. These are held within our stock of knowledge in varying modes of familiarity. Some of our previous experiences are clear and distinct while others are vague and intermingled with suppositions and prejudices.

Relevant typifications emerge as soon as there is some end in view. Whether we are planning a learning project for ourselves or a series of learning activities for others, we refer to our stock of knowledge for ingredients which are applicable to the project at hand. If a current project confronts us with a large expanse of unfamiliar terrain, then we tend to consult acknowledged experts in the area and other appropriate resources. However, from the outset our reference to typified elements in our stock of knowledge provides us with an index. Throughout the entire process, we make judgments about what is appropriate for the task at hand. This obviates the need to incorporate definitive and prescriptive formulations such as coping skills curricula. There is surely something remiss when adult educators forego the challenge of engaging themselves and their clients as the major resource in designing their own learning projects. The systematic design of learning projects arising from typified ingredients which point the way, via purposive planning, to appropriate resources requires effort and is sometimes difficult. But it is the *best* we can do.

INTENTIONALITY

Edmund Husserl considered intentionality to be the central insight into his phenomenological analysis of consciousness and the outstanding topic of phenomenological research. Consciousness is always directed towards something. It is always consciousness *of* something.

All of our experiences, as they manifest themselves within our stream of consciousness, are referred to the object or event experienced. Thought, expectations, fears do not exist as such. Every thought is thought *of*, every expectation is expectation *of*, every fear is fear *of* the entity that is thought, expected, feared. I am always conscious *of* something. What appears to me in reflection is the *intentional object* which I have thought of, which I expect, which I fear, and so on. Not only is my experience characterized by the fact that it is a *consciousness*, but it is simultaneously determined by the object to which my consciousness refers.

An *intentional object*, then, is the object or event singled out by an individual for cognitive attention. The act of experiencing an intentional object (which may be an object or event of either the physical world or the mind) is designated as the *intentional act*. Cognitive "constitution" of the object or event within an individual's stock of knowledge is achieved via the intentional act.

Any phenomenology of adult learning would need to focus its investigations on both the constitution of the intentional object and the intentional act. However, for our present purpose, it suffices to note that the intended object (or event) is not conceived as an already existing entity which awaits the act of intending. It emerges from the intending act. *Intentionality, then, refers us to the purposive experiencing of objects and events in which individuals bestow meaning on their activities.*

From the foregoing account, we can see that the notion of intentionality sets forth an entirely different orientation to that of behaviorism which still undergirds much of curriculum and program planning approaches in adult education.

For behaviorism, consciousness is a product of external events. We are conscious in the sense of being under stimulus control. Purpose or intention is merely a bodily reaction to reinforcement received from the environment. Intentional analysis, on the other hand, enjoins us to uncover the meaning and consequences of our actions which are purposive rather than merely reactive. An observation by Edmund Husserl is instructive in this context:

> I can question every intentional event, which means that I can penetrate and display its horizons. In doing this I disclose, on the one hand, potentialities of my existence, and on the other I clarify the intended meaning of objective reference.[6]

This all too brief account of the concept of intentionality reinforces observations already made in this essay with regard to program planning and evaluation, the facilitating of adult learning projects, and needs' assessment in adult education. It is apparent that there is theoretical support for claims that adult learners should have a real stake in all these phases of the adult education endeavor.

CRITICAL REFLECTION

Reflection as an observing of the mind and its operations incorporates the object *reflected upon (noema)* as well as the *reflecting itself (noesis)*. These correspond to the *intentional object* and the intentional act referred to in the previous section. Reflection is of paramount importance to the phenomenological method and to all those contemporary philosophical approaches which are linked with Husserlian phenomenology. In his delightfully readable book entitled *What is Philosophy?*, José Ortega y Gasset has this to say:

> Living is for the moment a revelation, a refusal to rest content with sheer being unless one sees or understands what one is, a process of inquiry, of informing oneself about oneself. It is the incessant discovery of the world around us.[7]

As a rule, we do not grasp the meaning of an action while we are caught up in its performance. Rather we turn back in reflection upon the flow of action to capture its meaning. In order to understand the meaning of my experiences, I have to pause, as it were, and glance backward on my acting. Through a deliberate process of recollection and retention, immediate experiences overlap with those of the past.

Meaning is imparted to on-going (future) projects through *anticipative reflection*. We can rehearse our projects as a kind of experiment and carry them through to completion in our imagination, reflecting on relevant retentions (past experiences) and on anticipations (foreseeable outcomes). Hence, I may rehearse a number of projects in my imagination before committing myself to a particular line of conduct.

An emphasis on critical reflection as an on-going evaluative dimension of adult learning activities brings an entirely new perspective to program planning. In reflecting, we become aware of how the original meaning of a project is modified by ensuing acts. This pre-empts the notion that a project can be adequately circumscribed by a number of definitive behavioral objectives (or 'competency' statements) prior to involvement of the participants. Attempts to grasp the meaning of what has transpired in the learning situation (project) by retroactive reference to initially prescribed behavioral objectives only adds to the artificiality of such an approach. In presuming that we can know what is to be experienced before the learning project begins, it fails to account for intervening events and significant shifts in meaning.

A reflective attitude allows for the fact that all our life-world projects are, to some extent or other, explorations during which we inevitably encounter novel situations. These take us beyond predelineated eventualities and the habitual occurences of past experience, opening up further possibilities for purposive action.

Through anticipative reflection we can systematically engage in futuristic research in adult education. As we have indicated, *anticipative reflection* permits us to experiment with all manner of possible future projects, weighing their consequences and referring them back to relevant typifications of past experiencing. The process is deliberative and reminds us, at a time when many adults seem overwhelmed by the tide of events, that we do have a hand in shaping the future. From this perspective, our subsequent behavior is planned rather than determined by forces external to ourselves. The scenarios of the futurist are, in effect, projected plans of action conceived in a moving present time which connects past experiences with anticipations of the future. In this regard, adult education faces a challenge to make futurists of us all through facilitating a learning society in which reflective inquiry is preferred to the prescriptive formulations of standardized curricula.

In a more immediate sense, investigations into our own experiencing through reflexive inquiry can add immensely to our insights into the adult learning process. Reflections on the various ways in which we experience the events of our life-world can yield worthwhile reports for those concerned with adult counseling and adult psychology. It would necessitate a temporary suspension, at least, of those well entrenched concepts (for example, life-stages) through which we interpret the flow of mental events. From direct reference to our own modes of experiencing and those of our contemporaries, as we grow older together, can emerge a more penetrating discernment of the aging processes and adult learning.

REFERENCES

1. Richard M. Zaner, *The Way of Phenomenology: Criticism as a Philosophical Discipline.* (New York, N.Y.: Pegasus, 1970), p.30

2. Alfred Schutz, *Collected Papers, Vol. 3.* (The Hague: Martinus Nijhoff, 1973), p. 100.

3. Richard M. Zaner, *op. cit.,* p. 35.

4. Edmund Husserl, *Ideas: General Introduction to Pure Phenomenology,* Translated by W.R. Boyce Gibson. (New York, N.Y.: Collier MacMillan, 1962), p. 171.

5. Alfred Schutz, *On Phenomenology and Social Relations,* Helmut Wagner (ed.), (Chicago: The University of Chicago Press, 1970), p.15.

6. Edmund Husserl, *The Paris Lectures,* "Introductory Essay," translated by Peter Koestenbaum. (The Hague: Martinus Nijhoff, 1964), p. 19.

7. Jose Ortega y Gasset, *What is Philosophy?* Translated by Mildred Adams. (New York, N.Y.: W.W. Norton & Co., 1964), p. 216.

Sherman M. Stanage (1927–   ), is Presidential Teaching Professor of Philosophy at Northern Illinois University, where he also holds a joint faculty appointment in the Department of Adult Education. He received his Ph.D. from the University of Colorado at Boulder. Besides serving on the faculty at Northern Illinois, Trinity University, and Bowling Green State University, Stanage has been a visiting professor at the University of Texas at Austin, Hamline University and the University of New Mexico.

Stanage's specializations include phenomenological investigations in ethics, value theory, and social and political philosophy. His numerous publications, including *Adult Education and Phenomenological Research: New Directions in Theory, Practice and Research* (1987), have applied these specializations to problems in adult education. His current work focuses on what he terms the subject matter of adult education, the "adult eductions of *person.*" Stanage is currently completing a book titled *Meaning Through Action: General Theory of Adult Education.*

In the following article, "Lifelong Learning: A Phenomenology of Meaning and Value Transformation in Postmodern Education," Stanage offers a phenomenology of meaning and values which he argues must be addressed by any theory of adult or lifelong learning. These phenomena of meaning and values are characterized by processes which are not linear or predictable, and which may be interpreted in vastly different ways within a postmodern perspective. The article carefully examines and distinguishes among (a) "postmodern adult education," (b) adult education in a "postmodern world," and (c) a "postmodern definition of adult education," and focuses primarily on the first of these distinctions.

SHERMAN M. STANAGE

24 Lifelong Learning: A Phenomenology of Meaning and Value Transformation in Postmodern Adult Education

INTRODUCTORY REMARKS

This paper offers a brief phenomenology of meaning and values which must be addressed by any theory of adult learning and by any theory of lifelong learning. These phenomena are constituted most essentially by process, change, alteration. But these processes, changes, and alterations are not linear, modular, or determinable and predictable. These phenomena are transformations in meaningfulness and valuation which are central and pivotal to those vital, rededicative perspectives which sometimes are called "second chance" opportunities for adult learners.

These opportunities are frequently viewed as crises or crisislike moments necessitating choices between periods of relative stability. However, the phenomena of transformations of meaningfulness and valuation must be interpreted in a vastly different way when these are intuited through a postmodern perspective.

What I have laid out for us this morning is surely a tall order for a brief presentation. But perhaps enough can be discussed at this time for each of us to refashion relevantizing, vitalizing, transformative, and rededicational ways whereby we can move through further reflective stages in our own lifelong learning as professionals. This recreating of our person is the core of the professional life of a person.

I shall move through the main points of this presentation in reverse order. Doing this will allow us to reflect together on the term, the concept, and the phenomena referred to as postmodern and postmodernism and thereby clarify them in the very beginning.

POSTMODERNISM

The term postmodernism has come into widespread use in literature, literary criticism, art, music, architecture, history, and philosophy, among many other areas of human creativity, invention, and discovery. It has become a familiar term and concept in human science approaches to anthropology, economics, psychology, sociology, and in many other social sciences. Some new ways of viewing physics, chemistry, and biology have sometimes been termed postmodern.

It is not difficult to cite a number of the most central figures in this conceptual upheaval: Edmund Husserl, Martin Heidegger, Karl Jaspers, Jean-Paul Sartre, Simone de Beauvoir,

Max Horkheimer, Theodor Adorno, Hans-Georg Gadamer, Jurgen Habermas, Michel Foucault, Jacques Derrida, Thomas Kuhn, and Paul Feyerabend, among so many others. In this brief listing I have included only philosophers who increasingly have become major sources of new conceptualizations for adult educators most interested in theory construction and in research models.

In all of these disciplines and fields of expression cited, and in the writings of each and every one of the persons named, postmodernism refers to the process of undercutting any and all absolute and certain starting points, any and all firm foundations for establishing meaning and for interpreting values. Postmodernism is a term which refers to a lifeworld, or lived world, in which persons through their literature, art, music, philosophy, and sciences call into serious question all claims to any absolute and certain value and truth which previously had been perceived, and conceived, to emerge from meaning based on absolutely firm foundations. The foundationalism provided in the modernism of Rene Descartes, himself the "father" of modern Western philosophy, for example, may have run its course.

Postmodernism articulates non-causal reasoning and argument, distinguishes between originations and beginnings, and claims that although it might be possible to trace out originations, it is not possible to establish firm, absolute, and causal-foundational beginnings. For example, Gerald Graff claims that

> In its exclusively literary sense, postmodernism may be defined as that movement within contemporary literature and criticism which calls into question the claims of literature and art to truth and human value. As Richard Poirier has observed, 'contemporary literature has come to register the dissolution of the ideas often evoked to justify its existence: the cultural, moral, psychological premises that for many people still define the essence of literature as a humanistic enterprise. Literature is now in the process of telling us how little it means. (Graff, 1984, p. 38)

The critical mass of personal and cultural phenomena referred to as postmodern and postmodernism did not suddenly begin; it did not beguile a modern world absolutely pristine in its foundational innocence. These phenomena have been structured through many sources, even as far back as the earliest "romanticism and the rise of romantic alienation and despair" (Graff, 1984, p. 39). It is rarely possible to experience the actual beginning of an intellectual and spiritual upheaval, or fully to understand originations and beginning as they take their places in our lives. This is as true of an individual person's life as it is of the life of a culture. In fact, separating strains of originations from actual beginnings is the historian's central work. This is the task of intellectual and social history.

R. G. Collingwood, as philosopher of history and historiographer, called this key focus of history the essence of metaphysical thinking. In doing so, he described what could be characterized as postmodern metaphysics. "People are not ordinarily aware of their absolute presuppositions" he said,

> and are not, therefore, thus aware of changes in them; such a change, therefore, cannot be a matter of choice. Nor is there anything superficial or frivolous about it. It is the most radical change a [person] can undergo, and entails the abandonment of all of [this person's] most firmly established habits and standards for thought and action.
>
> Why, asks my friend, do such changes happen? Briefly, because the absolute presuppositions of any given society, at any given phase of its history, form a structure which is subject to 'strains' of greater or less intensity, which are 'taken up' in various ways, but never annihilated. If the strains are too great, the structure collapses and is replaced by another, which will be a modification of the old with the destructive strain removed; a modification not consciously devised but created by a process of unconscious thought. (Collingwood, 1940, p. 48)

But we must go back to "modernism" for a moment. The "modern" authors, for example, included Reiner Maria Rilke, James Joyce, Paul Valery, W. B Yeats, Marcel Proust, T. S. Eliot, and William Faulkner, among many other "greats." These authors seemed to be deliberately creating, or attempting to create, values "in an inherently valueless world" (Graff, 1984, p. 39). We should remember that this "valueless world" was constructed in the earliest decades of the 20th century in large part by the mechanistic materialists and the logical positivists with their passionate, value-laden, and fixated beliefs in the materialistic and logical foundation of the (valueless) world.

We should not forget that much of adult education research (specifically of the hypothetical-deductive, behavioristic, neobehavioristic, and statistical varieties) over the past four decades or so has been very much gounded in the earlier foundationalism of the logical positivists. And modernist adult education is adult education which takes place within a world still perceived as a world in which foundations for it all will be found . . . in principle . . . sometime . . .

In the face of this foundationalism of materialism and logical positivism, the beliefs of the modernists (in literature and in literary criticism, for example) in the constitutive power of the

> imagination which supported romantic and modernist writers, their confidence in the order and meaning repeated in high cultural tradition as a means of rescuing themselves from the fragmentation of·a mass, industrialized society, appeared suddenly to have run its course by the mid-fifties. Since then, art and literature have increasingly incorporated a sense of irony and skepticism toward art's traditional pretensions to truth, high seriousness, and the profundity of meaning. (Graff, 1984, p. 39).

POSTMODERN ADULT EDUCATION

A distinction must be made between (1) postmodern adult education, (2) adult education in a postmodern world, and (3) a postmodern definition of adult education. My emphasis in this discussion is primarily on the first of these distinctions, postmodern adult education.

Two attitudes within the creations, inventions, and discoveries of postmodernism which are of great importance to adult education include the *apocalyptic attitude* and the *visionary attitude* (Graff, 1984, p. 38. The *apocalyptic attitude* expresses itself through the theme of the domination of the death of literature, with criticism in the arts acknowledging the futility of its own enterprise. There is no greater realization in all of adult education thinking than the realization of the utter futility of our enterprise "in staying our present course" in the face of catastrophic global misery and need. Each and every one of us clearly intuits this maximizing sense of failure any time and every time we meditatively attend-to our tasks as adult educators.

The *visionary attitude* expresses itself as "hopefulness for revolutionary changes in society through radical transformations in human consciousness" (Graff, 1984, p. 38). It seems clear enough that the adult education conceptual emphases on empowerment and transformation are derivable from these two all-pervasive traditions within postmodern thought. Hence, empowerment and transformation are clearly postmodern themes of great motivating force and power in adult education theory, practice, and research. But why do so many adult educators argue against the presence in persons, groups, and cultures of, and the motive power of, the clearly identifiable phenomena of empowerment and transformation?

A paradigm case of postmodern adult education, it seems to me, has been the work of Paulo Freire. I have argued elsewhere (Stanage, 1989) that the essence of Freire's most seminal theories, research, and practices articulating the transformation, empowerment, and liberation of the *person* of all persons clearly manifests originating influences from postmodernist sources. These sources include Husserl's phenomenology, Heidegger's hermeneutics, the existentialism of Jaspers and Sartre, and the unique concepts of Mounier's personalism and the liberation theology of Third World expressions of Roman Catholicism.

Although it is probably impossible to establish a beginning of postmodern adult education, if one were to try to fix such a beginning, Paulo Freire and his praxis (reflection and action) would emerge as a prime candidate marking such a beginning. In fact, viewing Freire's praxis as a clear and distinct watershed between modern adult education and postmodern adult education would go a long way toward helping us all to understand and to appreciate his work much more thoroughly. It might even be possible then to apply it to the transformation, empowerment, and thus to the liberation, of persons anywhere in the world who are caught in phenomenologically unique webbings and spiralings of hegemonic forces. And, truthfully speaking, who among us completely escapes these hegemonic forces?

There are many more postmodern strains in adult education. In the time available I can only point briefly to some of the most important ones. These strains relate to the ways in which we are committed to dealing with a number of very familiar problems:

(1) *The problem of defining adult education.* It is not simply the case that adult education is difficult to define, or that very bad definitions traditionally have been constructed. In contemporary adult education, more and more persons have simply given up the task of trying to define the key terms "adult" and "adult education." They have walked away from this seminal task.

(2) *The problem of whether adult education is a discipline.* Adult education in higher education contexts normally is treated as if it were a discipline, but clearly the phenomena supposedly constituting adult education as a discipline are not circumscribed as a distinct branch of knowledge or instruction. And adult educators have walked away from this cluster of problems as well.

(3) *The problem of explanation versus understanding.* This is perhaps the central issue for Critical Theory Adult Education. Critical theorists make explicit use of many of the most important postmodern figures and their theories and concepts in their approaches to adult education.

(4) *What is a person?.* The mere enumeration and description of contradictory models of what a person is in the context of adult education theory, practice, and research raises countless questions about how anyone is to approach the phenomena constituting adult education.

(5) *The problem of foundationalism in adult education.* This is the problem of adult education trying to provide—from within itself—a firm foundation for all of its work, or trying to ground it firmly within the context of an interdisciplinary matrix of the more traditional arts and sciences. Notoriously, adult educators borrow their theories, concepts and research programs from more established arts and sciences. There is nothing wrong with this borrowing, except when those theo-

ries, concepts, and research programs are grabbed at in non-reflective, haphazard, helter-skelter ways, such that their faddish and fashionable acceptance for a short time constitutes their only legitimacy and justification.

In other places I have argued that adult education can become the most rigorous of the human sciences (see Stanage, 1987, *passim*). An adult educator who does not see immediately the obvious relevancy of this claim might well still be committed to the fixated belief that the only kinds and degrees of science, scientific method, rigor, and precision are still those of the old logical positivism. But this habituated fixation to long-outmoded ways of professional work is definitively contradicted by the everyday world of work of practicing scientists (although not by teachers of science or "school approaches" to "scientific method" who have discarded the foundationalism and versions of absolute certitudes, exact meaning, and value-free sciences.

I know of no other kind of inquiries and practices (praxis) in which the subjects of the praxis are both the theorizers and those who are theorized about; are all themselves practitioners; and who are both researcher and the researched. In this special context of relevancy science and its rigor are not dictated by the exactness and sterility of logical positivism. Science (scientia) is any rigorous and systematic investigation of a determinate subject-matter.

The subject-matter of adult education is the adult "eductions" of *person* (Stanage, 1987). The rigorousness is the strict, undeviating, attending-to each and every one of the actual and possibilized adult eductions of *person*. The rigorousness is the thoroughly committed and scrupulous investigation of each and every possible adult eduction of *person*. This is the proper sense of "rigor" in scientific inquiry.

In this case, although it is not possible to separate theory, practice, and research in adult education, they must be distinguished for purposes of special phenomenological investigation. What I have just said itself constitutes an important claim in postmodern adult education. But even if someone asserts that this sort of thing is often done in other areas of human inquiry (in anthropology and sociology, for example), this assertion itself further supports my claim that we are now dealing with a postmodern adult education, since possible examples closest to what I am offering are the contemporary human sciences (in this case, the "social sciences" more humanized) which have been most influenced by postmodern praxis.

There are many more problems within adult education, as I have said, which articulate distinct postmodern strains. These include the ubiquitous and very familiar problems of: hegemonic professionalization and institutionalization; the hegemonic cooption of the young members of the profession who constitute the principal human resource as carriers of meaning and values within adult eduction; the proliferation of professional jargon (and with this the much-needed deconstruction of the text of this jargon); and the veritable flight from thinking so common in adult education contexts. Perhaps it is not so much a flight from thinking as it is the failure to make time available for reflection within the midst of the typical practitioner's everyday world of work.

CONCLUDING REMARKS

I now move back to the very beginning of this paper, and ask (in the postmodern vein) the question of whether the concepts of meaning and value have life today. If they do, their lives are surely different than they were, say, before the first world war, or perhaps the first four decades of this century. That was a period when most disciplines were still building upon firm foundations, still reaching out from their commitments to exactitudes of meaning, from the bases of their hopes and expectations of certitude; a period during which inevitable and completely unimpeded progress was the industrialized Western world's most important product and exportation.

But now, in this late period of the twentieth century, in the words of Jean-Francois Lyotard,

> **Postmodern** science [my emphasis]—by concerning itself with such things as undecidables, the limits of precise control, conflicts characterized by incomplete information, 'fracta,' catastrophes, and pragmatic paradoxes—is theorizing its own

evolution as discontinuous, catastrophic, nonrectifiable. It is changing the meaning of the word *knowledge*, while expressing how such a change can take place. It is producing not the known but the unknown. And it suggests a model of legitimation that has nothing to do with maximized performance, but has as its basis difference understood as paralogy. [Note: "Paralogy" is the term Lyotard uses to refer to "the return of narrative in discourses of legitimation. Examples are: the study of open systems, local determinism, antimethod. . . . " In this same passage Lyotard cites P. B. Medawar as claiming that '*having ideas is the scientist's highest accomplishment . . .* ' and that there is no 'scientific method' (Lyotard, 1979, 1984, pp. 60 f). Shades of Charles Sanders Peirce's **abductive inference**! But Peirce offered this idea to the world more than one hundred years earlier!].

And our own John Ohlinger, in reminding us that "wisdom is as hard to hold onto as a friendly butterfly but as basic to a good life as nutrition," once again demonstrates his own great, and always relevant, wisdom in reminding us that the information revolution may be an illusion since only certain kinds of knowledgable specialists may be able to access it; "public information when packaged in a computer is no longer public" because of a recent Supreme Court decision; biological information is lost forever with the extinction of species at the rate of 1,000 per year; and "the loss of cultural information due to the de-population of our rural areas is far greater than all the information accumulated by science and technology in the same period" (Ohlinger, 1989).

All of this is surely the stuff and substance of postmodern adult education. In the light of the needs of persons existing within a lifeworld (lebenswelt) rapidly becoming the product of postmodern creations, inventions, and discoveries, adult education necessarily must—in fact will—view itself quite differently than it did, say, before the Freirean revolution. For example, change will not be viewed as a period of crisis, upheaval, or mere transition between stable periods, with homeostasis, stability, and quietness being the "natural" and preferred states of existence of persons with whom adult educators might generally work. Instead, transformations, empowerment, and struggles against each and every degree and kind of hegemonic force will be among the essential structures of *person*, and in turn the lifeblood of adult education.

Thus it is that I claim that the phenomena constituting meaning and values are always processive and never static. Any reflection on them necessarily reveals them to be transformative and empowering of the *person* of persons. They are central and pivotal to vital, rededicative perspectives within lifelong education. They too articulate the lifeblood of adult education. Performing a phenomenological investigation of these phenomena is simply the clearest and most direct way of digging through modernist approaches to these archaeological insights.

When these phenomena are viewed from the perspectives of postmodern adult education, however, a quite new theory of adult learning emerges: Learning is the process of fusing the relevantized, antecedently present, meaningfulness of the lifeworld of one's own adult eductions of *person* as feeling(s), experiencing(s), and/or consciousing(s) with new meaning(s) and with new possibilization(s) of the world, of oneself, and of the sense of one's own adult eductions of *person* within the world.

A theory of adult learning consistent with this definition would have to offer a clear account of all of the key notions in the definition (of which there are many, and all are laid out in Stanage, 1987). When this is done the account could be turned around, and one could then say that the definition flows from the theory itself.

The contents of both of these points are the products of what Charles Sanders Peirce, as phenomenologist, (1839–1914, and as the founder of pragmatism, the only truly indigenous American movement in philosophy) called abductive thinking. He claimed that abductive thinking is quite different from inductive and deductive thinking. More importantly, Peirce claimed that abductive thinking was much more important than either of them since it is only through abductive thinking that the most seminal and crucial hunches, ideas, and hypotheses can emerge.

Finally, you can now see how it is that my presentation of adult education as postmodern adult education is a thought experiment, a research project in the mode of abductive reasoning. Has it helped you, in your own self-reflections to see adult education with new eyes, with new meaning and new values, as transformative and empowering?

NOTES AND REFERENCES

Collingwood, R. G., 1940. *An Essay on Metaphysics*, Oxford: The Clarendon Press.

Graff, Gerald (1984). The Myth of the Postmodernist Breakthrough. In Manfred Putz and Peter Freese (Eds), *Postmodernism in American Literature* (pp. 37–58). Darmstadt, Thesen Verlag Vowinckel and Co. Graff's analysis of some essential features of postmodernism is rich, incisive, and trenchant. He concludes, for example: "A radical movement in art and culture forfeits its radicalism and impoverishes itself to the degree that it turns its back on what is valid and potentially living in the critical and moral traditions of humanism. In a society increasingly irrational and barbaric, to regard the attack on reason and objectivity as the basis of our radicalism is to perpetuate the nightmare we want to escape" (p. 58).

Lyotard, Jean-Fracois, 1979, 1984. *The Postmodern Condition: A Report on Knowledge*, Minneapolis: University of Minnesota Press.

Ohlinger, John, 1989. And the Truth Shall Make You Laugh. *Adult and Continuing Education Today*, Vol. XIX, Number 14, July 17, 1989.

Stanage, Sherman M., 1987. *Adult Education and Phenomenological Research: New Directions for Theory, Practice, and Research*. Malabar, Florida: Robert E. Krieger Publishing Company.

Stanage, Sherman M., 1989. Freire and Phenomenology: *person*, Praxis, and Education for Infinite Tasks. An unpublished paper presented during the Critical Theory Preconference to the 30th Annual Adult Education Research Conference at the University of Wisconsin, Madison, WI, April 26–30, 1989.

R. W. K. Paterson (1933–   ) has advanced degrees in education and philosophy from the University of St. Andrews in England. He has held faculty positions at Bromsgrove College of Further Education, University of Manchester, Holly Royale College, and he is currently in the Department of Adult Education at the University of Hull in Hull, England, where he has taught since 1962.

A frequent contributor to the British journals *Adult Education* and *Studies in Adult Education*, Paterson is interested in existentialism, phenomenology, and more recently, psychical research. His major work, *Values, Education and the Adult*, published in 1979, is a major contribution to the philosophy of adult education. In this book, Paterson presents a well-reasoned analysis of many concepts, issues, and questions central to adult education. Paterson analyzes the terms "adult," "adult education," "teaching," "learning," and "educational objectives." He also explores the relationship of adult education to the society in which it takes place, the "right" of adults to education, and the social relevance of adult education. Like his contemporary, K. H. Lawson, Paterson argues that adult education must be a value-free, neutral activity, one that is committed to knowledge and truth rather than to social causes.

In the following selection, Paterson analyzes the concept of "adult." He argues that adulthood is a normative concept based on chronological age and status in society. Adults have certain rights and responsibilities not afforded children. Even though an adult may not be morally or emotionally mature, others can *expect* adults to be mature under the assumption that adults have had time to become mature. "Adults are adults," Paterson concludes, "because they are older than children."

R. W. K. PATERSON

25 Adulthood and Education

It is significant that we distinguish adult education from other forms of educational provision by reference to the nature of its clients. Primary, secondary, further, and higher education are differentiated from one another in terms of notional stages in the unfolding of the educational enterprise. Technical, physical, and moral education are differentiated from one another and from legal or medical education in terms of their distinctive contents and objectives. But, if nomenclature is any guide, the vast assortment of activities which are collectively styled 'adult education' derive whatever common

character they have from the character of the clients, actual
and potential, on whose behalf they are initiated. Naturally,
within this heterogeneous collection of activities different
levels of operation are recognized, and the multitude of programmes of study evince a multitude of distinguishable objectives and spheres of concern. However, if for most purposes we
marshal this astonishing miscellany of activities under the
generic name of 'adult education', this is solely because they
are felt to partake of a common identity rooted in the
characteristic needs, claims, and circumstances of adults as a
distinct genus of educational beneficiaries. To elucidate the
concept of 'adult education', then, we require to elucidate the
concept of an 'adult'.

This is by no means as straightforward as it may seem.
We use the term 'adult', as noun or as adjective, in different
contexts with differing overtones and emphases. Thus, when
an anthropologist speaks of the average height and weight of
the adults in some society, he does so in a context where the
accent is on processes of physical growth and development.
When a critic refers to an adult novel or play, he is claiming
that it solicits a certain maturity of response from the reader or
spectator. When a newspaper advertisement promises that a
forthcoming pantomime will be heartily enjoyed by adults, it
is acknowledging that the entertainment is principally devised
for the benefit of children. When a man tells his sixteen-year-
old son that he is not yet an adult, he may be reminding him
that some of his claims and expectations are inappropriate
because premature. And in a wide variety of contexts the term
'adult' is put to a wide variety of uses, with continuously changing implications and readily discernible shifts of emphasis.

Common to all these uses, of course, is the focal contrast
of the adult with the child. What is adult is contrasted, in this
or that respect and for this or that purpose, with what is adoles-
cent, juvenile, or infantile. An adult has been a child but is no
longer one. Adulthood is a state into which he has passed, from
a state of childhood which he has quitted. His passage into
adulthood is not conceived as a bare movement through time,
however, for central to the concept of an adult is the idea that
this state is attained by a process of *growth*. Adults are what
children grow up to become. To be an adult is to have reached a

certain stage of development, and, moreover, to have reached a
stage which is thought of as in some sense final, an end-stage
of a process of development which confers meaning and direction on the earlier stages of the process. Within the state of
adulthood, as within the state of childhood, there may be
earlier and later phases, from young adulthood to senility, but
one does not pass from adulthood into some altogether distinct
and novel state, at least within the bounds of our natural lives.
'Second childhood' is a condition which only adults can suffer.
Once an adult, in short, always an adult.

Although in recognizing that someone is an adult we are
recognizing that he has reached a certain stage of development,
it does not follow that the concept of an adult is a straightfor-
wardly empirical concept. In saying that someone is an adult
we are not simply saying that his physical development is
complete, or that his mental capacities and attainments, his
qualities of character, and his social awareness and skill have
developed to some given degree, for we might say all this of a
precocious child. Indeed, we are not necessarily saying
anything about his degree of physical, mental, and social
development, for we acknowledge that many adults are
physically stunted, mentally retarded, or socially backward.
The stage of development which the adult has reached cannot
be equated with any particular stage of physical, mental, or
social development. In calling someone an 'adult' we are not
claiming that he has any one empirical characteristic or set of
empirical characteristics. We are not describing, however,
vaguely, his appearance, state of mind, or behaviour. In calling
someone an 'adult' we are rather ascribing to him a certain
status, a status which derives its significance from contrast
with the status of a child and which he gains only after relinquishing the status of a child. If adulthood represents an end-
stage of development, this is because it unalterably revokes the
previous status of the individual who has now attained
adulthood, and it can never itself be revoked in favour of any
higher status into which the individual may pass from
adulthood.

Now, the concept of 'status' (while it may need empirical
criteria for its correct application) is preeminently a *normative*
concept. It enshrines valuations, priorities, estimates of

regard. Enfolded within the concept of 'status' there are all kinds of prescriptions and prohibitions, licences and requirements. In particular, a person's status comprises the ethical requirement that he act in certain specific ways and be treated by others in certain specific ways—and indeed the precise specification of these ways in large measure yields the precise specification of the status he enjoys. To be an adult, then, is to possess a certain status, with inherent proprieties and forms of comportment, inherent obligations and rights. When we consider someone an adult, we consider that there are distinctive compliances, modes of respect, which he may rightfully demand of us, and that there are natural dispositions, qualities of concern, which we may rightfully demand of him.

Among the various rights and duties of adults, there are some which have little direct relevance to the adult as a participant in education. A man has a duty to keep any promises he has made, and he has a right to choose his own friends, but it can hardly be claimed that the application of either of these principles seriously affects the scope and character of his educational needs and interests. There are other rights and duties of the adult which are of more direct relevance to his participation in education, but which he has in common with children and which therefore have no special implications for adult education in particular. It is in virtue of his general status as a moral agent, not in virtue of his special status as an adult, that he has a duty to tolerate the expression of opinions different from his own, and that he has a right to equality of consideration along with others.

However, inherent in the status of adult there are numerous valuations and requirements which do have considerable significance for the adult as a participant in education and which do not apply in anything like the same degree to children. Thus an adult is expected to take a full share in the tasks of society to which he belongs, and to bear some measure of responsibility for the internal life and external acts of his society. He is expected to play his part in actively bettering his society, in raising its quality of life and in making it a wiser and more just society. It is to the adult that we ascribe the duty of recognizing and caring for those things which are enduringly valuable in our civilization and in the natural environment, for we rightly believe that natural beauties and works of art, bodies of knowledge and insight, economic and technological advances, social institutions and freedoms, in short everything worthwhile that can be preserved and transmitted by intelligence and care is held by the present generation of mature men and women in trust for future generations. The adult, moreover, is in an important sense charged with caring for himself: we ascribe to him the duty to be mindful of his own deepest interests, to cultivate whatever talents he may possess, and to accept responsibility for his moral character and conduct and for the development of his qualities as a person.

The adult is also distinguished from the child by his enjoyment in high degree of various entitlements and prerogatives, many of which also have the greatest significance for his participation in education. An adult has a right to share in the making of decisions which affect his wellbeing. As a full member of the community, he has a right to share in the making of many decisions which affect the wellbeing of others, even when his own wellbeing is not directly involved. He is entitled to frame his life and conduct his personal affairs as he alone thinks fit, provided only that his obligations to others are met and that in his free initiatives he does not injure other men's legitimate interests or infringe their spheres of liberty. An adult is entitled to consult with whom he chooses, on whatever topics are of moment to him; he is entitled to seek opinions from whatever quarters he pleases, and to accept or ignore these according to his own free decision.

Unlike many of the 'rights' which are ascribed to children, the rights of adults are fully rights: they are discretionary claims, which he may choose to exercise or not to exercise according to his own unconstrained wishes and judgment. The fact that in some societies many adults are prevented from exercising their rights, and perhaps in addition absolved from performing some of the duties which rightly pertain to their status as adults, in no way affects the character or limits the scope of these rights and duties, which depend solely on certain properties inherent in the status of adulthood, not on the contingent circumstance of these proprieties being recognized. And the fact that in our own society individual adults may be debarred from exercising certain rights or exempted from performing certain duties, usually on grounds of incapacity, in no way diminishes their validity, which like the validity of all norms is always subject to a variety of relevant conditions being satisfied.

When we characterize someone as an 'adult', then, we are ascribing to him various prima facie rights and duties, which may in exceptional circumstances be rescinded but which are normally operative, just as a debtor may sometimes be released from his debts or a creditor denied his rights of recovery if good cause can be shown, although this by no means impairs the prima facie duties and rights inherent in the status of 'debtor' or 'creditor' as such. The proprieties which reside in the status of adult qua adult may and do lapse in individual cases, when they are overridden by more fundamental ethical considerations, but this does not in the slightest alter the general requirements which we hold to be intrinsic to the status of an adult as such.

On what grounds, however, do we feel it necessary to distinguish and identify these properties, these rights and duties, which constitute the status of the adult? We distinguish some men as 'debtors' and others as 'creditors' in virtue of an actual economic relationship, involving the objective exchange of money, goods, or services, and we identify individual debtors and creditors by reference to observable transactions which have taken place, from which their status as 'creditors' or 'debtors' flows. By reference to what actual characteristics do we distinguish those individuals on whom we correctly confer the status of 'adult'? In virtue of what objective qualities or relationships do we correctly ascribe to some human beings, but not to others, those rights and duties which are intrinsic to 'adulthood'?

Adults are not held to be adults because they have larger bodies than children, or because they have greater intelligence, since this is often not in fact the case. Nor is it because their bodies and intelligences have ceased developing: physical and intellectual growth commonly ceases before adulthood is reached, and in any case we would continue to consider someone aged thirty or forty an adult even if at that age he made a belated spurt of physical or intellectual development. It is not because a man has wider knowledge than a child that he is considered to be an adult, for some children are more knowledgeable than some adults. Nor is it because he makes a more tangible contribution to society: elderly or disabled adults make little or no tangible contribution to society, while some adolescents may be doing hard and dangerous work or performing essential services.

Perhaps, since adulthood is a status, with inherent ethical requirements, we should expect to locate the criteria justifying the conferment of this status a little nearer to the realm of the ethical. Perhaps our judgment that someone is an adult rests on our judgment that he possesses certain moral qualities, certain qualities of character, which coalesce to form a distinctive body of claims to adult status: to evince such qualities as prudence, self-control, patience, fortitude, tolerance, and objectivity, is, we might think, to have good claims to the dignity of adulthood. Kindred to these moral qualities there are deeply personal qualities which have an undeniable cognitive dimension but which are intimately interwoven with the individual's capacities for emotion and feeling—mature human insight, the perceptiveness of compassion, the imaginative understanding of another's situation, an unembarrassed responsiveness to the needs of others, a capacity for forming meaningful, stable, and realistic relationships: we might well judge that such personal qualities of balanced concern and involvement, when manifested in sufficient degree, constitute excellent grounds for the ascription of adulthood. No doubt our recognition of these moral qualities and personal capacities depends in part on valuations, appraisals, normative judgments, but equally there is no doubt that these qualities and capacities are objective characteristics discernible in the observable character and conduct of actual men and women. We might well want to take into account, also, the network of responsibilites—in the family, in the community, at work—which the individual has undertaken to carry, for we expect an adult to be able and willing to shoulder many different types of responsibility and to discharge them efficiently and without fuss. Finally, we might consider that an individual's title to adulthood rests in part on his length and breadth of experience, not in the sense of a mere catalogue of passively received impressions, but 'experience' in the sense of actively lived experience which has refined and at the same time strengthened the individual's relations with the world and with his fellows.

The trouble is that very many people who are unquestionably adults do not come anywhere near to satisfying these criteria. Many adults are foolish, weak, impulsive, self-deluding, or egotistical, and by comparison with many adolescents and even quite young children their qualities of character are meagre and inglorious. By the side of some perceptive and sympathetic children, who may show surprising quickness and depth of understanding, many adults appear emotionally obtuse, lacking in insight and sensitivity, and neither self-aware enough nor self-forgetful enough to make real connections with other people. They may shrink from responsibility, or prove woefully inadequate to discharge the responsibilities they have reluctantly incurred. And in too many cases age may not even bring instructive experience, but merely an increasingly mute mass of repetitive and undifferentiated commonplaces.

Yet we are surely right in surmising that the status of adulthood is very closely connected with these moral qualities and personal capacities, with the acceptance of responsibilities and the building-up of a meaningful body of experience. It is not so much that an adult must *actually possess* attributes and competencies of these various kinds. It is rather that an adult is someone whom we may *justifiably presume* to possess them. If we treat our neighbour as an adult, with the rights and duties intrinsic to that status, this is because we feel entitled to presume, for example, that in appropriate circumstances he will show restraint and impartiality, concern and understanding in some sufficient degree, and that he will accept a certain amount of responsibility and prove capable of drawing on his relevant experience with some measure of sense and skill. We do not normally feel entitled to presume any such attributes and competencies on the part of our neighbour's young child. Unless we have reasons to the contrary, that is, we shall form one set of expectations of the father and a quite different—and much more limited—set of expectations of the child. In the event, we may be disappointed in the father and pleasantly surprised by the child, but unless there are good reasons obviously annulling our original expectations of the father (an exonerating handicap, for example, or perhaps his exceptionally adverse circumstances) we shall feel and be *justifiably* disappointed in him. We do have justifiable presumptions concerning the attributes and competencies of different categories of people, and although we are often disappointed or surprised in individual cases, those cases in which our disappointment or surprise is justifiable at least demonstrate the justice if not the accuracy of our original presumptions. We may in the event be mistaken about individual soldiers, policemen, or doctors, but we are justified in expecting soldiers to be alert and courageous, policemen to be helpful and fair-minded, and doctors to be skilled and solicitous, all in their characteristic ways and in appropriate degrees. Similarly, we are justified in expecting a very much larger category of people to exhibit certain very basic moral and personal attributes and competencies, and it is because these very basic expectations are just (whether in individual cases they are accurate or not) that we are justified in ascribing to this large and assorted body of people all the rights and duties which are instrinsic to the status of adulthood.

An adult, then, may not *be* morally and emotionally mature, but we are entitled to expect him to be so, and he is an adult because he is a rightful object of such expectations. We are still left, however, with the unanswered question: on what *grounds* are we entitled to form these expectations of one individual, the father, but not of another, the child?

The answer to this question is, I think, deceptively obvious. It is, quite simply, because the father is older than the child. Adults are adults, in the last analysis, because they are older than children. For legislative purposes, of course, most modern states use age as the criterion for distinguishing adults from children, and it might seem as if age is used merely because it is administratively the easiest criterion to apply on a large scale though in itself purely arbitrary as a criterion of adulthood. This would be erroneous, however. In point of fact, age is not administratively the easiest of criteria to apply (height would be considerably easier), and while no doubt there is a margin of arbitrariness in adopting a particular age for the criterion of adulthood and applying it right across the population, the choice of age as such is completely in tune with what we intuitively perceive to be the permanent human realities underlying and underwriting the concept of an adult. If it is on grounds of age that we rightly form one set of expectations of the father and a different, more limited, and less demanding set of expectations of his son, ascribing to one the status of adult and to the other the status of child, this is because we correctly deem their difference of age to have *in itself* the greatest ethical and existential relevance.

Of course, we do in fact observe a fairly close correlation between a persons's age and his degree of actual moral and emotional maturity, and our general experience that older people do in fact tend to be in varying degrees more mature leads us to 'expect' them to be more mature in that purely descriptive sense of 'expect' in which we expect it to snow in January. However, there is a normative sense of 'expect', the sense in which even known liars are expected to tell the truth and are only blamed because we rightly expect them to do what we anticipate they will probably not in fact do; and it is above all in this normative sense that we expect moral and emotional maturity from older people, justifiably ascribing to them the status of adults in this legitimate expectation. In and of itself, we feel, age *ought* to have recruited an appropriate combination of those moral and personal attributes and competencies in presumption of which we consider older people to merit the status of adulthood with all its intrinsic proprieties.

There is nothing arbitrary or paradoxical in our judgment that a persons's age, the mere fact that a certain period of time has elapsed since his birth, should of itself generate fresh dimensions of moral identity. In human life the mere passage of time may create new situations, making new demands and offering changed potentialities. As conscious selves, we are aware of our being as mediated by time, we are aware of our being as inescapably rooted in time, and it is across time that we necessarily seize the meaning of any human eventuality or project. Brute objects, physical things, may be in time, but there is no time *for* them. Whether changing or unchanging, things simply are; it is persons who *act*, and in acting announce their consciousness of temporal transition. A conscious self, a person, is a fount of action as well as a centre of consciousness, and of course consciousness itself is essentially an activity, an ongoing and ceaseless manifold of conscious acts. While a wholly static and eternally unchanging physical universe is perhaps conceivable, the irruption of consciousness into such a universe would necessarily import a principle of change merely by virtue of the successive (and consciously successive) acts of the scrutinizing consciousness. The mode of existence of conscious selves, personal existence, is fraught with the recognition of its own temporality, and it is across the horizon of our temporality that we grasp and disclose ourselves and the world. The passage of time both encloses and liberates us; time limits as it frees; but in all its workings it is a primordial and overarching condition of human existence.

A person's age states his relationship to time. It states that a certain time has elapsed since his birth and that the time of his death is in the measure nearer. Only with the passage of time can there come use, habituation, inurement, for it takes time to get used to anything, and it takes the arriving consciousness time to get used to the structures and possibilites of existence. Only with the passage of time can there come real urgency, deepening seriousness, more intense concern, for it is as the hour of departure wings nearer that we become conscious of necessarily lessening opportunities and unavoidably altering priorities, and as the time remaining grows shorter we become increasingly alert to what remains of significance and value.

Quite apart from the changing circumstances it brings in its train, then, the mere passage of time in itself is of central importance to the life of a conscious being, critically affecting our key valuations and transforming our attitudes and expectations at their focal points. Thus we consider the postponement of a benefit to be in itself a deprivation, and the deferment of an evil to be in itself a grace. The duration of a friendship or of any relationship profoundly affects its inner quality, for better or worse. The length of a man's service, his seniority, confers upon him changing rights and responsibilities. Priority in time may establish moral entitlement, as in the principles of 'first come, first served' and the 'right of the first occupant'. We see periods of time as requiring division and distribution on principles of justice, as when we judge that a man has enjoyed some benefit for long enough and it is time he made way for others. The passage of time may in turn be a factor influencing the application of other principles of justice, as when the lapse of a considerable time between an offence and its punishment is adduced as a ground for merciful treatment. We consider the attainment of a great age—not only in human beings but also in the case of many inanimate objects, such as buildings or manuscripts—to be a proper theme of wonder, awe, reverence. And in general the past, qua past, comes before us as a dimension with which we are forced to come to terms; while we are conscious of the future, qua future, as the indefinite dimension which awaits us but which will not await us indefinitely.

Thus there is nothing arbitrary or paradoxical in our judgment that a persons's age, his objective relationship to time, of itself engenders objective presumptions of moral and emotional maturity. If a child's transition to adulthood is always more than a bare movement through time, this is because the mere passage of time, the very process of growing older, in itself creates new validities and altered expectations. Whereas we rightly expect a man of forty to display qualities of prudence, self-control, and perseverance, it would be quite unfair to expect a boy of ten to possess these qualities in anything like the same measure. We are entitled to expect people above a certain age to show tact and self-awareness in personal relations, and to respond with understanding to the emotional needs of others. We are entitled to expect them to assume a measure of responsibility in several different spheres. We are entitled to expect them to be in possession of an adequate body of experience, ready to use it, and capable of modifying and extending it. There is, in short, a wide but recognizable spectrum of moral qualities and personal capacities, habits of outlook and modes of conduct, which we consider to be distinctive of 'maturity' because we consider that the passage of time, and therefore the attainment of a certain age, is peculiarly relevant to the degree and manner in which a person may be expected to exhibit them. After reaching a certain age, a person who fails to show a sufficient degree of mental, moral, and emotional maturity is rightly regarded as blameworthy (unless there are exonerating circumstances), for we rightly judge that a person of this age *ought* to be thinking, feeling, and acting in ways appropriate to his age.

It is, then, because we may justifiably presume in someone of a certain age a sufficient measure of those attributes and competencies distinctive of maturity that we correctly ascribe to him the various rights and responsibilities which constitute the status of 'adulthood'. To say that someone is an adult is to say that he is entitled, for example, to a wide-ranging freedom of lifestyle and to a full participation in the taking of social decisions; and it is also to say that he is obliged, among other things, to be mindful of his own deepest interests and to carry a full share of the burdens involved in conducting society and transmitting its benefits. His adulthood consists in his full enjoyment of such rights and his full subjection to such responsibilities. Those people (in most societies, the large majority) to whom we ascribe the status of adults may and do evince the widest possible variety of intellectual gifts, physical powers, character traits, beliefs, tastes, and habits. But we correctly deem them to be adults because, in virtue of their age, we are justified in requiring them to evince the basic qualities of maturity. Adults are not necessarily mature. But they are supposed to be mature, and it is on this necessary supposition that their adulthood justifiably rests.

Maurice L. Monette (1946–   ) has graduate degrees reflecting scholarly interests in philosophy, religion, and adult education. In addition to an M.A. in liturgy, and an M.Div. in theology, Monette has two masters in adult education (Boston University, Columbia University), and an Ed.D. in adult education from Teachers College, Columbia University. Monette is also a Roman Catholic priest and a linguist, having learned five languages (French, Spanish, Portuguese, Latin, Greek) in the course of his studies.

Most of his professional experiences have been in the area of religious education. He has been a director of religious education for churches in Colorado and Massachusetts, as well as a consultant in religious education in New York and Illinois. More recently, he has been director of the Catechetical and Pastoral Institute of Loyola University in New Orleans, Louisiana, associate professor of religious education at Loyola, visiting associate professor at Catholic University, and a staff member of the Center of Concern in Washington, D.C.

While most of his publications are in the area of religion and religious education, his several articles in *Adult Education* represent an important contribution to philosophical thinking in adult education. Monette's approach is that of analytic philosophy, a value-free philosophical activity in which language is analyzed in order to bring conceptual clarity to policy and practice. In "The Concept of Educational Need: An Analysis of Selected Literature," Monette analyzes the concept of "need" as it is used in adult education. The uses of need as they appear in the literature can be categorized as basic human needs, felt and expressed needs, normative needs, and comparative needs.

MAURICE L. MONETTE

26 The Concept Of Educational Need: An Analysis of Selected Literature

ABSTRACT

This study explores the concept of need in adult education literature in view of assessing its usefulness for practitioners and clarifying the issues which remain to be debated by researchers and practitoners alike. Several major uses of the term need are highlighted and McKinley's classification of diagnostic models summarized. The following key issues are raised and discussed: whether need refers properly to both individuals and systems; who can best perceive need; the problem of shifting needs; and the critical relationship between needs and the operational philosophy of an institution. It is concluded that need assessment literature stresses technological at the expense of philosophical and normative considerations: that need assessment based solely on felt needs or on prescriptive needs is generally ineffective; and that need assessment procedure generally favors adjustment and not education for transformation.

INTRODUCTION

Among the concepts most widely used in the literature of adult education, the concept of need undoubtedly ranks high. Its popularity has been traced to Dewey by way of Bergevin and Lindeman (3:210). Its current favor, as London (17) notes, may be due in large part to the predominance of the Tyler (23) rationale in curriculum theory. In any case, this reviewer's observations concur with the opinion (3:210) that "much of the popular thinking about needs has been rather fuzzy." This review of the literature is an attempt to highlight the major uses of the term need in order to assess its usefulness for practitioners and to clarify the issues which remain to be debated by researchers and practitioners alike.

This review is based on a computer search of ERIC materials,[1] a review of major texts in the field (4) (10) (13) (22), and a survey of articles published in *Adult Education*. An effort was made to exhaust every publication which has dealt with need in adult education. A vast amount of literature was uncovered. Much of it was repetitive. Only the most salient contributions are discussed here.

[1] *The following descriptors were used and retrieved 330 accession numbers: (Achievement Need or Need Gratification or Status Need or Educational Needs or Financial Needs or Health Needs or Individual Needs or Information Needs or Psychological Needs or Needs or Self Concept or Self Esteem or Interests or Educational Interest or Interest Research or Interest Scales or Interest Tests or Personal Interests or Reading Interests or Student Interests or Vocational Interests or Hobbies or Curiosity or Student Motivation or Recreational Activities or Role Conflict or Role Perception or Developmental Tasks) and (Adult Education Programs or Adult Students or Adult Learning or Adult Vocational Education or Professional Continuing Education.)*

The key issues around the concept of need will be developed by way of an overview of major definitions of the term and a classification of assessment models. Subsequently, the following will be discussed at length: whether need refers properly to both individuals and systems; who best perceives need; the problem of shifting needs; and the crucial relationship between needs and operational philosophy.

DEFINITIONS OF THE TERM NEED

The implicit and explicit definitions of the term need in adult education literature may be sifted into four major categories: basic human needs, felt and expressed needs, normative needs, comparative needs and variant uses of the term. Each of these will be explicated in order to highlight key issues around the concept of need.

In the first sense, the term need indicates a deficient state that initiates a motive on the part of an individual or a non-observable or inferred bio-psychological state rather similar to a "drive." This condition may be understood as a tension state of some kind which causes gratification-seeking behavior. Need in this sense denotes an innate, unlearned condition which is "natural" to all. Thus, when Maslow (18) speaks of a need for security he is using this construct to help explain why most people seek personal safety and protection. This conception of need is subject to much controversy. Evidence for such covert tension states varies from person to person and from society to society. As James points out (11:19), such needs of themselves do not preclude any particular form of satisfaction: "The society in which an individual lives must add to the need a value which indicates its avenue of satisfaction." There mere existence of such a need, innate (security) or acquired (occupational achievement), in no way lessens the educator's task of goal delineation and selection. In the end, the vague, general and debatable nature of basic human needs does not facilitate the educational and ethical decisions which the educator must make.

The term need is most commonly used in the sense of an individual "want" or "desire" or "felt need," for example, a person's need to learn woodworking. In this context, need suggests a means of gratification (for example, a course in woodworking) and implies an ultimate goal (for example, "to qualify for employment as a carpenter"). A course in woodworking is appropriate for the learner inasmuch as it is instrumental in achieving the desired end. Although the demand for such a course clearly indicates the task of the educator, a cafeteria-type program based on "felt needs" does not obviate the necessity of his making value judgments. The educator must weigh the merit of wants, especially when they range away from practical skills toward human relations kinds of categories. Providing a course in strategies for overthrowing the government might require some justification. The educator must also choose which wants among many and by what means they are to be met. This issue will bear more discussion later. The want or felt need alone is an inadequate measure of real need in that it is limited by the perceptions of individuals, that is, their awareness of services available, their own self-awareness, and their willingness to depend on services. The felt need can also be inflated by those who request a service without really needing it. Furthermore, a felt need may or may not be expressed in terms of a demand for services. When expressed, a felt need can be taken as a measure of unmet need. However, waiting lists for a service are generally considered poor measures of real need.

A need may be called normative when it constitutes a deficiency or gap between a "desirable" standard and the standard that actually exists. The individual or group that falls short of the desirable standard is said to be in need. In a training program for teachers, for instance, one might speak of a need for knowledge about educational psychology. A normative need like this one is not absolute. It may not necessarily correspond with need identified by other standards. Standards set by various experts may be conflicting. That someone is in need is not a simple empirical fact, but rather a value judgment entailing three propositions: namely, that someone is in a given state, that this state is incompatible with the norms held by some group or by society, and that therefore the state of that someone should be changed. The value of such a need is instrumental in terms of the criteria set by a particular group or society. The value orientation of the educator may influence the normative definition of need insofar as the educator must judge the amount of resources to be devoted to meeting the need and whether or not the available resources can solve the problem. Evidently, normative standards also change with time depending on developments in knowledge and changes in the values of society.

Need is also measured by comparing the characteristics of those in receipt of a service with others who are not. If these others exhibit the same characteristics and are not receiving the service, they are said to be in need. Standardized provison, however, may still not correspond with need. The question of what level of supply is adequate remains to be answered. Comparative need, by itself, is not an adequate measure of real need.

Other variants of the term are in use. Needs in program planning may be called general or specific depending on whether they refer to a comprehensive program or to a specific learning activity. Both of these may further be distinguished (13:123) as operational or process needs (e.g., budget requirements, space and time considerations, learning materials) or as educational or learning needs (e.g., skill in woodworking or knowledge about U. S. foreign policy). Generally, need assessment is concerned with learning needs. Labeling a need as educational implies that it is capable of being satisfied by means of a learning experience which can provide appropriate knowledge, skills or attitudes.

There is yet another use of need that should be mentioned. The term is very often encountered in the form of a slogan. Usefully vague, it may appeal to program planners responsible for formulating policy, to the educator defending a certain program or a particular approach, or to someone called upon to inspire commitment (e.g., "Our programs meet the needs of people"). To be sure, slogans do have their place, but it is important to distinguish the slogan use of "need" language from its more analytic uses.

DIAGNOSTIC MODELS

Precise meaning of the term need is blurred both by the confusing variety of settings in which it is used and by the plethora of need assessment procedures suggested in the literature. Happily, a succinct and inclusive classification of diagnostic models has been proposed by McKinley (19). He divides existing models into three "families," the first two pertaining to the individual and the third pertaining to systems (i.e., societies, communities, institutions and sub-systems of these).

Mass approaches to identifying self-fulfillment needs are what McKinley calls Individual Self-Fulfillment Models. These include random appeal and selective appeal models. The first of these refers to efforts aimed at discovering the needs (usually defined as interests or wants) of individuals in a community which are potent enough to attract them to educational activities and to make a program financially self-supporting. The appeal to learners is on the basis of filling individual needs, not on the basis of improving the performance of the community as a system. The product of such a diagnosis is the cafeteria-type program often sponsored by educational institutions with continuing education programs. The second model in this family, selective appeal, focuses on the presumed needs of a known segment of the population, e.g., functional illiterates, women, retirees. Such programs are generally not based on local diagnosis, but rather on research data, packaged materials, and program formats already tested with the specialized population. McKinley cites two of the more systematic diagnostic approaches in this area of programming: Hertling's (9) adaptation of marketing techniques and Hand's (8) three community study approaches.

Individual Appraisal Models are those in which the clients are usually consciously involved in determining their own learning needs, either collaboratively or non-collaboratively. Collaborative models include both one-to-one approaches (as between client and counselor) and group approaches. The self-appraisal model is non-collaborative diagnosis, although the solitary learner may choose to use scales and other instrumented exercises, or a group setting (as in value clarification), or performance analysis techniques to determine training needs (sometimes also used collaboratively).

System Discrepancy Models are those used to discover the educational needs of social systems. These are termed discrepancy models because they assume or try to identify the gaps between what is and what ought to be in a given system. They aim either at solving system problems or at attaining some desired specified end-state. The first type is designated as the problem-need model and the second as the goal-identification model. The problem-need model of diagnosis leads to the development of programs that are remedial in nature, since educational needs, and therefore the derived educational objectives, are related directly to diagnosed difficulties in the client system. The goal-identification model results in an educational program with a general improvement thrust rather than a specific remedial focus. Bypassing the needs terminology of the problem-need model (19:77), "it assumes that educational objectives which are carefully derived from the official goals of the client system, will reflect desired learning outcomes that some educators would term 'needs'."

KEY ISSUES

As noted above, much of the fuzziness around the term need seems to be due to its indiscriminate application to society, communities, institutions, and groups, as well as to individuals. Knowles (13:91), for example, refers to "three types of need," namely those of individuals, of organizations or institutions, and those of the community or society at large. Knox (14:3), on the other hand, prefers to use terms like "social problems, or goals, or dislocations, or trends or even situational imperatives" when referring to societies or communities. The question before us is whether the term might properly refer to one reality under different manifestations or to more than one reality. The term will be examined first as applied to indiviudals and then as applied to social systems (as defined above).

When applied to individuals, need is used in two senses: on the one hand it is used interchangeably with "want" or "desire" and is often called "felt need," implying intentionality. The term interest is often used interchangeably with need or "felt need" in this sense, although it is clearer that an interest is best known by the individual. Generally the term interest does not cause confusion since it is used in reference to one's curiosity, enjoyment or leisurely pursuits (15).

On the other hand, the term need may refer to some lack in the individual, a gap in knowledge, attitude or skill measured according to some objective criterion. In contrast to the felt need, this concept is often called "real need"—"real" apparently indicates that some outside observer is utilizing some criteria which are not necessarily the individual's.

These specialized uses of the term need (i.e., felt and real) have emerged from the debate over the question of who can best assess the needs of the adult learner. As Knox (14:5) points out, some educators believe that a need is a need only when it is recognized by the potential learner as a need, thereby providing motivation to close the gap. Others he says, hold that the major step in problem solving is the recognition of an existing problem, so that the most pressing needs that people have are ones that are better recognized by others. Hence come the specialized uses of need: the adjective "real" emphasizes the fact that the lack really, objectively exists, that it is not only thought to exist. Akin to the meaning of interest, the "felt need" is conceived as a conscious desire. The adult learner is said to have "real" needs of which he or she may not be aware. Part of the learning process, therefore, ought to involve the testing of felt needs so as to uncover the real needs. The term "sympotomatic," although closely related to "felt," is used to describe that need which is considered real by a person but in actuality is only a manifestation or symptom of a deeper, real need (2).

The question of who can best determine an individual's needs does not require an either/or answer. The perspectives of both the adult learner and others can help identify the gap. Individuals often have a wealth of information and understanding concerning their needs. Because learning is essentially an internal process, only learners themselves can, in the end, decide to learn and to act upon their learnings. Persons other than the adult learner (program planners, experts) can in some cases specify objective standards to which individuals can compare themselves in order to determine the nature and magnitude of their need. Where such standards are absent or minimal, facilitators who are knowledgeable in a given area might supplement or even provide alternative reference points. Learners may also be helped to anticipate some learning needs that could arise in the future as a result of social trends or changes in the life-cycle.

Parenthetically, the anticipation of possible needs raises an important point. None of the authors mentioned deals adequately with the problem of the shifting character of needs and goals which Mezirow points to in "Program Analysis and Evaluation: An Alternative Approach":

> When education is interpreted as an independent variable, it almost always violates the requirement of homogeneity, constancy and disparateness. Amount, type and quality of learning resulting from student interaction, changes in instructional pace, style, tempo, and goals, and the relationship and ordering of significant elements within this evolving process are only in part predictable. [21]

Needs often change rapidly, even during educational programs. Most of the literature suggests that the need-assessment process ought to be continuous or that evaluation should take place at regular intervals during a program. However, the same literature [13] [22] [23] also advocates the use of behavioral objectives more as prescriptions than as heuristic devices, thereby setting serious limits on the possibility of on-going assessment of needs. A more dynamic, change-oriented definition of needs and goals may be required. Perhaps a need-assessment procedure can be explicated from the alternative model of evaluation suggested in the aforementioned article. In any case, this is another area of needed research.

To return to the question at hand, the adult educator is sometimes called upon to assess the "needs of systems" as such in order to improve system performance through some educational programs. It is immediately obvious that systems in themselves do not have needs in the sense of desires, wants, interests, or felt needs. The individuals within the system have such needs, some of which may be closely related to the performance of the system. Nevertheless, the needs of a system are not the sum total of the needs of the individuals within it [20]. Systems have problems as well as ends to which they are ordered; however, and this is what needs-talk masks, systems as such cannot be educated. Education properly refers only to individuals and only by analogy to systems. What a system is said to need is basically what an observer needs or wants for the given system. If the performance of a system is to improve, the *individuals* within the system must act upon themselves and upon their system.

Given the variety of uses to which it has been subjected, the concept of need may soon become worthless for program planners unless it is defined more narrowly. Perhaps educational need might be defined either from the point of view of the individual learner, as a desire/want/interest; or, from an external perspective, as an objectively determined deficiency in knowledge, skills, or attitudes.

VALUES AND THE CONCEPT OF NEED

This author found very little needs literature that deals with the question of values or the role of normative considerations. Knowles (13:125) refers to "a philosophic screen" in *The Modern Practice of Adult Education.* In the adult education literature, only James (11) (12) deals directly and at length with the issue.[2] Yet, as Atwood and Ellis (3:212) points out, "values are so inextricably involved with needs that some attention to them seems to be required." The importance of value considerations is most obvious when the educator is faced with the question of choosing among conflicting or contradictory needs which are to be met or the question of which needs should be dealt with among the nearly infinite number or the question of which course of action for meeting needs is to be selected. It becomes apparent that the concept of need has no meaning without a set of norms and that it is therefore impossible even to identify needs without them. The concept of need is an attractive one in adult education because it appears, by its straightforward appeal to empirically determined facts, to obviate the educator's responsibility for making value

[2]*In the curriculum and in the social work literature concerning need assessment, the question of values is approached by Archambault (1), Komisar (16), and Bradshaw (6) among others.*

judgments, thereby escaping arguments about values. As James concludes:

> Efforts to use "needs" to define goals frequently amount to an attempt by the educator to relieve himself of one of the duties assigned to him by society—which is to delineate and define goals of educational institutions. Such use of "needs" is a consequence of misinterpreting the nature of social learning and a misreading of the goal of educational leadership. (11:26)

Values are learned by social interaction and are shaped by society through many agents, one of whom is the educator. The voluntary nature of adult participation and the democratic ethos of our society complicate the role of adult educators. They cannot ride rough-shod over the values of adults even if these are judged ill-considered, and yet they must direct the traffic of values and ideas through educational programs and, at times, take stands that may oppose prevailing norms.

Needs literature often implies that diagnostic procedure is politically neutral, or that it must assume the values of the client system, or that the so-called self-fulfillment models are self-justifying. These assumptions are challenged by Freire's contention (7) that education is political, that is, that education is utilized either for individual adjustment to a given system or for the transformation of a system to the ends of the individuals involved. His point becomes apparent in the discussion about who is to determine "real needs." If it is assumed that the educator is the final arbiter of real need, does this not constitute an imposition of the educator's world view upon the learner? If it is assumed that needs assessment is solely the function of the educator, is this not a denial of the freedom and self-determination of the individual? Manipulation by the educator may be determined by the extent to which the educator justifies his teaching on the ground that this or that is "good" for the student, by the extent to which the student is allowed to participate in educational planning, and also by the extent to which the educator exposes his own assumptions and world-view, hence engaging himself in dialogue with the world-view of the students. The so-called individual-fulfillment procedures or the implementation of programs on the basis of felt needs can easily disguise subtle and perhaps unconscious manipulation on the part of the educator whereby cost-benefit or system-maintenance or the educator's personal preference becomes the sole criterion for the sponsorship of educational programs.

Manipulation is avoided neither by those adult educators who follow a line of adaptation to the felt needs of the learners and limit action to stimulating their demands, nor by those who disregard the aspirations of the learners by substituting more "desirable" learning objectives which have not come to the learners' attention. Freire (7:85, 109) suggests, as an alternative, that the educational process begin with the felt needs of the constituency, pose the meaning of these needs as a problem, and thereby promote dialogue between the educator and the learner to the end of mutual liberation.

The foregoing discussion around James's critique of the supposedly value-free use of "wants" to identify educational goals ought not to blur the necessary mutual relationship between needs and the functional philosophy of an institution, which includes that institution's goals. On one hand, the needs of the community are reflected in the goals of the institution if that institution is at all relevant. On the other hand, institutional goals influence the kind of need assessment done as well as the outcome once the needs have been analyzed and prioritized. Needs do not exist "out there," well-defined and obvious to any observer. The experience of need proper to individuals is mediated by the qualitatively and quantitatively limited perspective of the observer, including his goals, his philosophy, and his language. That explains the critical role of dialogical relationship between educators and their constituency and the resultant bankruptcy of a supposedly value-free concept of need.

CONCLUSION

Perhaps the literature on needs can best be summarized by the following statements pertaining to areas of needed inquiry and to implications for practice.

1. There appears to be general consensus in the literature on need that felt needs or wants *per se* are inadequate for defining educational objectives.

2. Likewise, prescriptive needs ("real needs") *per se* are inadequate to the task.

3. The various needs approaches to educational planning (felt needs, prescriptive needs, basic human needs, and combinations of these) are by no means value-free, that is, they do not obviate the educator's responsibility for making judgments of value.

4. In practice, need language is used both as slogan and as articulation of an approach to program development. It is important to distinguish one use from the other.

5. Need might best be defined from the educator's perspective, that is to say, as prescription. Because of its stress on intentionality, the term want might best replace need as motive.

6. The term need, except perhaps in slogan form, always implies more or less directly, some standard or valued state of affairs or certain social norms against which need is measured. Such standards are generally taken for granted and left unchallenged by need assessment procedures. Need assessment basically favors "adjustment."

7. The discussion of needs mostly revolves around technological or scientific questions. Rarely does it involve relevant philosophical questions in the realms of ontology, epistemology or axiology. No analysis which is purely scientific can determine the desirability or "need" of anything.

8. As Knowles and Knox both point out, needs must be sifted through the "philosophical screen" of the sponsoring institution for the defining of objectives. Given the paucity of attention to philosophical and normative considerations in adult education literature, and the critical role of both of these in any discussion of need, it is perhaps fair to say that the key variable in need assessment, as presently conceived in the literature if not in practice, is the strength of the educator's conviction of the acceptability of given needs.

REFERENCES

1. Archambault, Reginald D. "The Concept of Need and its Relation to Certain Aspects of Educational Theory." *Harvard Educational Review* 27, (Winter 1957): 38-62.

2. Atwood, H. Mason. "Diagnostic Procedure in Adult Education." *Community Teamwork* 19 (March April May 1967): 2ff.

3. Atwood, H. Mason, and Ellis, Joe. "The Concept of Need: An Analysis for Adult Education." *Adult Leadership* 19 (January 1971): 210-12, 244.

4. Bergevin, Paul. *A Philosophy for Adult Education.* New York: Seabury Press, 1967.

5. Blakeley, R. J. "Adult Education Needs a Philosophy and a Goal." *Adult Education* 3 (Fall 1952): 2-10.

6. Bradshaw, Jonathan. "The Concept of Social Need." *Ekistics 220* (March 1974): 184-87.

7. Freire, Paulo. *Pedagogy of the Oppressed.* New York: Herder and Herder, 1970.

8. Hand, Samuel. *Community Study as a Basis for Program Planning in Adult Education.* Tallahassee, Fla.: Florida State University, 1960.

9. Hertling, James. "Market Research: A Guide to Adult and Continuing Education Program Planning." *Adult Leadership* 21 (January 1973): 217-20.

10. Houle, Cyril. *The Design of Education.* San Francisco: Jossey-Bass, 1972.

11. James, Bernard. "Can 'Needs' Define Educational Goals?" *Adult Education* 7 (Fall, 1956): 19-26.

12. James, Bernard, and Montross, Harold W. "Focusing Group Goals." *Adult Education* 6 (Winter 1956): 95-100.

13. Knowles, Malcolm. *The Modern Practice of Adult Education.* New York: Association Press, 1970.

14. Knox, Alan B. "Critical Appraisal of the Needs of Adults for Educational Experiences as a Basis for Program Development." (Mimeographed.) Teachers College: Columbia University, 1968.

15. Knox, Alan B. "Interests and Adult Education." *Journal of Learning Disabilities* 1 (April 1968): 220-29.

16. Komisar, B. Paul. " 'Need' and the Needs-Curriculum ." In *Language and Concepts in Education*, pp. 24-42. Edited by B. O. Smith and R. H. Ennis. Chicago: Rand McNally and Co., 1961.

17. London, Jack. "Program Development in Adult Education." *Handbook of Adult Education in the United States*, pp. 65-81. Edited by Malcolm S. Knowles. Chicago: Adult Education Association of the U.S.A., 1960.

18. Maslow, Abraham. *Toward A Psychology of Being.* New York: D. Van Nostrand Company, 1968.

19. McKinley, John. "Perspectives on Diagnostics in Adult Education." *Viewpoints* (Indiana University) 49 (September 1973): 69-83.

20. McMahon, Ernest E. *Needs—Of People and Their Communities—and the Adult Educator.* Washington, D. C.: Adult Education Association of the U.S.A., 1970.

21. Mezirow, Jack. "Program Analysis and Evaluation: An Alternative Approach." *Literacy Discussion* 5 (Fall 1974).

22. Miller, Harry L. *Teaching and Learning in Adult Education.* New York: MacMillan, 1964.

23. Tyler, Ralph, *Basic Principles of Curriculum and Instruction.* Chicago: University of Chicago Press, 1950.

Kenneth Lawson (1928–   ), now retired, holds an honorary post as special professor in the Department of Adult Education, University of Nottingham, England.

After serving an apprenticeship in the aircraft industry during World War II followed by military service, he became a student at Ruskin College, Oxford in 1951. As an undergraduate at the University of Oxford, his first degree was in philosophy, politics and economics. He was later awarded a Ph.D. by the University of Nottingham where he was variously an administrative officer in the Department of Adult Education, warden of the University Adult Education Centre, and later, assistant director of the Department of Adult Education. He has taught extensively in diploma and higher degree courses in adult education and has published numerous papers and articles. His main book is *Philosophical Concepts and Values in Adult Education* (1979).

Having argued for a neutral concept of adult education, he now accepts that both the practice and the philosophy of adult education reflect dominant social and political philosophies and values. He is currently interested in the influence of liberal political theory as expressed by such writers as J. S. Mill, John Rawls, R. Nozick and R. Dworkin. He is interested in conceptual problems in adult education and in the implications of semantic theories of truth, relativism and postmodernism. He believes that the field of adult education is now too fragmented to permit the formulation of general theories.

In the following selection, "Equal Rights, Equal Opportunity and Equal Chance" from *Analysis and Ideology: Conceptual Essays on the Education of Adults*, (1982) Lawson argues that, while equality in education is an ideal condition, the concept itself is problematic since there is no such thing as equality in general. Without "particularization," that is, specification of the kinds of equality desired, and consideration of "what the term means, and what policies will make the idea a reality," he suggests that educational equality remains abstract and largely unachievable. Lawson discusses the concepts of equality, fairness and rights and their relationship to politics and resource distribution. He concludes that the serious issues related to equality in education "impinge upon the idea of the kind of society people want and educators too are expected, perhaps more than most, to be involved in the debate."

KENNETH LAWSON

27 Equal Rights, Equal Opportunity and Equal Chance

The frequently discussed issue of making special adult education provision for various 'disadvantaged' groups may be seen as evidence of a concern for fairness and justice. The various arguments put forward can be put into a context of a group of ideas associated with the concept of 'equality' and especially with the idea of 'equality of educational opportunity'. What this term means, and what policies will make the idea a reality, has been the subject of much debate, much of it in the context of schooling. Unless the discussion is rooted in specific examples, it remains abstract and removed from the making of policy, but even in theoretical terms, the idea of 'equality' has to be particularised. In this sense, 'equality' is rather like the idea of 'freedom'. Both terms generate strong emotional responses from most people and few are likely to deny explicitly that they are against either as an ideal, but what they are in favour of might be far from clear. 'Freedom' unspecified is virtually meaningless and political campaigning is usually intent upon securing particular freedoms. As rallying points, the banners of both 'freedom' and 'equality' have their uses, but with the latter, as with the former, we need to know and to specify the area of equality that we seek. It would seem that there is no such thing as 'equality' in a general unqualified sense. What this essay attempts, in the context of adult education, is to explore some of what might be called the 'logic' of the concept of 'equality' and to consider the implications in relation to the arguments in favour of special adult education provision.

EQUALITY AND FAIRNESS

It is a frequently made point that 'equality' is closely associated with thinking about 'fairness' and 'justice' and the beginning of a concern for equality might be found in an awareness that some state of affairs, such as the distribution of wealth, is unfair or unjust. There is a sense of dissatisfaction with distributive matters in relation to the 'goods' of society. Another area of concern might be with alleged inequalities of treatment by bureaucracies or before the law. The discussion, therefore, focuses on such things as the establishment of 'rights'.

Whatever the specific area of concern, the issues involved have to do with authority, power and frequently with resources. There is dissatisfaction with the manner in which these things are used, and persuasion and power are used in order to influence or bring about change. The framework, therefore, may be described as 'political', and this description may be used of both practical and theoretical considerations. Even when dealing with analysis of the concepts involved, we are dealing with issues that have a political importance.

EDUCATION AND POLITICS

This brings us to a consideration of 'equality' in relation to 'education' which is also a political matter. Changes are sought in the administration, organisation and perhaps also the purpose of educational institutions. There is a concern for such things as conditions of access, selection procedures, the allocation of resources and probably with the curriculum. The question of whether educators *per se* have any responsibility for these matters is immediately raised, and I find it difficult to argue that they are or should be neutral, because even if they defend what exists as being the embodiment of educational values and principles, they are taking a political stance. To say nothing in the face of change reduces educators to technicians concerned with teaching, but not with the framework

and its accompanying values in which they teach, or with what
they teach.

If the view is adopted that education is concerned with
'the worthwhile', it can be argued that logically and not merely
from contingent inclination, educators are politically committed. What is 'worthwhile' may or may not be self-evident, but
when defined, and an educator is sure of what is entailed by
the notion of 'education as the transmission of what is worthwhile', he then has a duty to defend it, if any impending
changes put the notion at risk. The duty follows from the commitment to the 'worthwhile'. If the idea that 'the development
of persons' is also built into the concept of 'educaiton' as a
worthwhile thing to do, then this seems to carry additionally
a commitment to ensuring fairness of treatment to all persons.
Moreover, the development of one person cannot be conceived
apart from relationships with others, therefore the consideration of such things as fairness seems to be logically entailed.
This does not necessarily make every educator an egalitarian,
but it does seem to give them a responsibility for ensuring
that everyone shall be dealt with as fairly as possible, and this
on occasion could involve considering equalities and inequalities. On this view educators must make judgements on a range
of social, ethical and political issues, and they cannot take ref-
uge in matters relating only to knowledge.

FAIRNESS AND RIGHTS

The notion of 'fairness' and the concept of 'rights' are
interrelated ideas used when considering the distribution of
society's 'goods'. If we discover that someone has received a
'prize' by cheating, we are entitled to say that he has no right
to it and that in receiving it, he is being unfair to others who
have observed the rules. Those who have observed the rules
may be said 'in fairness' to have a right to certain things which
the rules of the game entitle them to. A right is an entitlement
which is specified is some way, either as part of a moral code
or a legal code. It is seen as 'fair' or 'just' that people are given
what they are entitled to. Those who uphold the system have
a duty to ensure that no entitlement is unreasonably withheld.

The concept of a 'right' presupposes acceptance of the ideas of fairness and justice in dealing with the administration of rights. At the same time, we can use the concept of a 'right' to justify or explain why we should be fair to people, and both terms have to be presupposed in systems of rules and laws. In such systems, people are deemed to have a right to fair treatment.

This group of ideas provides a starting point from which to analyse the idea of 'equality of educational opportunity', which is derived from a moral and political judgement that people have a right to education. Such judgements form part of the total 'package' of entitlements within a given society.

Given that there is a law which specifies that all citizens over a certain age have a right to education, it might be asked whether this means an equal right. We say, in everyday speech, such things as 'people have (or should have) an equal right to health, freedom and education', but it can be argued, as by Mary Warnock[1] that the creation of a right in itself confers that right equally upon all those upon whom the right is conferred. The notion of 'rights' includes or presupposes the idea of 'equality'. If we wish to exclude any individual of group of individuals, that is to say if we wish to deny them equality of treatment, we exclude them from the right which has been created. Thus that we could say that although everyone has a moral right to health, only those who hold a British passport have a right of access to the British National Health Service.

The specification of 'equality' becomes meaningful when we wish to legislate for the distribution of whatever 'goods' are involved or to legislate for the manner in which people shall be treated. Thus, in wartime, it might be said that everyone has a right to an adequate diet within the limit of available food supplies. It is then a further question whether the actual ration of food shall be the same (equal) for everyone. In the event, there might be a larger ration for manual workers and a smaller one for sedentary workers. Children and nursing mothers might be allowed a ration which contains more calcium, and a whole range of similar distinctions could be made. Each decision of this kind recognises the existence of the basic right but there are legitimate differences in the allocation and distribution of food.

In education, similar issues are involved, and as Mary Warnock also shows, the establishment of a right to education has to be accompanied by further rules or clauses which specify whether or not there is also to be a right to an equal education.[2] As in the case of wartime rations, various arguments may be adduced on the basis of which the 'distribution' of education can be planned, and both quantitative and qualitative considerations have to be taken into account. There can be equality and inequality in respect of access to and the use or resources, or in respect of the kind of education which those resources provide, although it might be said that 'differences' rather than 'inequalities' is the more appropriate term to use when referring to kinds of education. To say that there were inequalities inherent in the secondary modern and grammar school curriculum rather than differences between them, represents a more persuasive and more politically loaded form of expression.

SPECIFICATIONS AND CATEGORIES

A point to be noted is that if greater equality is thought to be desirable as an object of policy, the area in which there is to be equality has to be specified. We might be concerned with food, incomes, education and many other things, but there is no such thing as 'equality in general', any more than there is freedom in a general sense. We have to specify particular freedoms, and particular kinds of equality. With education there is the problem also of defining the sense in which we want educational equality.

Whether we are talking about equal shares or equal treatment, there is also the problem of which group is to be taken into account for the purpose of comparison. A right to education might be specified in such a way that it is given to all members of a society. It might also be confined within a particular age group, and such a situation might be said to apply in Britain at the present time, when adult education provision is cut because the statutory duty to provide it is not clearly or sufficiently defined.

Where a right is deemed to be applicable to everyone, membership of that society is the sufficient criterion for inclusion in the group which has the right. There is a duty to ensure that the right is made operative, and access to education cannot, without denying the right, be made conditional upon other criteria such as wealth, race or intelligence. In some sense there has to be education for all. The right could be extended to all foreign nationals living in the country, or to their children only and a range of possibilities of a similar nature might be considered. What is at issue is the definition of appropriate criteria for categorising people in respect of a particular right. Once defined, other criteria such as wealth and social status are ruled out as being irrelevant. In arriving at such decisions, conflicting views are likely to be expressed and few if any criteria are likely to be regarded as self-evidently acceptable. Many disagreements in relation to questions of equality are, therefore, reducible to disagreements about classifications: who shall be included and for what purposes.

Social and political values are reflected in decisions made and in the case of education especially, theoretical views are also to be found. An example of this may be seen in the Foreword to the *Newsom Report* in 1963 when Edward Boyle claimed that 'all children should have an equal opportunity of acquiring intelligence'. This view is dismissive of the idea that intelligence is a criterion for admission to education. Measured intelligence ceases to be a criterion by which children are to be categorised for selection purposes and acquisition of intelligence becomes an aim of education. The validity of such a view has to be established, especially as it can lead to other more contentious theories such as those which lead to the idea of 'positive discrimination' which claims that certain groups of people should be treated differently or unequally in comparison with others.

This brings out the Aristotelian point that justice and fairness require that while equals should be treated equally, unequals should be treated unequally. Equal distribution of food between people who are dissimilar in their dietary requirements would be unfair, because they would benefit differently from an equal ration. Unequal rations on the other hand might be seen as a way of equalising benefits. Once again the classification of people is seen to be an issue because they have to be grouped together for the purposes of comparison and distinction. Manual workers might be compared with manual workers, but clearly not with children, but then there might be relevant distinctions between manual workers depending on whether they are employed in steelmills or in light industry.

The principle of unequal treatment between unequals follows from the point that there can be no equality in a general sense and that as each specific area of equality is defined, corresponding inequalities are produced.[3] The example of equal rations and differential benefits is a case in point. The imposition of an expenditure tax ensures that everyone who buys a given article rated at 10% pays the same amount of tax, but it represents unequal percentages of income unless everyone earns the same amount.[4] We cannot have equality in every respect and it has to be decided which respect is most desirable. In the case of taxation the argument may be in favour of inequality in the amount paid, but a levelling out in terms of the percentage of income paid and the decision may be made in favour of direct taxation which takes away an equal proportion of everyone's income. This of course leads to inequality not only in the amount paid but it still leaves the better-off with larger amounts of money after tax. A further decision to introduce progressive taxation in order to even out differences in after-tax incomes might then be made, but we cannot have equality in all directions.

Once the decisions about categories and kinds of equality have been made, fairness demands that, within each group, treatment must be equal and further differences such as the colour of a person's skin or the school that he went to are regarded as inadmissible differences. In most case, the decisions arrived at will represent compromises between different requirements and between conflicting ideals and it is not likely that there will be any single 'best' solution. Indeed, on Rawls' 'difference principle'[5] we might have to judge between having equal distribution of wealth and low levels of investment, or inequalities of wealth and high investment and the latter might be chosen if it is seen to lead to a higher standard of living for the least well-off. Socialists, on the other hand, might claim to prefer a lower standard of living for everyone in order to reduce inequalities between people.

EQUALITY AND ADULT EDUCATION

We now turn to a more direct consideration of the preceding arguments in relation to adult education. Here, as with education generally, a concern for greater equality can mean a number of things and even expressing our interest in terms of 'equality of opportunity' is not very precise.

There is the question of access, and equality may be conceived in relation to opportunities to engage in education. In this respect, the various 'disadvantaged' groups are seen as being unfairly treated because they do not take part in adult education, and this is interpreted as evidence of unequal opportunities. Beyond this may be seen a related inequality in respect of the alleged benefits of education, such as access to power, social status, income earning potential or to a better quality of life. Whether or not education, and particularly adult education, is in fact empirically related to these by-products is a matter which requires demonstration but the assumption that there is a relationship sometimes sours our thinking.

Barriers to access may be presented in organisation and institutional terms and high course fees which bear more heavily on the less well-off, is a clear example. Greater equality in this respect is, therefore, sought in differential fee scales weighted in favour of certain groups, and once again we have an example of a preference for inequality of one kind (unequal fees charged) in order to achieve greater equality of another kind (more equal participation rates between groups).

A more educationally fundamental problem, however, may be seen in the presentation, conduct and content of adult education and in its goals. Novel forms of organisation and new concepts such as 'community education' can be cited as one kind of attempt to deal with these problems, as can special programmes of workers' education. These might not be seen explicitly as attempts to secure greater educational equality but they can be interpreted as such.

In drawing attention to these issues, I wish to draw attention also to an idea which is implicit in the claim which is sometimes made, that adult education represents a 'second chance', and the notion of 'chance' as discussed by M. Warnock.[6] It seems to be a useful term to introduce into the discussion.

A right to an equal opportunity for education can be established by law. Even if this right is taken to imply only an opportunity for access, certain groups such as the bedridden, mothers tied down by large families or those who are inhibited by previous experience, might be said to have a poor or unequal chance of taking up their rights. In some respects, the distinction between 'opportunity' and 'chance' in this context is purely verbal, but the distinction does at least draw attention to the necessity for expanding and amplifying the more limited notion of a legally established 'right to equal opportunity'. Further steps have to be taken in order to ensure that the prescribed opportunities can be made a reality, and in order to achieve this, positive discrimination in the form of extra resources or special provision might be necessary.

The idea of adult education as a 'second chance' also draws attention to the more fundamental point that education is seen not only in terms of opportunity for access (although adult education as a 'second chance' provides that) but also in terms of opportunity for success. This may be linked to the idea that education is a competitive process and that adult education provides a further opportunity to succeed. There might have been equal opportunity to take part in education, but as in a race there are unequal chances of winning because of variations in ability, which in turn might be influenced by differences in social background and so on. In races we handicap in order to equalise the chances of winning and in education a similar principle can be seen in 'positive discrimination' to ensure a greater chance of success. It also entails the provision of a greater chance of winning if the prizes obtained by educational success are limited, as are places in higher education or positions of power and highly paid jobs. Be evening out the chances of success and providing for greater equality in that sense, we do not provide equality in the achievement of success if some people still have to be losers. Nevertheless, a more even distribution of the chances of failure might seem to be more just.

Such views of education seem to presuppose progression upon a ladder with complete success going to those who reach the highest level. For the rest, their relative achievements are measured on the same scale. An attempt to break away from this view is represented also in the *Newsom Report* which declares that 'every child has an equal chance of developing his interests and personality irrespective of intelligence, and that might mean giving more education to the subnormal than to the brilliant child'. This could be construed as not merely giving more, but also something different to some children, and such a view emerges in some of the so-called 'radical' thinking about adult education. If the chances of successful outcome or achievement in education are to be both maximised and equalised, two possibilities present themselves. Either the standards of achievement are made so low that everyone can count as having succeeded or different kinds of achievement are expected of different groups of people. The latter view is found in Bantock's proposals for different kinds of education for two cultures[7] and in proposals for a specially conceived 'workers' education' of the kind suggested in *Adult Education for a Change*. In its most extreme form, a wholly student centred approach is the logical outcome, with learning and achievement related uniquely to each individual. All then have a chance of success within their own parameters. There can be gross inequality in what counts as education, but equality in the rate of success, although it is achieved at the cost of weakening the concept of education and its value.

The less extreme proposal, to strengthen the idea of equal education opportunity by tailoring education to meet subcultural needs and interests, has its attractions. Academic knowledge is made available to those who recognise its worth and can cope with it, and more pragmatically, useful knowledge is designed for those with other kinds of ability, needs and interests. There is equal opportunity for adult education but not for equal adult education implicit in *Adult Education for a Change*,[8] where we also find examples of the choices that have to be made between the kind of equality and its concomitant inequalities which are to be the object of policy. More people might have a chance of success but they are involved in different games, each with its own rules. Once again the problem of deciding on the different games and defining who shall be eligible for each also has to be faced.

Once such decisions are made we have to face the possibility that different kinds of curriculum and forms of organisation might have different status and also correlate differentially with non-educational success. It might, therefore, be a hollow kind of equality which gives everyone a medal but which overlooks the fact that some medals have a higher value than others. But judgement on specific decisions is not the purpose of this essay. Instead I have tried to show something of the nature of the problems which have to be faced in connection with educational equality and the decisions which have to be made. In the end we have to define those areas of equality which are valued and the areas of inequality which seem to be less important and can, therefore, be tolerated. The degree of equality is judged between cases of a similar nature and deciding what areas of similarity are significant and relevant is perhaps the most difficult task. This is not only because of inherent technical difficulties but because of the social values and political interests and goals that have to be taken into account. The whole idea of equality is value based and fraught with the possibility of disagreement on aims. It raises moral and legal questions of fairness and justice and above all it has political implications. Moreover, it is inconceivable that there can be a society in which these issues are not present, or that there can be educators who can claim to have no concern for them within education. Who is to be taught, what and how they are to learn, their chances of success, are questions inherent in education and especially adult education, where there is much freedom to choose. These questions impinge upon notions of fairness and justice because they impinge upon the idea of the kind of society that people want and educators too are expected, perhaps more than most, to be involved in the debate.

REFERENCES

1. Warnock M., *Schools of Thought*, Faber, 1977, p. 27.

2. Ibid., p. 26.

3. This principle can be seen to be making no more than the tautologous claim that a rule applies to whom it applies. People expect to be treated according to rules which are appropriate to their circumstances and that people in different circumstances shall be treated in accordance with different rules. The central problem is that of deciding the grounds on which people shall be classified for the purpose of determining which rules apply to them.

4. A formal proof of this point is given by D. E. Cooper in *Illusions of Equality*, Routledge and Kegan Paul, 1980, p. 14.

5. Rawls J., *A Theory of Justice*, Clarendon Press, 1972, p. 328.

6. Warnock M., op. cit., pp. 37–38.

7. Bantock G. H., *Culture, Industrialisation and Education*, Routledge and Kegan Paul, 1968.

8. Thompson J. L. (ed), *Adult Education for a Change*, Hutchinson, 1980.